WHITE-C[

Frank Jones is a journalist, columnist and award-winning former foreign correspondent for the *Toronto Star*. He is of Welsh origin and spends part of the year at his home in the Brecon Beacons, and the rest of his time in Toronto, Canada. His previous true-crime books include *Murderous Women* which was published by Headline in 1991.

Also by Frank Jones

MURDEROUS WOMEN:
True Tales of Women Who Killed

WHITE-COLLAR KILLERS

True Stories of Unexpected Murderers

Frank Jones

HEADLINE

Every reasonable effort has been made to trace the copyright
holders on material contained within this book. However, if there
has been any accidental omission, the author and publishers would
be glad to rectify it in future editions of the book.

Copyright © 1992 Frank Jones
The right of Frank Jones to be identified as the
author of the Work has been asserted by him in accordance
with the Copyright, Designs and Patents Act 1988.

First published in Canada
by Key Porter Books Limited, Toronto, Ontario

First published in Great Britain in 1993
by HEADLINE BOOK PUBLISHING PLC

First published in paperback in Great Britain in 1994
by HEADLINE BOOK PUBLISHING LTD

10 9 8 7 6 5 4 3 2 1

All rights reserved. No part of this publication may be
reproduced, stored in a retrieval system, or transmitted,
in any form or by any means without the prior written
permission of the publisher, nor be otherwise circulated
in any form of binding or cover other than that in which
it is published and without a similar condition being
imposed on the subsequent purchaser.

ISBN 0 7472 4204 6

Phototypeset by Intype, London

Printed and bound in Great Britain by
HarperCollins Manufacturing, Glasgow

HEADLINE BOOK PUBLISHING LTD
A Member of the Hodder Headline PLC Group
Headline House
79 Great Titchfield Street
London W1P 7FN

CONTENTS

INTRODUCTION

A priest commit murder? A doctor? A lawyer? A dentist? An airline pilot? A policeman? Even a Mother Superior? All murderers?

Indeed, and who better equipped! Because each of these professionals, whether New Hampshire teacher Pam Smart instructing students in self-reliance or Eastern Airlines pilot Richard Crafts flying tourists into La Guardia, are people we have been taught to trust.

And each of them – Sister Godfrida tending the sick and the aged by night, lawyer Herbert Rowse Armstrong acting as clerk to the magistrates – possessed, in one form or another, special advantages in the area of homicide. In the unusual case I have called 'The House on rue Saint-Hubert', Abbé Adélard Délorme repeatedly invoked the protection of his cassock in resisting police attempts to bring him to book for murder. The lawyer who turns to murder starts out with a knowledge of the law, an intimate acquaintance with the workings of the police force, and a greater insight into the minds of judges and jurors than you and I are likely to have. And when, in rare instances, policemen turn to murder, count it an inside job, committed with a perfect knowledge of how the circumstances will appear to their colleagues investigating the crime.

Above all, it is doctors we should fear. From Billy Palmer, who used poison in the 1850s to compensate for his bad luck on the racetrack, to John Baksh, who poisoned one wife and came within an ace of poisoning a second in a London suburb in 1986, doctors, of all the professionals, have the highest incidence of murder among their number.

The most obvious explanation is that physicians have the knowledge and the means at hand to commit murder with a good expectation of getting away with it. But there must be more to it than that, because any list of the most notorious murderers of the last century and a half has to include the names of a dozen or more doctors, and during the second half of the nineteenth century homicide became almost a medical speciality.

The 1970s and 1980s were the era of what anthropologist Elliott Leyton has called 'the rise of the modern multiple murderer'. But it's worth remembering that rogue physicians long ago led the way. Palmer may have disposed of sixteen, most of them his own illegitimate offspring; Dr Neill Cream, who graduated from Montreal's McGill University, in 1876, murdered at least eight, most of them prostitutes to whom he dealt out an excruciating death with doses of strychnine.

In more modern times, Dr Marcel Petiot, under cover of the German occupation of Paris during the Second World War, murdered an uncounted number of Jews after offering to help them escape to South America. And the most notorious killer of them all, Jack the Ripper, judging by the skill he showed in dismembering and disfiguring his victims, was almost certainly a doctor. What is especially intriguing is that, where Leyton, in his landmark study *Hunting Humans*, found that modern mass and serial murderers were almost invariably insecure misfits, the medical murderers were, almost to a man, exuberant extroverts.

Why, then, did they turn to murder? Part of the answer may be that entry requirements for the medical profession in the last century were so lax that any scoundrel could qualify. Methods of detecting poisons also did not become sophisticated until towards the end of the nineteenth century, so there was a good chance of getting away with murder before that time. In the last century, too, as the case of Dr William Henry King, the homoeopathic doctor, shows, people were quite accustomed to dosing themselves with arsenic and other poisons for medicinal reasons, making it difficult to separate deliberate murder from ignorant self-medication. Even in modern times, as the story of Dr John Bodkin Adams illustrates, it is almost impossible to draw the line between intentional homicide and the humane act of 'easing the passing'.

The book has yet to be written to explain just

why doctors among all the professionals, even allowing for their opportunities, make up the over-whelming majority of professionals who murder. It need hardly be said that physicians generally have only the well-being of the patient at heart. But, is there something in the practice of medicine that attracts the potentially homicidal individual? Or is there something in medical training that dehumanizes and conditions that one person in a thousand, making him or her capable of killing?

The answers will have to wait. What is certain is that doctors, just like the other professionals I have written about here, are likely to be the last to be suspected. The most effective cloak under which to commit murder, we learn again and again, is education, an affable public persona, and a position in life in which one is looked up to and admired.

To be in that happy situation is enough for most people, and they would not dream of jeopardizing their position by so much as stealing a chocolate bar, let alone committing murder. When the unthinkable occurs, and such a person turns to murder, it is not surprising that he or she applies all the charm, the skill, and the organizational abilities that ensured success in the legitimate world to secret, nefarious schemes. The result can be a baffling mixture of black and white, the best example of which I came across in the court pro-ceedings against Dr Arthur Warren Waite, the dentist who murdered his in-laws, but who was caught before he could wipe out other family members.

Dr Morris J. Karpas, a psychiatrist (or 'alienist', as they were then called) testified that he had found Dr Waite writing poetry in prison. The dentist told him he loved nature in all its forms; enjoyed watering flowers, 'so that May should not die' and, on a voyage home from South Africa, had often paced the deck, looking at the stars and weeping. He complained to Dr Karpas that his wife, who would undoubtedly have been next on his hit list, 'was not soulful. She was not romantic. I wanted her money, and expected to accomplish great things with it.'

He was amazingly frank about his motives: 'I have always been for myself, and never cared for others. If I wanted money, I got it. I am a coward, and whenever I have been in a hole, I took the easiest way out. My life consisted of lying, cheating, stealing, and killing. My personality was that of a gentleman, and I went in for music, art, and poetry – as far as I thought it was required by my vocation.'

Some vocation.

In writing about these sinners, I can report I generally met only saints who gave their assistance often quite unstintingly. The few names that I have room to mention: Brian Lane, founder of The Murder Club; Kate Clarke, of Hay-on-Wye; Simone Gerson, of Toronto; Patrick O'Neill, of Newtown, Connecticut; Arthur Herzog, of New York City; Dr Gerhard Falk, of Buffalo; Detective-Sergeant Ed Stewart, of Toronto; Scotty Broughton, of Brighton, Ontario; Doug Lucas, of the Centre for Forensic

Sciences, Toronto; Edwina Morgan, of Rugeley, Staffordshire; Dr Tony Norton, of Toronto; and Dr Madhu Baksh, of Bromley, Kent.

HOT FOR
TEACHER

She arrived home from the school-district meeting
around ten o'clock, parked her nifty little silver
Honda CRX – the one with the 'Halen' vanity plate
named after her favourite rock group – then let
herself into their rented townhouse at 4E Misty
Morning Drive. Greg, still in the business suit he'd
worn to the Metropolitan Life sales meeting earlier
in the evening, lay dead in the hallway, the blood
drying now from the single bullet wound in the
back of his head.

Pam Smart must have stood a moment, watching
to make sure he wasn't still breathing. So, this was
it. It was finally done. She noted the disconnected
stereo speakers standing by the door, as if they'd
been left there by fleeing burglars, and the drawers
and furniture strewn around to support the idea of
a robbery. So, this was it. She wouldn't have been
human if she hadn't allowed herself one small
moment of triumph. Then she took a deep breath
and prepared to go next door to raise the alarm.

Patrol officer Jerry Scaccia arrived at the cream-coloured townhouse complex, a few steps from the giant Hood Commons shopping mall, at 10:10 p.m. By then Pam Smart was at the neighbour's. Officers, guns drawn, quickly established the killers were no longer in the house. Entry had been made, apparently, through a back door leading to the basement that had been carelessly left unlocked. A CD player and jewellery belonging to Pam and worth about $300 were among the paltry few items stolen.

Greg must have blundered right into the robbery scene, Pam, petite, cute, and twenty-two, told the police. As an ambulance took away the remains of her twenty-four-year-old husband, the officers watched and listened and said little. Something, they knew, wasn't right.

'From the start we didn't think it was a burglary,' Captain Loring Jackson, the man put in charge of the investigation, told me later. Burglaries in Derry, a New Hampshire town of 31,000 some forty miles north of Boston, happen during the day, when people are out working, not in the evening when everyone's home, he said. 'And this was a high-density condominium complex with lots of people around.'

Even putting aside the odd circumstance of Greg Smart having been shot from the rear with the gun held to his head, execution style, rather than from the front as he would have been if confronting an armed robber, the whole gun business didn't make sense, said Jackson. 'A burglar's whole instinct is to run if he hears someone coming. And in this state burglars don't carry guns, because if they're armed, there's a mandatory additional sentence tacked on.'

The next day, 2 May 1990, Jackson interviewed the attractive young teacher. She told him she was media co-ordinator at Winnacunnet Regional High School in Hampton, thirty miles from Derry, in charge of videos and other visual aids. She also taught courses on self-esteem and on the perils of drug and alcohol abuse. Did Greg have any enemies? Did anyone have it in for him? She was surprised at the question. It didn't make sense. This was just a burglary gone wrong, a mindless thing almost like a traffic accident. Greg just happened to come through the door at the wrong time. Jackson explained his reasons for believing this was anything but a burglary, but she still looked sceptical. Who on earth would want to kill Greg, a guy everyone liked? It was especially tragic, she told him, because they would have celebrated their first wedding anniversary the following week. 'He planned a big party. He was taking me down to Florida.' There was a double reason to celebrate: Greg, who had joined Metropolitan Life just the year before, to sell life insurance like his dad, had just been named regional sales rookie of the year.

Pam Smart, Jackson noted, shed a few tears, but seemed subdued, reserved. You'd never have thought her husband had just been brutally slain.

'But people react very differently to grief,' he said.

In the days and weeks that followed, no clues turned up to suggest the identity of the killer. There were no tell-tale fingerprints at the crime scene, and local underworld sources could throw no light on the crime. Meanwhile, Pam Smart was putting the heat on the cops. On what would have been her wedding anniversary, she called the Manchester television station WMUR (where she had earlier applied for a reporting job and been turned down) to offer to go on air about Greg's death. Why hadn't the police found his killer, and why did they persist in believing it was not a robbery? she wanted to know. How was she coping? 'I can't figure out where the strength is coming from,' she said with an easy composure. 'But it seems like it's coming from inside. Maybe it's a part of Greg that's helping me go on with everything.' She told a newspaper reporter the killing was undoubtedly the work of 'some jerk, some drug-addict person looking for a quick ten bucks'.

A month had gone by and the murder was still unsolved. Then, one day, a man named Vance Lattime, Sr., arrived at the Derry police station with a .38-calibre Charter Arms revolver. It was his gun, he said, but he believed it had been used by his seventeen-year-old son, Vance 'J.R.' Jr., in the Greg Smart killing. Lattime, Sr., had wrestled with his conscience for twenty-four hours after Ralph Welch, also seventeen and one of his son's best friends, had come to him with a story that J.R. and another friend, Patrick (Pete) Randall, sixteen, had confessed to killing Smart.

Ballistic tests would show the gun was indeed the one used to fire a particularly lethal hollow-tipped bullet into Greg Smart's skull. And Welch, who had accompanied Lattime, Sr., to the station, proved only too eager to cooperate with the police – he now feared for his life at the hands of his friends. He'd heard rumours that Randall and Lattime, as well as a third friend, William (Bill) Flynn, sixteen, all of them students at Winnacunnet High, had carried out the killing. One day, at the Lattime home, he just out and asked Vance and Pete if it was true.

'Who told you that?' one of them asked. His cousin, Ray Fowler, had told him. Was it true?

Pete and J.R.'s answer was to slam the bedroom door on Ralph – for a conference of war. Undeterred, Ralph crept to the door and pressed his ear against it. 'Bill's going to be pissed,' he heard one of them say, referring to Bill Flynn's likely reaction on hearing the secret was out. 'And you know who's going to be next.' Ralph took that to mean they might kill Ray Fowler for telling. As he burst in through the door, it didn't occur to him they could have meant him.

'I can't believe you guys actually killed someone,' he said. Pete Randall told him to sit down and cool it. Then, in a monotone, he related the details of the murder. 'But, to kill someone!' exclaimed Ralph at the end.

'That's what they do in the Army. They do it

11

every day,' said Pete coolly. And, full of bravado now: 'Yeah, big deal. I figure I'll be a hired assassin some day. Good money.'

'I couldn't believe it didn't even bother them,' Ralph told the cops. 'I couldn't believe my best friends actually killed someone. Pete told me they even said some prayers before doing it. Like that made it OK.'

After listening to Ralph's story, there was nothing for the cops to do now except arrest the three youths and write finis to another sordid little juvenile crime. Except that Ralph Welch had one more fact to impart, a fact that would bring reporters scurrying to New Hampshire from around the world, set off a feeding frenzy among New York book publishers and literary agents, and light up the conference lines in Hollywood. His three friends, Ralph said, had been put up to killing the young insurance salesman by his wife, Pam. She had seduced Bill Flynn when he was only fifteen, and then had immediately started pressuring him to dispose of Greg.

It is, of course, the dream of every bored high-school kid. What else is there to think about during those numbing English classes! What if? What if Ms Hotpants got up from behind her desk at the front, came sauntering down the aisle, and undid more than just the top button of her blouse. Whew! What if, just as you were leaving class, Mrs Pucker-lips said, 'Randy, would you mind coming round to my place after school? I've got something that needs fixing.' Wow!

Pam Smart's favourite group, Van Halen, even has a song about it: 'Hot for Teacher'. Maybe that's where she got the idea. Maybe not, because the fact is that sexual tensions between students and teachers are one of the great unmentioned constants in schools everywhere. And, according to Victor Ross, a Colorado school superintendent and author of *The Forbidden Apple*, a book on the subject, the fantasies are played out in real life more often than people realize. It can start with the well-muscled school football hero standing just a bit too close to a female teacher not much older than himself. Or with a male teacher who always finds it necessary to lean over and help that particularly attractive co-ed in the third row. In most cases people try to ignore it. Sometimes that's impossible, and in many teaching jurisdictions where such contact is forbidden – including New Hampshire – teachers regularly have their certificates revoked.

However it started, Billy Flynn was to have his fantasies realized to an extent he couldn't have imagined. A tall, skinny kid with fair hair down over his collar, he had never been to bed with a girl when he reported for Project Self-Esteem, a mandatory programme for Winnacunnet freshmen in which Smart was an adult leader. She was something – beautiful, full of zip – and he was smitten. Then Flynn, a guitar player himself, found out she was a heavy-metal fan who liked Van Halen and his ultimate favourite, Mötley Crüe. He and J.R. soon found themselves student counsellors in the programme, and one day Smart invited Billy over to her office and showed him perhaps her dearest possession: a photograph of herself with guitarist Eddie Van Halen, taken backstage at a concert at the Tampa Stadium.

Bill was hopelessly, haplessly, flattered and in love. He dreamed of nothing but Pam Smart. But, of course, she was a teacher. In real life nothing could happen.

He was in her office on 5 February 1990 when she said the words he'd never expected to hear. 'Do you ever think of me when I'm not around?' Had he heard right? She was looking at him in kind of a soft way. He turned a deep red. 'Yeah,' he stammered. Yeah, he did a whole lot. Thought about her. A whole lot. She reached her hand across the desk towards him: 'Because I think about you all the time.'

To all outward appearances, Pamela Ann Wojas Smart was the daughter every American mother dreams of from the moment the doctor tells her, 'It's a girl.' Ambitious, pretty, and smart as her name, she was aiming at a career as a television newsperson, and didn't hesitate to tell people she planned to be 'the next Barbara Walters', referring to the reigning queen of the network interviewers.

She lived and worked in New England, but her style and outlook owed more to Florida, where, the second daughter of the three children of a Delta Airlines pilot, John Wojas, and his wife, Linda, she had spent her early years. The couple lived in Miami – not in the seething Latino capital of the headlines and movies, but in one of those anonymous middle-class suburbs called Pinecrest-Palmetto, thirteen miles south of the city centre, where the water sprinklers hissed all the night long and aquamarine backyard pools winked up at planes passing overhead.

In an atmosphere where family break-up was common and teen drugs a nagging problem, the Wojas family, in their stucco rancher, seemed almost old-fashioned. The kids were well-behaved, there were no spats, and Pamela in particular was seen as bright, clever and involved, making her way through public school and junior high without a ripple.

John Wojas, though, became increasingly concerned about crime impinging on the neighbourhood, and when Pam was in eighth grade he moved his family to a $225,000 house in Windham, a golf-and-country-club kind of community north of Boston. Pamela, the good little trooper, adjusted well to the move, and, after a year at Windham Center School, sailed through Pinkerton Academy in nearby Derry, as honour-roll student four years in a row. Energetic, nearly always with a smile, it was almost as if she was ticking off items for some future job résumé: homeroom rep, football cheerleader, Winter Carnival organizer, activist in

Students Against Drunk Driving. And if Pam Wojas sometimes seemed a little, well, manipulative in getting what she wanted and in projecting the right image – dating the co-captain of the football team, for example – that only confirmed the feelings of those around her that she was heading for big things in life.

At heart she was still a Florida girl, and in 1985, with several of her friends from Pinkerton, she enrolled at Florida State University at Tallahassee, where she studied media performance as a preparation for a career in TV. At that point there were two preoccupations in Pam's life: becoming another Barbara Walters, and giving her undying allegiance to the Van Halen heavy-metal rock group. Those two themes came nicely together when she put up a proposal to the university radio station, WVFS-FM, that she should host a two-hour weekly, late-night heavy-metal show called 'Metal Madness'. It was the high point of the week for her to go on air with her familiar sign-on: 'You're listening to the Maiden of Metal on Metal Madness.'

Returning home to New Hampshire at Christmas during her junior year, she found a third preoccupation, Greg Smart, who had an unglamorous job as an assembler of truck booms in a local plant, but who, with his long hair, bore a passing resemblance to the rock performer Jon Bon Jovi. At first Pam, courtesy of her father's airline flying privileges, would fly home frequently to spend time with

Greg. But it got to be a drag. 'Why don't you give up that dumb job and come down to Florida?' she'd urge him. Greg didn't need much persuading. With his parents, Bill and Judy, tagging along in their little Toyota – just to make sure he didn't run into trouble – Greg drove his Mercury Cougar south, with his belongings piled in back, and the couple set up house in a refurbished motel unit.

They were busy times. Pam, in addition to her studies, was working part-time as a news intern at a local TV station, WCTV, and also had a job as errand girl in a government office; Greg got a job on a landscaping crew while studying for the life-insurance industry exams. There was still time to attend rock concerts, and at the 'Monsters of Rock' show at Tampa Stadium in June 1988, Pam, using her rock-show pull, managed to get backstage and have that picture taken with Eddie Van Halen that was to have its uses later.

Beneath the long hair, Greg was an old-fashioned boy who told their friends his big idea was to save up and buy Pam a diamond solitaire. In January 1988 they became engaged, and now Greg had another priority: to get Pam back to New Hampshire. He couldn't stand the Florida heat, and while other Northerners lapped up the Florida sunshine, Greg was dreaming of skiing. When she graduated a few months later, completing the four-year course in three years, Greg presented Pam with a cuddly and very expensive brown and white Shih Tzu puppy. His name? What else? Halen.

The couple returned to New Hampshire on a high. Greg had passed his exams and was going to work with his dad. Pam didn't get the TV job she wanted, but settled for the media co-ordinator post at Winnacunnet High. A few months later, a Florida television station phoned and offered her a job as a starter reporter. Pam bit her lip and said, sorry. After all, in May 1989 she and Greg were going to have a big wedding at Sacred Heart Church in Lowell. Every girl owes herself a decent wedding once in her life.

What was it that Pam Smart saw in lanky Bill Flynn? When the three boys eventually appeared in court, it was Pete Randall, stocky and handsome, who seemed the likeliest candidate for romance. Vance Lattime had a murky complexion and thick glasses, while Bill Flynn, in the words of Tammi Plyler, a reporter in court that day, 'had kind of a gentle face, an air of vulnerability'.

Perhaps Smart saw in him a youth who could be easily swayed, especially because Bill Flynn and his two friends were considered at Winnacunnet High to be outsiders. While most of the kids at the school came from swanky Hampton, Hampton Falls, and North Hampton, the three came from Seabrook, a tacky, depressed one-time fishing village, the model for cartoonist Al Capp's Dogpatch, the fictional locale of the Li'l Abner strip, that today exists under the shadow of a nuclear-power station. At Winnacunnet High, Seabrook kids simply didn't cut it.

That didn't make Bill, J.R., and Pete punks. Bill's dad was killed in a car crash in 1987, shortly after the family moved from California, and his mother told Bob Hohler, of the *Boston Globe*, that it was Pete and J.R. who drew Bill out in the bad year that followed. J.R. used to help his grandmother serve a Thanksgiving meal for the poor and, for their willingness to shovel snow for the elderly in Seabrook, the boys were known as 'The Three Musketeers'. There was another side to them: although none had a criminal record, each had already been involved in minor drug and burglary incidents.

Pam Smart now had to find a way to give the romance some momentum. Teachers don't simply hang around in the school-yard, smooching with students. So, she came to Billy's house. An orange-juice commercial they were making for a contest (first prize: a trip to Disney World) was excuse enough, and while Bill's mom was working in the kitchen, she joined him in his bedroom, where he put on Mötley Crüe's 'Starry Eyes'.

'Are you going to kiss me?' she asked, as he lay on the bed, hands behind his head.

'Yeah.'

'Well do I have to come over there and make you?'

Bold now: 'Yeah.' So she did.

It was her husband, Greg, who was the big problem, she told him. He was mean to her, had even hit her. And he was seeing someone else. She seemed near to tears. 'One night he locked me out of the house. In winter, too, and all I had on was my nightclothes.'

One day at school, she had good news for Bill. Greg was going to be away overnight. Why didn't he spend the night with her? She drove him first to the video store, where they picked up three videos, including the Kim Basinger–Mickey Rourke steamer, *9 ½ Weeks*.

Billy swallowed hard as, nestling on the leather couch, they watched Basinger snap off a pointy little pepper between her even, white teeth, pop strawberries suggestively between her lips, and spill a glass of milk down her chin while Rourke massaged syrup into her thighs. 'I always wanted to dance like that for someone,' Pam murmured in his ear, as Basinger did a bump and grind for Rourke to Joe Cocker's throaty 'You Can Leave Your Hat On (Take Off Your Dress)'. 'But there was never anybody I could do it for.'

The movie over, she left him for a few moments, then he heard her voice calling him. Van Halen was thumping on the stereo – 'Black and Blue'. She had on only a filmy turquoise négligé, through which he could see her nipples. Billy's mouth felt parched. 'Come here,' she said.

Later, he would say, she told him to fetch some ice cubes from the kitchen. The trick was to hold them in your hand until they melted, just the way Mickey Rourke had done in the movie, then allow the water to fall, drip by icy drip, on her neck, between her breasts, around her nipples until it pooled in her navel, then ran in rivulets down her stomach.

20

Next morning Billy was like the guy who won the lottery. Boy, wait 'til the guys heard this. This was the kind of stuff you only read about in those books on the top shelf at the milk store. Jeez, Billy was still too young to even get into movies where they showed this sort of thing.

But as she drove him the thirty miles to school she seemed sad, unhappy. He thought he detected a tear. 'What's up? What's the matter?' he asked, figuring maybe she was regretting the whole thing.

'Oh, Bill, I do love you. I love you truly,' she said, gripping the wheel and staring straight ahead.

'I . . .' the words sounded awkward in his mouth. 'I love you too.'

She turned towards him and her eyes were moist. Then she shook her head. 'No, I can't ask you that.'

'Ask me what? I'll do anything, Pam. Honest. Just ask me.'

'It wouldn't be fair. No, I can't.'

'Tell me, tell me what's bothering you.'

'The thing is, Billy, we can't go on seeing each other like this.'

'Can't . . . ?'

'Not while Greg's around. It's too dangerous.'

'Well, why don't you divorce him? You don't love him.'

She sighed. 'I wish I could, pet, but I can't. You see, he'd get everything. The furniture, the dog, the car, everything. It's all in his name. I'd have to move back in with my mother.'

'Why d'you marry him in the first place?'

'Back then,' she said, as if referring to some other era in history rather than just a year earlier, 'it was the thing to do.' Billy nodded. 'So, you see, there's no future for us while Greg's around.'

'Whad'ya mean?'

'I mean Greg's got to be gotten rid of.'

'You mean . . .'

'I mean killed.'

Now he was way out of his depth. He nodded as if she'd just put forward an airtight argument for going out for burgers and fries. 'Yeah, I see what you mean.' They were a couple of blocks from the school.

'I better drop you here,' she said, stopping the car.

'Pam, I . . .' he began.

She held his collar and pulled his face towards her. 'Don't say anything, sweetheart. Just think about it, will you? Think about it. It won't be difficult.'

She didn't mean it, he told himself as he walked towards school. She'd have forgotten it by tomorrow. She was just pissed off with Greg. It'd blow over. Meanwhile, wait 'til the guys heard what he had to tell them. Shee-it!

A few days later – a tribute to those marvellous Japanese engineers and the amount of space they manage to build into a microcar – Billy and Pam had it off in a state park in her little CRX. But he'd barely zipped up when she returned to her theme. If she divorced Greg, he'd never give her any peace, she said. He'd be forever following them. Had he thought how Greg could be disposed of?

'But I got no gun, no car, nothing,' he protested.

'Billy, unless Greg is gotten out of the way, I can't see you again, and that's that.'

'Don't say that, Pam.' His years were showing. He was going to blub like a baby any minute. 'Please.'

'There must be someone you know. What about your friends, Pete and J.R.?'

'Why would they do it?'

'I'd pay them, that's why. See, there's two policies on Greg's life. I checked. It's a total of $140,000. I'd be willing to pay, say 10 per cent. Fourteen thousand dollars.'

Finally it was making sense. He felt his heart thumping in his chest. 'I'll talk to them,' he said.

J.R. and Pete didn't have to think about it very long. It appealed to their sense of self-esteem. To be hit men, well that was quite a promotion from being petty thieves and joy riders. OK, so later Pam said she'd pay them only $500 each, and they never did see that, only a pair of lousy speakers out of Greg's Toyota truck, but bumping off a guy – think what that would do for their reputations. Who knew where it might lead! And the nice thing was, they'd be doing their friend Billy a favour, just ensuring that he held on to his piece of ass. Viewed from every angle, it was a neat deal.

So now there were four conspirators. But Pam Smart knew she had to keep up the pressure so the boys would carry through. She didn't want it to be just a talkathon. She wanted action.

For his sixteenth birthday in March she bought Billy a subscription to *Guitar* magazine. Where were they going to get the gun, she wanted to know. 'I'll have to buy one. It'll cost maybe two hundred bucks,' he told her. No way was she paying for that, she said. In the end J.R. said he knew where he could lay hands on one. He didn't want to say it was his father's, in case she vetoed that idea. And Pam came through with $30 for Billy to buy hollow-point bullets, which he'd heard were 'quick and painless'.

She and Billy regularly performed Honda acrobatics – in a factory parking lot and in a wood behind the ballpark in Seabrook, among other places. But it was always the same theme afterwards. 'He hits me, Bill. He grabs my hair and throws me down,' she told him, showing him a bruise on her arm. To keep him at boiling point, she sent him a steady stream of love letters, some of them quite explicit, which he was pleased to share with his friends in a class called 'Crime and Punishment'. One day in her office, she turned the phone speaker on, called Greg, and the boys listened in while they argued. At the end Greg said, 'Well, if you want a divorce, that's fine with me.'

Pam turned to them. 'Now you see why I have to have this done,' she said.

By 1 May she had the Three Musketeers psyched up for the job. The plan was that they would borrow

J.R.'s grandmother's car in Haverhill, Massachusetts. Driving over there in the CRX, J.R. took the wheel, and Pete sat in the passenger seat, while Pam and Billy lay in the back, their feet between the front seats. By now she was feeling panicky. 'How should I act when I find the body?' she asked them. Her voice was shaky. 'Should I scream, or run out of the house or call the cops?' Just act normal, they told her. Maybe she should go to a neighbour's.

Perhaps to shock her a little, they started talking about how they'd kill Greg. A knife would be quick and easy, less noise than the gun. 'Oh, Christ no,' she said. 'I don't want you to get blood all over my white leather couch.' She thought suddenly of Halen, her little dog. 'Put him down the basement first,' she told him. 'I don't want him traumatized.' And they should be sure to wear dark clothes and gloves, she told them before leaving them. Bill should tie back his hair, she said, so that he could not be as easily recognized.

Shortly before nine o'clock that evening J.R. sat waiting in the car in the shopping plaza around the corner from the Smarts' townhouse, stabbing plastic soda bottles with an Exacto knife and singing to relieve his tension. Inside the house, Bill and Pete, waiting behind the door, were arguing whether to stab Greg with a butcher knife they'd found in the kitchen or hit him over the head with a candlestick. Either method would be preferable to using the gun, which Billy now had, because

25

ballistics might trace the gun back to J.R.'s father.

The sound of Greg's truck pulling up put an end to the argument. Their hearts thumped as they heard him put the key in the lock. Greg had no time to react. Pete grabbed him by the hair as he came through the door, and slammed him against the wall. Suddenly Greg found himself on his knees, the knife held to his throat. 'Gimme that ring,' rasped Pete. Incredibly Greg said, 'No.'

'Why not?'

'It's my wedding ring,' he said. 'My wife would kill me.'

The remark broke Pete's nerve. The knife trembled. He couldn't do it. Billy pulled out the .38 and rammed it into the back of Greg's head. He, too, waited what seemed like minutes. He thought of the only thing that could make him do it – Pam. 'God forgive me,' he said, then pulled the trigger.

In the car Billy was laughing. They decided to drive over to Hampton Beach, see if they could buy some cocaine with the gold chains they'd grabbed in the house. J.R., at the wheel, was singing 'Shoo Fly Pie' at the top of his voice. 'Shut up!' yelled Pete. 'I hate that fucking song.'

After hearing the boys' stories, Captain Jackson at the Derry police had a problem. If they went into the witness box and claimed a teacher had put them up to murdering her husband, they'd be laughed out of court. It would look like a too-obvious attempt to shift blame. Did anybody else know about the plot? Well, there was Cecelia Pierce, the boys told him. She was Pam's sixteen-year-old intern or student assistant, and she knew about the scheme maybe a month before Greg Smart got knocked off. She'd even come into the bedroom at the Derry townhouse one day when Pam and Bill were having sex on the floor.

Cecelia, after a talk with the police, was a very frightened young person. Knowing about the murder ahead of time – even if she hadn't thought they would really go through with it – could land her in court, she now realized. Three days after that talk, Cecelia agreed to make phone calls to Pam which would be taped and, even scarier, to wear a body pack to record conversations with Pam.

And, finally, Captain Jackson, sitting in a surveillance van thirty yards from the school parking lot where Cecelia and Pam sat talking in the little Honda, heard the authentic voice of Pam Smart making admissions no jury would have believed if they had not been on tape.

'If Raymond [Fowler, another teenager who had told police about the murder plot] hadn't run his fucking mouth off, this would have been the perfect murder,' Pam was telling Cecelia this sunny day, 13 July. And then there was that other snitch, Ralph Welch. 'The problem is, my heart is like, shit, having a heart attack, like I can't even fucking believe this because why would they tell Ralph? If they never would have told Ralph, you know . . .'

Then she looked into Cecelia's face. 'I'm afraid

one day you're gonna come in here and you're gonna be wired by the fucking police and I'm gonna be busted.'

Naw, never happen. Not her, Cecelia assured her.

If the police did question her, Pam advised, 'You're better off lying. If you tell the truth you're gonna have to send Bill, you're gonna have to send Pete, you're gonna have to send J.R. and you're gonna have to send me to the fucking slammer for the rest of our entire life.'

As she felt the cops closing in, she was still confident that she would never be convicted of helping murder her husband. It would come down to who the jury believed, a person like herself, 'with a professional reputation and a course that I teach, and a sixteen-year-old facing the rest of his life in the slammer. They are going to believe me.' As for the stuff about having sex with Billy, 'Why would a twenty-two-year-old woman like me be having an affair with a sixteen-year-old high-school student! That's just ridiculous, and people will not believe that.' And then there were moments of fear: 'I don't know what to do, you know what I mean. I feel like shit. But it's not my fucking fault.'

If Cecelia thought what she was doing was potentially dangerous, Pam gave her no reassurance. 'What good is it going to do if you send me to the fucking slammer,' she told the student. 'Because if you think that's going to be the end of your problems . . .'

Later in the transcript she explains that, in that case, Cecelia's family would face heavy legal costs if she went to the police. But was that all she meant? After Smart's conviction in the murder plot, a further charge against her of attempting to get a fellow prison inmate to murder Pierce was dropped.

Television satellite vans were clogging the parking lot of the Rockingham County Superior Court, some one hundred reporters from as far away as Japan were in attendance, and people had been lining up since 2:00 a.m. for the few public seats in the courtroom when Pam Smart went on trial as an accomplice to murder in March 1991. The proceedings were carried live on WMUR-TV, the station that had once turned down Pam Smart for a job; the case was featured on *Entertainment Tonight*, the network show-biz magazine; and even Greg's father, Bill, said he was contemplating a movie contract, although he insisted he wanted to keep 'creative control'. Even before the trial began, Cecelia Pierce had received several thousand dollars for TV appearances, and had signed a $100,000 movie contract with Once Upon a Time Films.

Asked in court if he thought it was OK to make money from the death of his best friend, Brian Washburn, who had been close to Greg, shrugged and said, 'Everyone else is.'

In January, Bill Flynn had pleaded guilty to second-degree murder, J.R. and Pete to being accomplices to murder. Facing life sentences with no possibility of bail, all three had agreed to testify against Pam in return for lighter sentences. Pete Randall's courtroom account of how Greg Smart pleaded for his life before he was shot was so harrowing, Judge Douglas Gray called a recess so that the dead man's mother could be taken, sobbing, from the courtroom. There were tears, too, among family members when, during his testimony, Bill Flynn got down on his knees to show Greg's position before he was shot.

The one person who never showed a hint of emotion was Pam Smart, who, wearing feminine pinks and flowing skirts, sat in the dock, quietly taking notes, 'almost like a princess', one awed young male spectator told the *Boston Globe* reporter. In the witness box she was insistent that she had played no part in the murder.

'They murdered Greg,' she said, meaning the three youths. 'They're the ones who broke into the house. They waited for him. And they're the ones who brought him to his knees and brought a knife to his throat. I didn't force anybody to murder Greg.'

Of her affair with Billy, she said, 'I loved him at one point.' Yes, she had sent him two photographs of herself wearing a frilly bikini and striking provocative poses, but a week before the murder, she claimed, she told Bill, 'There's absolutely no way I could live with this any longer and I was going to tell Greg.' When she told her husband and said she was sorry, 'he asked me if I loved him, and I told him I did. I loved him.'

And the taped conversations with Cecelia Pierce? 'When someone you love is murdered, you do things you maybe wouldn't have done beforehand,' she said. 'I was totally obsessed with finding out who had murdered my husband. In my mind I thought I would play a game with her and pretend I knew more about the murder – to get information.'

In his summation to the jury – an unusually well-qualified group headed by a nurse and including, among the seven men and five women, a software engineer, a graduate student from Harvard and a retired banker – defence lawyer Paul Twomey argued that the three youths were simply thrill-killers who had blamed Pam Smart in order to reduce their sentences. 'They have not a shred of moral decency in them. They came in here and lied to you,' he said.

But the assistant attorney-general, Paul Maggiotto, had a convincing three-layer argument to offer. Even if the jury did not believe the three boys, he said, there was the word of Cecelia Pierce and, most important, the tapes. And even if they had doubt about Cecelia, he said, there was still Cindy Butt, another student with no connection to the plot, who had testified that, a month before the murder, Cecelia had told her she had a friend named Pam who wanted to have her husband murdered. 'If anyone in the jury room talks about fabrication, talk about Cindy Butt,' he advised the jurors.

In fact, jury members would say later, it was the

tapes that ultimately convinced them of Pam Smart's guilt.

After Smart was sentenced on 22 March 1991 to spend the rest of her life in the New Hampshire State Prison for Women, without the possibility of parole, Greg's father announced he and his wife were going to visit his son's grave. 'We're going to tell him, by God, she did it,' he said. His mother had felt there was something wrong from the moment Pam returned Greg's belongings to them in plastic bags – even his picture and his favourite house plants – three days after the killing. 'She got what she deserved,' said Judy Smart.

In the summer of 1992, Bill Flynn, by then eight-een, was sentenced to twenty-eight years to life for his part in the murder. The judge ignored the plea of his mother that, 'Bill was a fifteen-year-old child, Pam used sex, lust and the threat of abandonment to get what she wanted done.'

Pete Randall received a similar sentence; Vance Lattime, Jr. was sentenced to eighteen years to life; and Raymond Fowler had earlier been sentenced to fifteen to thirty years.

Speaking from prison as she started her lifelong sentence, Pam Smart was admitting nothing. 'I feel like I'm in Russia,' she told the *Boston Globe*'s Bob Hohler. As for the criticism that no one had ever seen her shed a tear for Greg, 'I'm sorry if I reacted wrong, but nobody gave me the twenty-two-year-old widow's handbook.'

So why did Pam Smart engineer the death of her

husband of less than a year? The reasons put forward seem laughable – the disparity in their educations was causing friction; he had cut his hair and looked less a rock star and more the insurance salesman he really was; he preferred spending time with his buddies in the backwoods with his Toyota truck to going to concerts and gourmet restaurants with Pam. If these were reasons enough for murder, the graveyards would be full of young husbands.

The answer lies rather in Pam Smart herself. Like many of the professional people you will meet in this book, there was nothing in her middle-class upbringing to set her apart. But somewhere along the way, it was as if a gene went missing. Call it morality, call it knowing right from wrong. It used to be fashionable to call such people psychopaths, except that no one's quite sure what that term means any more. Education, good breeding, and important positions in life provide no immunity. They are people who will use any means at hand to achieve their ends and seem curiously blind to the consequences. They have always been with us, although today there seem to be more of them. In that sense, the Pam Smarts may be the wave of the future.

We will give her the last word. Speaking from prison, she was outraged at the media circus, the Pam Smart teeshirts and jokes about the case going the rounds. 'I don't know how anybody in the world could consider anything about this funny,' she said.

'People seem to have lost sight [of the fact] that someone is dead.' Indeed.

THE HOUSE ON
RUE SAINT-HUBERT

The body was found huddled beside a tool shed on a piece of vacant land in the suburb of Notre Dame de Grâce. It was discovered by two workmen arriving early Saturday morning to collect their tools, and it presented several unusual features. The young man's wrists were tied with a flimsy piece of string that would have been easy to snap, and the tails of his well-cut overcoat were pulled up over his head and secured with safety pins. When these were removed at the morgue, the head was found to be wrapped in a piece of quilting. There was no blood, either on the ground or on the shed, and no sign of a struggle having taken place. When police moved the body, they found the snow beneath was not melted, and although the man had been shot, people living nearby had heard no sounds in the night. It was not hard to deduce that he had been killed elsewhere and his body dumped in the vacant lot.

The identity of the corpse was quickly established: in his pocket was an envelope addressed to Raoul Délorme, 190 rue Saint-Hubert, Montreal. It was as though the killer had deliberately left a visiting card, Detective Georges Farah-Lajoie of the Montreal Sûreté thought as he went through the man's belongings at the morgue on 9 January 1922, the Monday following the discovery of the body.

'Take a look at his shoes,' Dr Wilfrid Dérome, the pathologist, urged him.

Farah-Lajoie – his colleagues in the Montreal police department called him 'The Arab' on account of his having been born in Damascus – picked up a shiny, brown leather shoe sitting beside the pile of clothing. 'Expensive,' he said, running his fingers along the smooth upper. 'And almost unworn,' he noted, turning it over. 'Certainly they were never worn outdoors. The nails are not even rusty. So,' he said, smiling at the doctor, 'where are the overshoes?'

'You've got it,' said Dérome. 'No overshoes. And look at the topcoat. Not a mark on it. No bullet hole. Yet there was a hole right through the poor fellow's jacket.'

'So, we know he was shot indoors.'

'And by a real amateur,' said the doctor, pulling back the sheet to reveal the roughly sewn-up torso. 'See, here, and here! It took six bullets to finish the poor fellow off. A real piece of butchery. My opinion, if you want it . . .'

'Tell me, doctor.'

'My guess is when you find the place this was done you'll find someone who has been busy with a mop and scrubbing brush.'

One hundred and ninety rue Saint-Hubert seemed to Farah-Lajoie, as he observed it thirty minutes later, a secretive house. It presented to the street a solid wall, three storeys high, pierced by a few disproportionately small windows and topped with defensive-looking battlements. Even the two small bay windows above the doorway seemed placed there more as look-outs than with any idea of letting in daylight, and the door itself was recessed and hidden at the top of a flight of steps. The very bulk of the Romanesque-style house near the corner of fashionable Dorchester Street suggested people who had money, although you'd have to think they were careful with it.

'An odd place for a priest to live,' said Farah-Lajoie, helping his obese colleague, Desgroseilliers, over the snowbank.

'Well, he's an odd guy to be priest. A real cold fish. You know, Georges, how people react when you bring them tragic news, but this guy . . .'

'We tell him we're from the Sûreté,' said Detective Pigeon, catching them up after parking the car. 'And ask him if Raoul Délorme lives there,' said Desgroseilliers. ' "Yes," he says, "He's my younger brother." And straight away he asks us if his brother is ill because he was sleeping away from home the night before.'

'So,' continued Pigeon, 'I give him the usual

story, tell him someone carrying identification in his brother's name is gravely injured, and he says, "Where is he?" At the morgue, I tell him. "Then he's dead," he says, like he's telling us. We told him we wanted him to come with us and see if he could identify the body. Didn't turn a hair. "Give me a few minutes so I can get dressed," he says, "and on no account tell my sisters, who live here with me." '

'So, how was he when he saw the body?' asked Farah-Lajoie, leading the way up the steps to the front door.

Pigeon shook his head. 'He just looks him up and down, like he was buying cabbages. "Yes," he says, "that's certainly my brother." No tears, nothing. Just gives him a quick benediction and turns away.'

Immediately after his first ring, as Farah-Lajoie would record in the small memoir he wrote on the case, Abbé Adélard Délorme himself, apparently cheerful, opened the door and, rubbing his hands, led them into his study. He was in his thirties, the detective judged, a little overweight, roundfaced with a shock of dark hair and grey eyes that regarded them blandly from behind wire-rimmed glasses. Abbé Délorme, Farah-Lajoie already knew, ministered to the poor as chaplain of a charitable institution, L'Assistance Publique, but looking around at the dark, expensive furniture and the Abbé's comfortable figure, he could see no sign that the priest shared any of his clients' discomfort.

'Gentlemen, cigars?' The Abbé held out a box.

38

Havanas, Farah-Lajoie noticed.

'No, thank you, Father. If you don't mind,' he said, taking a packet from his side pocket, 'I'll stick with my Pall Malls.'

'Go right ahead. Now how can I help you?'

'If it is all right with you,' said the detective, 'we'd like to go over the facts again concerning your brother. We don't like to bother you at a time like this, but, you see, sometimes something is forgotten, something important.'

'Of course. No bother at all.' The Abbé was all geniality. 'As I told the officers before, Raoul – he was really my half-brother, you know. My father remarried – Raoul left the house about three o'clock on Friday. He was going to the Princess Theatre. Then, at seven o'clock precisely, he telephoned me.' The Abbé indicated the telephone on his desk.

'Excuse me, Father. He called you on that phone, but may I ask what the other phone on the bureau there is for?'

'Ah, you are very observant, as a detective should be. That telephone is used only by my sisters. My sisters, Florence and Lily, and my half-sister, Rosa, they live here, too, you see, and that is where they receive their incoming calls.'

'And it was definitely to this phone on your desk that Raoul called?'

'I can't see that it matters, but yes, Detective, it was to this phone. He called to tell me he had met two old friends and they were going out together, I gather in some style. He told me he would probably not return home until the following morning.'

'Names?'

'No, he didn't mention who they were.'

'Where was he calling from?'

'He didn't say. He just said it was a pay box. And then – it was most mysterious – the telephone in my bedroom rang three times during the night, at two o'clock, at three and then again at four.'

'But there was no one on the line?'

'I don't know. Once I thought I heard groaning and sobbing. I was so annoyed the third time, Detective, I will admit I used a word quite unsuitable to my position, and then I called the operator to complain.'

'There is a third telephone in your bedroom, Father?'

'For emergencies, yes. Sometimes I am called out to minister to some poor dying soul. It is an extension from this phone on my desk.'

'Now, Raoul lived here with you, is that right?'

'Yes, except when he was away at university in Ottawa. He would have graduated this year, poor chap. He was just home for the Christmas holidays.' The priest put his hand to his mouth and, for the first time, betrayed signs of emotion. 'Only the day before I had been out with him to buy him clothes to go back to college.'

'You supported your brother, then?'

'You might say so. You see, gentlemen, my father, whose name was also Adélard like mine, was a building contractor. You have heard of him? He had done rather well, and when he died six years ago there was a good bit of property. Well, Raoul, who was only nineteen at the time, was too young to take responsibility, so naturally it fell to me as the eldest – I am thirty-seven now – to run things. My bishop very generously relieved me of my normal duties so that I would be free to administer the estate.'

Farah-Lajoie noticed that the priest gestured a good deal with his left hand. His right remained inside his cassock, except that, now, as he began going into details about the rents he had to collect and the paperwork he had to cope with, he for a moment flourished that hand before concealing it again.

'Excuse me asking, Father, but you seem to have hurt your hand.' Farah-Lajoie watched for a hesitation, perhaps a slight flush. There was none. 'Oh, that,' he said showing them the red mark on the wrist of his right hand. 'Most painful. You see, I fell on the ice on the way to mass on Saturday morning. Mademoiselle Morache, our concierge, advised me to put iodine on to to avoid infection.'

'Of course. You were very close to your brother?' The detective caught the priest's shrewd glance.

'Our relations could not have been more cordial. I was like a father to him. Last summer, for example, we went on a long motor trip together in the United States. Of course' – the Abbé smiled – 'as a single young man, his interests were rather different from mine. During the holidays he would go to the cinema nearly every day and often to the theatre. He would get up late every day, but then, isn't that the way with young people, Detective?'

'Did he have many friends?'

'To be honest with you, no. I have to say not a single friend came to the house during the Christmas vacation. That is why I was rather glad when he called me to say he was going out with friends on Friday night.'

'Girls?'

The Abbé laughed. 'I tried in my modest way to be a bit of a matchmaker. But when I mentioned certain young ladies who I thought were both pretty and virtuous, I am afraid he showed no interest.'

'How was he doing at university?'

'He was not brilliant, I have to admit,' replied the priest. 'But his professor told me that last term his marks were quite improved. As a matter of fact, Raoul told me he was looking forward to getting back to college.' The Abbé stood up, turned his back to them, and looked out of the window. 'His trunk was packed. He was due to leave on Saturday.' There was a small catch in his voice.

'Father,' said Farah-Lajoie softly, 'do you have a gun?'

For a moment, it seemed the priest had not heard him. But he was smiling when he turned. 'Of course. It is an old revolver that used to belong to my father. I keep it in the car for protection.'

'I see. Could I perhaps take a look at it?'

'Certainly. Why don't I show you over the house.' He looked over his glasses with an amused expression. 'You were going to ask, weren't you, Detective?'

The Abbé led the way into the kitchen, produced two keys, and unlocked a door opening on to a flight of stairs leading down to the garage. 'I am the only one who has access,' he said, leading the way and switching on the light. 'Here we are.' From the glove compartment of the large Franklin sedan he produced a Bayard automatic pistol. It did not seem especially old to Farah-Lajoie.

'Have you ever fired it, Father?'

'Only once. When we were travelling in the States. A dog frightened Raoul and I fired a shot to frighten it off.'

'I see a box of bullets there, too. Would you mind if we take them and the gun along for examination?'

Upstairs again, Farah-Lajoie asked for a description of Raoul's watch, which had been ripped from his waistcoat pocket, leaving only a piece of broken chain. 'Oh, that was not his watch,' the priest replied. 'His was at the jeweller's being repaired. I lent him my watch when he went out.'

'And the overshoes, Father. I believe you mentioned earlier buying him a pair of overshoes to return to college. Could I see them?'

'Here they are,' said the Abbé, opening the hall closet and producing a shiny, new pair of rubber galoshes.

'I see an old pair there. Are they yours?'

'I expect so. I have several.'

'Would you try them on for me, Father?'

The Abbé sat down obligingly on the hall bench. His face reddened as he tugged at the stubborn overshoe. 'What's so important about overshoes?' he asked, with a trace of irritation.

'Just details, Father. We have to look at everything or we get in trouble with the chief back at the office.'

On the sidewalk once again, the sun had come out and the glare on the snow momentarily blinded the three officers. 'A strange bird, our Abbé,' said Farah-Lajoie. 'What kind of a priest would carry a gun?'

'Well,' said Pigeon, climbing behind the wheel, 'I don't think he liked you very much either. When you went to the toilet, remember? He said, "I can read in that man's eyes, he is not a good Catholic, and he is also a flirt, a ladies' man. Isn't that so?" '

'My god,' said Farah-Lajoie, stroking the points of his moustache, 'I hope you agreed with him. I have my reputation to think of.'

At the Sûreté office the detective learned that a bloodstained cap, matching the description of the one worn by Raoul Délorme, had been found that morning in the street not far from where the body was discovered. Beside it, the snow in the road was stained pinkish-red. Several neighbours in the area, which was known for drinking, fights, and prostitution, had now come forward to say they had heard gun shots the night of the murder. But, although a picture of Raoul was circulated widely in the city, no one in the following days reported having seen him at any local theatre or restaurant the night of his disappearance, and none of his friends came forward.

Farah-Lajoie's investigations revealed that, when he died in 1916, Délorme Sr. had left a fortune worth $185,000, including twenty-one rental apartments or houses. The Abbé was the executor of the estate, although Raoul who, unlike his brother, could be expected to produce children, would inherit the bulk of the estate when he reached twenty-five. The detective was also intrigued to discover that, only a week before Raoul died, the Abbé had taken out a $25,000 life-insurance policy on his brother's life, and that the Abbé had split the sales commission with the agent. As to the Abbé's business methods, one large property owner told the police, 'He has given us landlords a bad name.'

Returning to the house on rue Saint-Hubert with more questions, Farah-Lajoie was surprised to find two uniformed officers posted at the door. 'Look, my friend,' said the Abbé, after offering him the customary cigar, 'look at these terrible letters I have been receiving. They are accusing me of the vilest things, of killing my brother. I am afraid for my own life. That is why I asked your superiors for protection.'

Had Raoul, Farah-Lajoie asked mildly, left a

will? 'I believe he wrote one last year when he had an operation for appendicitis,' replied the priest vaguely.

'Could I see it?' For once the Abbé appeared flustered. 'I don't know. I think it is still in Ottawa, at the college.' He seemed more willing to talk about the grand preparations for Raoul's funeral the next day. 'We are doing it with the greatest amount of pomp imaginable,' said the priest. 'You must come, Detective, and I am asking that for a special reason. Undoubtedly there will be large crowds there, and I am quite sure Raoul's assassin will be among them. I implore you to watch carefully because there might be an attack on my person.'

The detective left, saying he would likely have to make a trip to Ottawa. 'I hope Raoul did not forget me in his will,' said the Abbé in what might have been a weak attempt at humour. 'I was good to him.'

Farah-Lajoie was glad afterwards that he had attended the funeral. It was, as the Abbé had promised, a sumptuous affair. There had been no attack on the priest, and even though the Church of Saint-Jacques was packed, no suspicious characters had been spotted. But what the detective noticed was the utter fervour with which Abbé Délorme conducted the requiem mass, his voice sometimes breaking with emotion. Afterwards, though, as he accepted condolences, the priest seemed quite himself again.

Less was learned on the trip to Ottawa. Raoul, said the Oblate Fathers at the university, had taken the will home with him at Christmas. But awaiting Farah-Lajoie on his return to Montreal was more encouraging news. The owner of a gun store, Oscar Haynes, had volunteered the information that, on 27 December, the Abbé Délorme had come to his store and exchanged an old Ivor-Johnson revolver for a new Bayard automatic and had bought two boxes of bullets for it. When Farah-Lajoie showed Haynes the Abbé's gun, he readily identified it as the one he had sold. The only difference, he said, was that, when he sold it, the gun was properly oiled, and now it was oiled excessively, as if by an amateur.

Back at his office that evening, Farah-Lajoie turned out the lights, lit a Pall Mall, put his feet on the desk, and went over the facts as he had learned them. The following summer, significantly, Raoul would have been due to graduate and would have taken over the administration – and most of the profits – of the estate. Farah-Lajoie was certain now that the Abbé had lied about the gun and the will, and the bullets removed from Raoul's head had been identified as having been fired from the Bayard automatic.

The more the detective thought about events at the house on rue Saint-Hubert the day of the murder, the more it seemed to him that, from start to finish, they had been orchestrated by the Abbé. The priest, who led a surprisingly active social life, had turned down several invitations that day. Considering it was the Day of Kings, a Quebec holiday, that was unusual. However, he had bought three theatre tickets for a matinée performance for his sisters, and they had left the house after lunch. So, the Abbé was the only one to see Raoul leave, if he did leave, at 2:30 p.m. Shortly after 5:00 p.m. – around the estimated time of Raoul's death – various people had seen the Abbé around the neighbourhood, engaged in running errands.

But what about the phone call the priest claimed to have received from Raoul at seven o'clock sharp? Farah-Lajoie believed he knew the explanation for that. He had found a boyfriend of Florence's who said that he had phoned her at that time. The Abbé answered and told him she wasn't there and to call back in ten minutes or so. When he called back, the priest was all apologies. He had not realized his sister was at home, he said. He would get her right away. It was after the first phone call, Farah-Lajoie conjectured, that the Abbé had put down the receiver and told his sisters in the other room that Raoul had called to say he wouldn't be home that night.

And the three phone calls in the night, which the sisters dimly remembered hearing? Farah-Lajoie had an explanation for those, too. It was possible, he had discovered, to use the sisters' telephone in the study to dial the Abbé's line so that the phone would ring in the bedroom upstairs. As for the Abbé's claim that he had complained to the tele-

phone operator after the third call, none of the
operators on duty that night could remember
receiving such a complaint.

Suddenly it was daylight and Farah-Lajoie's colleagues were coming noisily into the office. His
ruminations, he realized, had occupied the whole
night. 'I didn't even have any breakfast coffee,' he
complained to Desgroseilliers. But he knew now
what he had to do.

An inquest into the circumstances of Raoul's
death had opened but had then been adjourned to
give the police more time to collect evidence. Now
Farah-Lajoie went to the coroner, a man named
McMahon, and laid out the facts as he knew them.
They pointed, he said, to only one conclusion: that
Abbé Adélard Délorme should be arrested immediately for murder. McMahon, who had the power to
issue the warrant, heard him out and then shook
his head. 'You know that you are dealing here with
a priest. The evidence is only circumstantial. You'll
need better proof than that.'

The following day, Abbé Délorme took the offen-
sive. He announced to the press that he was offering a $10,000 reward for the arrest and conviction
of his brother's murderer. He would even offer
$25,000 if he thought it would solve the case, he
said. The Abbé assured reporters that he was offering the reward with the approval of the Sûreté, and
that he was satisfied with the work of the detectives on the case. That didn't stop him complaining
privately to the reporters that he suspected Farah-

Lajoie of stealing a coat from the house during the course of a search.

Two days later, as the case commanded more and more interest in newspapers throughout North America, we find the Abbé, in an interview published in *La Presse*, refuting rumours of his own involvement in his half-brother's death. 'Is it reasonable I would have killed my brother when I have plenty of money?' he asked. 'I want to see the killer caught and punished. I want revenge for the blood of my brother.'

Suddenly the Abbé was seeing the police investigation as a plot against himself and the church. 'Let's arrest those dangerous people, those low people, the free-thinkers, the non-believers,' he declared. But he was not surprised at the turn events had taken, he insisted. Jesus, who it was his privilege to represent, 'suffered more than me'.

'L'Affaire Délorme' became the subject of a national debate, arousing fierce antipathies between Protestants and Catholics, and engaging the wits of private detectives, psychics and others claiming special knowledge. The Abbé did his best to keep things lively by writing letters to the Minister of Justice in Ottawa, the Premier of Quebec and the newspapers, claiming that he was the victim of religious persecution.

Farah-Lajoie spent his days following up worthless tips and meaningless clues. The blood on the cap which the Abbé had identified as belonging to his brother was in fact human, but the 'blood' on the road, to the amusement of newspaper readers, turned out to be horse urine. The reason for its pinkish-red hue was not explained. It was time for the detective and his colleagues to return to the house on rue Saint-Hubert, even if that meant further accusations from the Abbé that he was being persecuted.

They found him genial as ever, pressing them, as usual, with his cigars and raising no objection to their examining the automobile. This time the officers found small, suspicious stains on two pillows in the back, as well as chicken feathers on the seat.

'Ah, those!' exclaimed the priest. 'That was from the day I took a friend for a drive in the country and he bought some live chickens.' The police took away the pillows and the feathers, which bore evidence of some sticky substance.

On a suitcase against the wall of the garage, Farah-Lajoie made a further discovery. Beneath a pile of dirty laundry, he found a small square of quilted fabric similar to the cloth found wrapped around Raoul's head. In the basement he found string, seemingly of the type used to bind the dead man's hands.

Dr Dérome's tests showed the spots on the cushions were human blood, and the fabric and quilt stitching proved it to be identical to the piece found with the body. The Abbé showed surprise when, the following day, Farah-Lajoie arrived at the house with Dr Dérome, who said he personally wished to inspect the car. After finding suspicious spots on the upholstery, the doctor asked permission to take away the seats for tests – tests that would prove the further presence of human blood, although someone had tried to wash away the stains with soap.

'Every day you are taking something with you,' said the Abbé, smiling as the car seats were carried away. 'Eventually it will be my turn.'

The Abbé's next-door neighbours had all been away the day of the murder, but now Farah-Lajoie discovered a man living three doors away who remembered hearing the Abbé's car either entering or leaving the garage around nine o'clock and again about eleven o'clock that night. The priest had been quite definite in saying he hadn't used his car that day.

Now, finally, challenged by the coroner, Abbé Délorme admitted that Raoul's will was lodged with a notary public in Montreal, although he objected to it being read out at the inquest because it would place him, he said, 'in a peculiar position'. The will, read nevertheless, named the Abbé as principal beneficiary.

Another part of the puzzle fell into place when a yellow envelope arrived at the office of the head of the provincial police. It contained the gold watch, bearing the initials 'A.D.', that the Abbé had lent to Raoul the day he was killed. The watch was packed in a Pall Mall cigarette packet, perhaps in a clumsy attempt to incriminate Farah-Lajoie. But the handwriting on the envelope, although disguised, was later identified as that of the Abbé.

As the coroner still hesitated over issuing a warrant, the attorney-general, the province's highest legal officer, finally intervened. It was a reporter who arrived at the Abbé's door first with the news that he was about to be arrested. 'Are you crazy!' cried the Abbé wildly. 'Don't they know this is a cassock and that as a priest I am protected.' Then he became coldly calm: 'Let them come and arrest me,' he said. 'I had a gun in the car, yes, but I also have one here in the house. Believe me,' he said confidentially to the journalist, 'I have my agents too working for me. My boys are with me.'

Alarmed, the reporter informed the authorities the Abbé might be dangerous. To allay his suspicions, Chief Lepage of the Sûreté called the Abbé and invited him to his office 'to clear up a few questions'. When he arrived, Lepage assured him it was a ploy to protect him from those who might attack him. The Abbé was calm and contained as he was led into the final session of the coroner's inquest, which ended with a recommendation from the jury that the priest should be arrested for the murder of his half-brother. He merely gave a disgusted smile as he was led from the courtroom, flanked by police officers.

Next day, following a court appearance, it fell to Farah-Lajoie to drive the Abbé to the Bordeaux Jail, accompanied by Pigeon and another detective, Rioux. The priest was in mischievous mood. 'Hey,' he said to Rioux, 'didn't I see you on a certain evening recently with a woman, let's say, of some style. You know what I am talking about?' Rioux blushed beet red.

'So, Farah-Lajoie,' he said, turning to the detective, 'here we are, you and me!' He gave the officer a thump on the back that suggested anger more than affection, then peered into his face. 'Aren't you frightened?' Farah-Lajoie gripped the wheel tightly. 'No,' he said, 'I am not frightened.' After all, the detective had won – hadn't he?

When the trial opened 9 June 1922 the defence made an immediate attempt to have the Abbé declared unfit to stand trial by reason of insanity. The priest contributed to this impression by flourishing a bright silk handkerchief, laughing out loud at times, and at others muttering to himself, 'Bibi [his nickname for himself] has his cassock. Bibi has his cassock.'

After a procession of psychiatrists trooped into the witness box to claim the priest was unbalanced, the jury took only ten minutes to concur, and the Abbé was transferred from the Bordeaux Jail to the Asylum of Saint Michael at Beauport.

And that would have been the end of the story – if, very soon after, the Abbé had not made an application to the courts to regain control of the family estate, backing his demand with a certificate from the asylum's superintendent declaring that he was now sane. This was too much for the provincial government, and the Abbé was ordered to stand trial for the murder of Raoul.

In court, he was jovial as ever, and sucked pink and white peppermints throughout the proceedings. The evidence was damning: this time a witness had been found who claimed to have seen the Abbé returning home in his car at midnight the night of the murder, and an examination of the estate books showed $14,000 was missing. The Chief Justice of Quebec, Sir Francis Lemieux, who presided, delivered a powerful indictment of the accused. 'All men are equal before the law. You must have courage,' he told the jury. 'Justice must be vindicated.'

It was all in vain. The jury ended up hopelessly split, ten for conviction and two stubbornly against. A third trial ended with a similar result. It was clear that, in a heavily Catholic province, there would always be jurors unwilling to convict a priest no matter how suggestive the evidence. By the time of the fourth and final trial, the provincial government had clearly given up any hope of convicting Abbé Délorme, and, after a token prosecution, he was found not guilty.

We need not be as squeamish. What really happened that afternoon of 6 January 1922? If Raoul had survived only a few more months, Abbé Délorme would have had to hand over their father's estate and all the perquisites of wealth that went with it and return to being a humble priest. But his brother's death would bring him, the police estimated, $180,000. He had plotted the murder for some time. The easiest thing, he had decided, would be to stage an apparent suicide. It was certainly not unheard of for a young student to blow his brains out in a fit of depression. And, if it was suicide, there was no problem with using the Abbé's recently purchased Bayard automatic.

As Farah-Lajoie reconstructed the crime in the memoir he wrote to vindicate his reputation after the efforts made by the Abbé to impugn his honesty, Raoul would have been sitting, likely smoking his pipe, in his study on the second floor, perhaps listening to the gramophone, as he often did. The Abbé came up behind him and, with a sudden movement, clamped an ether-soaked rag over his face. Almost in the same moment, he held the revolver to Raoul's temple and fired.

His scheme would have succeeded – except for one detail. The Bayard has a peculiarity in that the barrel is three-quarters of an inch below the line of sight. Instead of penetrating the brain, the bullet smashed into the jaw, where, in fact, two bullets were found.

Raoul grasped instinctively for the gun, and a desperate struggle ensued. The Abbé knew if he faltered he was lost. He fired wildly and repeatedly. Only after the sixth shot was Raoul still. But now the suicide plot was useless. Who ever killed himself with six bullets? The Abbé had to think quickly, had to somehow come up with a new scheme to account for his brother's death.

He saw immediately that the first requirement

was that Raoul's body must be found elsewhere. He got his brother's overcoat, put it on him, then fetched the quilting and bound up the bloody head. He may have used the sheets from Raoul's bed to wrap the body or to clean up because the sheets were found next day to be damp, presumably washed. Undoubtedly he tied the hands in the garage to make transportation of the body easier, and left the body there – he, after all, was the only one with a key to the garage – for later transportation.

Then the Abbé attended to his alibi, making sure he was seen outside the house by several people shortly after five o'clock. When the godsend call came from Florence's boyfriend, the priest improvised brilliantly to convince his sisters that Raoul was alive and well at that time. By 8:45 p.m., when the sisters again went out, it was time for the Abbé to go to work.

To keep Raoul's blood from dripping on the car upholstery, Farah-Lajoie guessed he had propped up the body in the back seat with cushions and, garbed in his raccoon coat, he had climbed behind the wheel. To anyone on the street he would have seemed like any chauffeur driving his employer, who was sitting in the back seat. As an area where crime and violence were common, Notre Dame de Grâce was the ideal district to dump the body. He returned home around 11:00 p.m. and, after his sisters got in, staged the clever little telephone charade throughout the night to add a hint of mystery and intrigue to the story.

Considering how little time the Abbé had to concoct the scheme, and the panic any normal person would feel at the sight of the bloodied body lying on the floor, the priest's performance was remarkable. Small wonder he forgot a few details, like the overshoes, the overcoat with no bullet hole and the fact that the body having already chilled, would not melt the snow beneath it.

Ultimately, he won his duel with Detective Farah-Lajoie. After being found not guilty, he was relieved of his religious duties and assigned by his superiors to an institute for deaf-mutes. There, free at last from accusations and gossip – at least from his mute companions – he administered his substantial holdings, even adding to them by taking an insurance company to court and forcing it to pay up on the $25,000 insurance policy he had taken out on Raoul's life.

It would be nice to think that the Abbé felt at least a crumb of remorse every January, as the anniversary of Raoul's death approached. Because indeed, on 20 January 1942, two weeks after the twentieth anniversary of his brother's death, the Abbé, then fifty-seven, was found lying on the floor of his study, bleeding from the mouth after suffering a seizure, and died shortly after. But the timing was probably just a coincidence.

And the house on rue Saint-Hubert? It stood in reduced circumstances until 1988 when, following a fire, it was demolished.

BLOODSTAINS
ON THE CARPET

Policemen, for the sake of their own sanity, must sometimes develop a macabre sense of humour. Take, for example, the bathtub that serves as a drinking trough for horses at the stables of the mounted unit of the Lancashire Constabulary in Preston in the north of England. The tub was stained brown when I saw it, but the brass plaque above it shone brightly. It announced that this was the very tub in which Dr Buck Ruxton had, in September 1935, dismembered the bodies of his wife, Isabella, and the family maid, twenty-year-old Mary Rogerson.

Ruxton, you see, was rather out of the normal line of professionals who kill. Your average white-collar murderer tends to be a tidy fellow. He doesn't like a mess. So, his method of choice is likely to be a poison. Such is particularly true of doctors, who, in addition to being the most murderous of the professionals, have the necessary knowledge to use drugs effectively. But Dr Ruxton, born in India of a

French mother and Parsee father, applied a different area of his medical training to the beastly business of murder: surgery. And that's what makes his a horror story plain and simple.

You can still visit the handsome double-fronted Georgian house at 2 Dalton Square in the old city of Lancaster where it happened, although no one lived within these walls after the events of 1935, and it now houses the town's planning department. And it's easy to see how the central location, at the foot of a fine square dominated by Lancaster's Greek temple-style town hall, would appeal to the young Dr Ruxton, arriving in town in 1930 to set up practice.

As the first person of colour to occupy a prominent position in Lancaster, he, as you might expect, encountered prejudice. But, if the local establishment was cool towards the new doctor, the warm-hearted ordinary Lancashire folk took to him. He was soon known as 'the workingman's doctor', and he had the largest practice in town. Even today, you'll find older people in Lancaster who say he was the finest doctor they ever had.

A good doctor Ruxton may have been; as a husband he was a jealous tyrant.

Ruxton, who had changed his name by deed poll from Bakhtyar Hakim, arrived in England from Bombay in 1925. He had medical degrees from London and Bombay, including a Bachelor in Surgery, and it was while he was doing postgraduate work in Edinburgh that he was smitten by Isabella Kerr, a not-very-attractive Scottish woman with a long face and prominent teeth (of those, more later), who was managing a restaurant. She had formerly been married to a Dutch sailor from whom she was now divorced, while Ruxton, a handsome and highly emotional man, had a wife still in India.

They went through a form of marriage, and before and while they lived in Lancaster, they had three children – Elizabeth, Diana and Billy. But Belle, as he called her, soon discovered her husband was insatiably jealous. She had only to talk to a man for him to fly into a rage and accuse her of having an affair. Today, when we are more familiar with wife abuse, the pattern would quickly be recognized: twice Mrs Ruxton sought protection at the police station just a few steps away, across the square. 'I would be justified in murdering her,' Ruxton, who kept a revolver under his pillow, said on one of these occasions. A maid had seen him on the bed with his hands around her throat; another had seen him attack her, crying, 'You are a dirty prostitute', while her sister Jeannie said Isabella had tried to gas herself in 1931. He even told a police officer, 'My wife has been unfaithful, and I will kill her if it continues.'

In Lancashire there are local writers prepared to say on the basis of their research that Mrs Ruxton was flighty and gave Ruxton cause for anger. A play presented locally portrayed Ruxton as a victim of racial prejudice. To suggest that either factor justified what followed shows the cruellest insensitivity.

In the final build-up to tragedy, Mrs Ruxton, at

61

the beginning of September 1935, travelled to Edinburgh with the family of Robert Edmonson, a young solicitor-in-training, and they stayed the night in a hotel. Ruxton was convinced she had slept with the young man, though Edmonson denied it in court. On 14 September his wife, observing an annual rite, took the car and drove to the nearby resort of Blackpool, where she always met her sister to view the famous illuminations. It was a jolly evening – drinks, rides at the fair, a lot of laughs about when they were growing up – but when Isabella left them to drive home she was a bit worried that she would be home after 11:30, when she had told Ruxton to expect her.

What happened in the next six hours or so after Isabella Ruxton arrived home will never be known in detail. But let's see what can be deduced from the many comings and goings at 2 Dalton Square the next morning, a Sunday.

At 6:30 a.m., Ruxton calls on Agnes Oxley, who was supposed to clean house for him that day, and tells her not to come, as his wife and the maid, Mary Rogerson, have gone on holiday to Edinburgh.

At 9:00 a.m., Winifred Roberts arrives with the Sunday newspapers and rings repeatedly; when Ruxton finally comes to the door, he tells her the Edinburgh story.

At 10:00 a.m., it's the woman with the milk, and she notices the doctor's hand is bandaged. 'I jammed it,' he explains.

At 10:30 a.m., Ruxton goes to a service station, buys four gallons of petrol in cans, then buys a similar amount from another petrol station.

At 11:00 a.m., Mrs Isabella Whiteside arrives with her son, whom Ruxton is supposed to circumcise. He tells her he must postpone the appointment because his wife is away in Scotland and, 'there is just myself and the little maid, and we are busy taking up carpets.'

All the while, of course, Ruxton has to deal with his children, the oldest seven, as they wake up, demanding breakfast. At 11:30 a.m., though, he arrives at the door of his friends Herbert Anderson, a dentist living six miles away in Morecambe, and his wife, asking if they will look after the children for a while, as Belle has gone away on holiday. Mrs Anderson asks about the bandaged hand. Ruxton says he cut it opening a can of peaches.

At 4:00 p.m., whatever Ruxton has been doing in the house, he now feels it safe to bring in an outsider. He calls on Mary Hampshire, a patient who has not worked for him before, explains that his wife is in Blackpool, and asks if she will help him clean up the house, as the decorators are coming the next morning. 'Where is the maid?' she asks. On holiday, he replies.

What Mrs Hampshire saw when she arrived at the house on Dalton Square would be of crucial interest in the trial. The carpets in the hall and stairs were taken up, straw was littered everywhere, the bathroom was filthy, and the bathtub was stained a brownish-yellow colour. The doors to the bedrooms were locked, but she noticed that, in the lounge, supper for two was laid out, but uneaten. In the small, paved yard she noticed carpets, a shirt, and some surgical towels, all partly burned.

After she had swept out as best she could, her husband helped her scrub the stairs. As they were leaving, Ruxton gave Mrs Hampshire some carpets and a suit. 'You can have it cleaned,' he said. 'I had it on this morning when I cut my finger and it's badly stained.' The next day, haggard and unshaven, Ruxton asked Mrs Hampshire if she would do some more cleaning. Picking up the suit he had given her, he offered to have it cleaned. As he had been good enough to give it to her, the least she could do was have it cleaned herself, she said, at which point Ruxton asked for a pair of scissors to cut out the maker's label. When she went later to wash the carpet he had given her, the water came away red.

Mrs Hampshire was getting suspicious. When she arrived at his house that day, there was no cleaning to be done. 'I sent for you because you give me courage,' the doctor said oddly. Where was the mistress? This time he said she was in London. 'Doctor, you are telling me lies,' she said. 'Yes, dear, I am,' he replied without hesitation. 'I will tell you the truth. My wife has gone away with another man and left me with the three children.'

Ruxton told Mary Rogerson's parents an even

odder story: Did they know Mary was pregnant? 'Mrs Ruxton has taken her away to see if they can do anything about it.' Mary's father said he wanted her back regardless, and if Ruxton didn't bring her back he would go to the police. 'Don't go to the police,' he pleaded. 'I'll bring her back on Sunday.'

The signs that something grisly had happened at 2 Dalton Square were, you would think, unmistakable. The neighbours saw Ruxton carrying parcels from the house and saw fires burning in the little yard at the back; the dustmen noticed some of the carpets left out for them were bloodstained; and, when Mrs Oxley finally came to clean, she noticed a foul odour in the bedrooms, which were now unlocked. Why did no one call the police? Because a little blood would not be unusual for a doctor doing minor surgery in his own house and, as always, who would suspect a popular and able doctor of being a murderer?

It was on 29 September that Susan Johnson, on holiday just over the Scottish border in Moffat, in Dumfriesshire, went on a walk she would never forget. Crossing a bridge over a ravine on the Edinburgh-Carlisle road, she paused to admire the scenery. Glancing down into the valley below she saw, to her horror, a package out of which protruded what seemed to be a human arm and hand. She hurried back to fetch her brother, who opened the parcel. It was, in fact, an arm, and inside were other remains wrapped in a torn piece of sheet. Police immediately found another four bundles of assorted body parts decomposing and infested with maggots on the bank of the river, plus two heads wrapped in cotton wool, one of them tied up in child's rompers. Over the next few days, more than thirty parcels of remains were recovered from the ravine, some wrapped in a copy of the *Sunday Graphic and Sunday News*, dated 15 September 1935. A month later, a highway worker found a rain-sodden package beside the Glasgow-Carlisle road, five miles from Moffat. It contained a left foot. A week after that, another young woman out for a walk found a right forearm and hand wrapped in newspaper in roadside bracken half a mile from the ravine.

The dismemberment had been done by an expert; it was not even clear at first, apart from the fact there were two heads, how many bodies there were. One of the heads was clearly that of a young woman; the other was thought to be a young man's. Reconstruction and identification of the bodies would present one of the great forensic challenges of modern crime detection.

Just how tough a job it was becomes clear in a book published two years later, *Medico-legal Aspects of the Ruxton Case*, written by John Glaister, professor of forensic medicine at the University of Glasgow, and James Brash, professor of anatomy at the University of Edinburgh, the two men who led the team of scientists involved. It is one of the grisliest and yet most fascinating books in the field.

The usual hack-and-slash murderer, wanting to

dismember the body of his victim, uses a saw, and, to the expert, putting the parts back together is as simple as doing a child's jigsaw puzzle. In this case, though, the whole job had been done with a knife, the bones being separated at the joints. To make matching almost impossible, skin and flesh had been removed in many cases from the bone. But the very skill with which the job was done – the neat incisions, indicating a familiarity with joint construction – revealed that the murderer had medical knowledge.

Probably no murderer has ever done a more thorough job of trying to prevent identification. Noses, ears and eyes, as well as the skin on the faces and scalps of the two heads, had been removed, and some teeth had been extracted. One body was clearly female, but the torso of the other was missing, and the experts had to use bone measurements and skull characteristics to identify it as female. In the end, though, the murderer had outsmarted himself. In removing certain features of the bodies, he had simply drawn attention to them. A bunion had been removed from one foot, for example, in exactly the place where Isabella Ruxton had had a bunion. The tips of the toes of that body had been cut off – and Mrs Ruxton had humped toes. The woman's distinctive large front teeth were missing. Skin and tissue had been removed from a hand belonging to the other body – in exactly the place where Mary Rogerson had a scar on her right thumb.

Reassembled, the two bodies conformed in estimated age and height to those of the two missing women. Photographs of the two women matched when superimposed upon the skulls, and shoes belonging to the women fitted casts made of the dismembered feet.

The killer may have been an expert with the surgical knife, but in other areas he made elementary mistakes. A sharp-eyed policeman noticed that some of the pages of the *Sunday Graphic* in which body parts were wrapped were from a 'slip edition' intended for delivery in the Lancaster and Morecambe district. Both the child's romper and a blouse in which parts were wrapped were identified as coming from a parcel of clothing bought at a jumble sale and given to Mary Rogerson. Her stepmother even identified the patch she had put under the arm of the blouse. If there was even a shred of doubt, a comparison of fingerprints taken from the 'Mary Rogerson' corpse with prints photographed meticulously over a period of eleven days in Mary's bedroom in the Ruxton house established the identity once and for all.

In mid-October, even before identification of Mrs Ruxton was definite, Lancaster police chief Henry Vann phoned the doctor from his office just across the square, told him they had some news of his wife, and asked him to drop by. 'I've just put the children to bed,' said Ruxton. No problem at all, said the chief. He dispatched a burly detective to play babysitter while the interrogation of Dr Buck

Ruxton began. The doctor never returned to 2 Dalton Square. After two days of questioning, he was charged with the murder of Mary Rogerson.

On 5 November, appearing on remand, Ruxton was charged further with the murder of his wife. It was as if something snapped. 'It is impossible! It is a damned lie!' he shrieked. 'It is damned rotten. My religion would not permit it.' As he ranted on, the chairman of the magistrates called a five-minute recess.

Norman Birkett, the eminent lawyer who defended Ruxton at the Manchester spring assizes in 1936 (and who later sat in judgment at the Nuremberg trials), told an interviewer shortly before he died that the Lancaster doctor was one client in whose innocence he had difficulty believing. 'Nobody could read, as I read, all the facts the prosecution was going to prove without feeling, well, this is a very difficult case,' he said. 'But it didn't make me any less eager to do everything that I could for Dr Ruxton.'

As no fewer than 115 witnesses, from dustmen to eminent pathologists, made their way to the witness box, Ruxton kept up a steady stream of notes and suggestions to Birkett, waving his hand to attract his lawyer's attention. When Mary Hampshire fainted in the witness box and had to be helped out for fresh air, Ruxton, the concerned physician, said, 'She will be all right.'

On the eighth day of the eleven-day trial, Birkett sent Ruxton a note, pointing out that it was hopeless to call medical evidence against the over-whelming case put forward by the prosecution. His wish would be to put Ruxton on the stand, he wrote, although he would, of course, then have to face the fire of cross-examination. 'I entirely agree with you,' wrote Ruxton in reply. 'I wish to give evidence on my own behalf.'

Ruxton, although he sometimes seemed on the verge of tears, was a surprisingly good witness. Asked about his stormy marriage, he said, 'If I may put it in proper English, we could not live with each other and we could not live without each other.' He rather spoiled the effect by adding a French proverb, 'Who loves most chastises most.'

To the charge that he had murdered Mary Roger-son, he flared, 'It is absolute bunkum with a capital B, if I may say so.' He was weeping as he added, 'Why should I kill my poor Mary?' He still main-tained his wife had left him about 9:00 a.m. that fatal Sunday, taking Mary with her. The copious bloodstains throughout the house and in the drains? From his cut hand, he explained. Or per-haps from a miscarriage his wife had suffered.

Ruxton was calm and collected as he shrugged off the questions of the prosecutor, J. C. Jackson. Was his wife unfaithful? 'Yes,' replied the prisoner. 'It has been going on since 1932.' But, when cross-examination resumed the following morning, Ruxton went to pieces. Suddenly he couldn't remember a lot of the facts. He stumbled, postured and wept. When Jackson confronted Ruxton with a cleaner who was prepared to say the suit he had given Mrs Hampshire had been cleaned and returned to him only shortly before the murder, Ruxton stammered, 'My Belle does all the cleaning . . . I know nothing about it . . . I don't remember it.'

As Jackson badgered him, Ruxton shouted hysterically, 'Out of two hundred cases of confinement in Lancaster, Dr Ruxton has never written a death certificate.'

'It would be better for you and everyone,' the judge admonished him, 'if you listened to the questions and tried to answer.' At another point, Birkett had to rise to tell his client to keep quiet and answer the questions calmly.

Jackson's final question left Ruxton floundering. 'If that is the sheet from your wife's bed,' he said, pointing to the material that had been identified by an expert as coming from the Ruxton house, 'can you explain how it got around the bodies at Moffat?'

'How could it be, sir?' said Ruxton helplessly.

Birkett made what he could of the few gaps in the Crown case. If murders had been committed at 2 Dalton Square, how was it that so many people had come and gone that Sunday morning and on subsequent days without suspecting it? And why, if Ruxton had transported those grisly parcels of flesh in his car or another car he'd rented around that time, had no traces of blood been found?

But Mr Justice Singleton erased any doubts in the jury's minds by calling up the exhibits one by one – the bloodstained stair pads, the child's romper, the blouse. 'Doesn't this establish the case for the prosecution as a case was rarely established before on circumstantial evidence?' he said. It was the work of an hour for the jury to find Buck Ruxton guilty. 'I want to thank everybody for the patience and fairness of my trial,' said Ruxton, calm for once, before a judge sentenced him to death.

On the night of his execution, after his appeal failed, Ruxton wrote to Birkett: 'Thanks awfully, old man, for all you have done.' He left Birkett a set of silver fish knives and forks – perhaps not the most appropriate gift. Learned counsel gratefully declined.

The same night, Ruxton wrote to Vann, the police chief who had arrested him: 'May I make a dying request? Oh, please do be good to my children. You will not fail me, will you? Be a friend to them.' He ended: 'Dear Vann, I don't bear the slightest grudge against you. Shake hands. God bless you all.'

On 12 May 1936, a grey, overcast day, large crowds gathered outside Strangeways Prison in Manchester, many of them demonstrating against the death penalty, as Buck Ruxton made his last exit. The following Sunday the sensational *News of the World* published a signed confession in Buck Ruxton's handwriting. It said: 'I killed Mrs Ruxton in a fit of temper because I thought she had been with a man. I was mad at the time. Mary Rogerson was present at the time. I had to kill her.' It was dated 14 October 1935 – the day after he was arrested. A reporter from the paper had seen Ruxton at his home shortly before the arrest. It was when he visited Ruxton in prison that the doctor had supposedly given him the confession in a sealed envelope with instructions that it be opened only upon his death. If he was acquitted, it was to be returned to him. If Ruxton had any hope at all of being found not guilty, he had taken an incredible risk. Why? The note certainly shows no sign of Ruxton's florid verbosity. But it was rumoured the newspaper had paid Ruxton £3,000 for the confession, a sum that would tidily take care of Birkett's bill for £2,000, while leaving any money realized from the estate for the upkeep of the children.

A fund in fact was set up for the children and, says Vann, 'They all made good.'

As for Ruxton, many have felt some sympathy for this emotional man who was governed by his passions. If Mary Rogerson had not witnessed the murder of Belle Ruxton and the doctor had not disposed of the bodies in such a gruesome fashion, the case would have been no different from hundreds of crimes of passion – regrettable but apparently inevitable – committed every year.

I take a different view. A study of the detailed plans of the house and its furnishings put in at trial shows Ruxton slept in the largest bedroom, while his wife was crammed in a smaller room with the three children, one of them having to sleep on a

73

camp cot. This meant either that their marriage had, to all intents and purposes, ended, and she no longer slept with him, or that Ruxton was used to keeping his wife in a state of subservience. His threats and earlier assaults against her would be grounds enough for prosecution today.

But it was the events of that September night that reveal Ruxton for the monster he was. The police believed that Mrs Ruxton was strangled on the third-floor landing outside her bedroom door. Mary Rogerson, opening the door of her room, would immediately have been confronted by the sight of the doctor and his wife's body. If Ruxton had murdered in one blind moment of anger, wouldn't the natural thing be for him to feel remorse, to tell the maid to fetch the police? No, Ruxton's first thought was how to save his skin, and so he cold-bloodedly and viciously advanced on the cowering Mary Rogerson – his 'little Mary' – hit her over the head with some object, fracturing her skull; and then, judging by the copious amounts of blood on the landing and down the stairs, slit her throat or stabbed her.

Again, there was a chance for remorse, a chance to give himself up. Instead, he carried the bodies downstairs to the bathroom located on a half-landing halfway up the main staircase, and went about the ghastly business of draining the blood expertly from the bodies and reducing them to parcels of meat and bone, some of which, in the photographs produced in court, would not have looked

74

out of place on a supermarket meat counter. Doctors at the trial estimated it took a minimum of five hours to dismember each corpse. The packages were then stored in the bedrooms, no doubt among the children's things, while Ruxton made his preparations for the drive to Scotland and the dumping of most of the remains over the bridge.

Not the image of 'the workingman's doctor', not the charming bedside manner still remembered in Lancaster, not even the picture of the loving father thinking at the last of his children – none of this can erase those bloody images. People who grew up in the 1930s still remember that at school they would chant: 'Bloodstains on the carpet, bloodstains on the knife. Dr Buck Ruxton has murdered his wife.'

At the police stables, they told me that using Ruxton's famous bathtub as a horse trough hadn't turned out to be such a good idea after all. Many of the horses refused to drink from it.

A TALE OF
TWO LAWYERS

They were two men with a great deal in common.
Both Englishmen, they had come to small Welsh
towns to practise law. Both married women who
were, or considered themselves, a cut above their
husbands. And both men – something almost
unknown in the legal profession – would, within a
period of seventeen months, be charged with murdering their wives.

Harold Greenwood, short, with a droopy moustache and a gift of the gab, and Herbert Rowse
Armstrong, a tiny, precise figure with waxed mous-
taches who always insisted on being called 'Major',
never met, so far as I can discover, although they
lived a bare sixty miles apart. But each followed
the legal proceedings against the other with profound interest, knowing that, to a degree, their
fates were bound up together.

Even the towns of Kidwelly, in South Wales,
where Greenwood, a Yorkshireman, arrived with
his wife, Mabel, in 1898, and Hay-on-Wye, a Welsh

border town, where Armstrong, a Devon man, arrived in 1906, are alike in appearance, with narrow, winding streets and timbered Tudor houses. Greenwood had married Mabel, a member of the renowned Vansittart family, in 1896, and, in 1910, relying more on Mabel's private income than on the modest returns from Harold's law practice in nearby Llanelly, they bought Rumsey House, a large, ugly Italian-style mansion on the banks of the River Gwendraeth in the centre of Kidwelly. Armstrong, meanwhile, married Katharine Mary Friend, the unprepossessing daughter of a Devon printer, in 1907, and, in 1912, they bought Mayfield, a rather forbidding late-Victorian house on a hilltop in Cusop, a hamlet close enough to Hay that the Major could walk every day to his office on Broad Street. In a very short time, the names of both houses would be familiar to newspaper readers all over the world.

For both men, the events that were to propel them into the limelight began in the early summer of 1919. In May, Armstrong came home from his stint of First World War military service with hopes of a life rather different from that he had led with Katharine and their three children before going into the army. It was common knowledge in Hay that Armstrong had a difficult time at home. Even in their wedding picture, Katharine Armstrong, with mildly protruding eyes, looks like one of those stern Victorian missionaries, and she kept him on a short lead. 'Bath night!' she announced one day as Armstrong was playing at the local tennis club, and he went home without complaint.

But, during his war service, which saw him doing administrative work on the home front, with only a brief three-month period at the front in France, Armstrong had tasted a different life. He could smoke all he wanted – a habit he could indulge only in one room at home – he could drink in the mess, and he even had a tentative affair during the war with a woman named Marion Gale. But, if he had come home thinking life would be different, he was quickly disabused. 'No wine for the Major,' Katharine would announce at dinner parties, and she again resorted to telling him off in front of the servants.

If the Major, who now picked up the strings of his solicitor's practice and took his place again as clerk to the local magistrates, seethed, he showed nothing of it. His behaviour in public towards his wife was impeccable, and he was admired for his restraint. But, the very month Armstrong came home, Katharine went to see Dr Thomas Hincks, complaining of pain in her shoulder and right arm and numbness in her fingers.

In Kidwelly, the Greenwoods' marriage was a very different affair, with Mabel, whose brother, Sir Thomas Vansittart Bowater, was a former Lord Mayor of London, being seen as the martyr. Even though her health wasn't good, she was tireless in working for local charities and social organizations, while, behind her back, her insatiably gossipy Welsh neighbours wondered how she put up with that philandering husband. It wasn't as if Harold had been actually caught in an act of adultery, but, while he seemed to have no men friends, he loved the company of women and flirted freely. Mabel was especially jealous of his carryings-on with Mary Griffiths, the sister of their physician, Dr Thomas Griffiths, who lived with her brother, conveniently just across the street. 'That is Harold's weakness,' Mabel once told Mary Griffiths, who, local rumour had it, was once seen sitting on Harold's knee on a train. 'He is too fond of women.'

Yet, although a friend, Florence Phillips, a frequent visitor to Rumsey House, spoke of tiffs and disagreements, and Greenwood himself would admit his wife was jealous, to most outsiders their marriage appeared reasonably happy. It was only in the wake of the disturbing events of the weekend of 14 June, 1919 that tongues really began wagging.

For several months Mrs Greenwood, who was forty-seven, had been in declining health, complaining of her heart, fearing that she had cancer (the post mortem would reveal a weakened heart and a benign tumor). She had gone about her social duties as usual that week, although several noticed that she had difficulty climbing the stairs for an antiquarian meeting at the Town Hall on Thursday. On Saturday, though, after an early lunch with her husband, she announced her intention of taking the train five miles to Ferryside to attend a meeting of the local tennis club. Greenwood, protesting that she really wasn't strong enough to go, walked with her to the station, and, according to him, she rested a while on the way, complaining of heart pain.

But, to the vicar of Kidwelly, the Reverend David Ambrose Jones, who sat beside her as the little train clickety-clacked between embankments bright with honeysuckle and wild roses, Mrs Greenwood seemed her usual cheerful self, if a little wan. She walked the three-quarters of a mile from the Ferryside station and back, and took an active part in the meeting. As she left Kidwelly station, Mrs Greenwood was overtaken by her eldest daughter, Irene, twenty-one, who worked in a bank in Llanelly, and they walked home together. Late that afternoon, it would emerge, Harold Greenwood, who did not have a telephone at home, had gone to the town telephone exchange and put in a call to the office of the *Llanelly Mercury*, a local newspaper. The operator – one of those who made it her business to know everyone's business – said a woman's voice answered and that Greenwood told her, 'I am happy. I am satisfied now.' Greenwood, according to the operator, regularly made Saturday-afternoon phone calls to the same number, and the same voice always answered.

On Sunday morning, the Greenwoods – father, mother, Irene, and their youngest son, Kenneth,

81

ten (a daughter, Eileen, seventeen, and son Ivor, fifteen, were away at boarding school) – had a late breakfast and, as Mrs Greenwood was not feeling well, they did not go to church. Irene went to the kitchen 'to look after the pastry' (whatever that meant) and her mother wrote letters, while her father, assisted by the local cinema manager and car enthusiast, Tom Foy, worked on Greenwood's car. In the dining room, Hannah Williams, the eighteen-year-old parlour maid, was laying the table for the midday meal, and it is at this point that confusion begins.

Williams would say that Greenwood went into the china pantry just before lunch and remained there fifteen minutes. She remembered it clearly, she said, because, out of good manners, she didn't like to go into the pantry, and it held up her table-laying. Greenwood's account was that, when the gong sounded for lunch, he went into the pantry to wash his hands, as he always did before a meal, and was only there a few minutes. It was handier to wash there rather than to go up to the bathroom, and a roller-towel had been installed specially for him. Williams, who had worked at Rumsey House only a few months, said he invariably went upstairs to wash his hands.

She would also say she put out a bottle of whisky for Greenwood, and a bottle of port wine for his wife, and a red wine glass for each of them, and that she poured a glass of wine for Mrs Greenwood. Irene and Kenneth, she would say, drank water.

But everyone else – the cook and the Greenwoods – said Mrs Greenwood rarely drank port wine, and that it was a bottle of burgundy that stood on the table that day. A wine merchant would even say that Mrs Greenwood had bought a bottle of burgundy bearing the label 'Real Pure Wine' only the day before.

The family, and the servants after, had for lunch that day a roast – some remembered it as lamb, others beef – vegetables, and, most significantly, gooseberry tart and custard. Afterwards, Mrs Greenwood had a lie down, and later complained to her husband that she had diarrhoea. 'You had no business eating that gooseberry tart' was his unfeeling response.

Mrs Greenwood was well enough later to have bread and butter and a cup of tea with the family, and it was only shortly after 6:30 that she complained of heart pains and feeling sick. Her husband gave her brandy, and together, and with difficulty, he and Irene got her upstairs to her bedroom. Greenwood fetched Dr Griffiths from across the way, and he found her sitting on a couch, vomiting.

The doctor prescribed sips of brandy and soda, and later sent over a bottle of bismuth for the stomach upset. While Irene helped her mother get undressed and into bed, Greenwood walked around the garden with the doctor, then invited him to a game of clock golf. His intention, he explained later, was to detain the doctor, and, indeed,

Griffiths looked in on his patient before leaving and judged her slightly improved. Then, bustling on to the scene came Florence Phillips, who had been invited to supper with the Greenwoods but who, instead, after one look at the deathly ill Mabel, went scurrying to fetch the district nurse, Elizabeth Jones, who had cared for members of the family before. Miss Phillips would claim it was her idea to fetch the nurse, while Greenwood and his daughter would say it was theirs.

The nurse found Mrs Greenwood in a state of collapse and with a low temperature. Seeing the bottle of bismuth sent over by Dr Griffiths by the bedside, from which Mrs Greenwood had been given a dose, Nurse Jones thought it was heart medicine, and gave her a second dose before going home at nine o'clock for an hour to put her child to bed.

Seeing the patient no better on her return, Nurse Jones asked Greenwood to fetch the doctor again, and here a curious interlude occurs. Both Miss Phillips and Nurse Jones estimated the husband was away nearly an hour before he returned with the doctor. He had, in fact, been chatting with the doctor's sister, Mary. His wife, he told her, was gravely ill and would probably not recover. He seemed, she would say, in light spirits. Then he told her an odd thing: a fortune-teller, he said, had predicted he would soon be going on a honeymoon trip.

When he eventually arrived, the doctor was not

of much use. Although Mrs Greenwood was getting steadily worse, experiencing diarrhoea such as the nurse had never seen in her professional experience, he still put it down to a tummy upset caused by the gooseberry tart. The long-suffering woman probably did her cause no good by apologizing for creating all the trouble, and at eleven o'clock she insisted that Irene go to bed, as she had to go to work in the morning. Saying goodnight to Miss Phillips at the gate, Greenwood told her not to worry, that he had seen his wife much worse in the past. When Dr Griffiths, out for his bedtime stroll, asked him a moment later how Mrs Greenwood was, he replied, 'Easier' – a surprising statement considering that, when he had asked her how she felt a short time before, her reply had been 'Very bad.'

Soon after midnight, and with Mrs Greenwood asking now if she was dying, Nurse Jones again sent the husband for the doctor. He returned, saying he couldn't rouse him. The nurse, who would say later that by now she had her suspicions that 'things were not as they should be', went herself, knocked at the door, and the doctor came to the window right away. After seeing Mrs Greenwood again, the doctor prescribed two pills, which he sent over to Rumsey House with Greenwood. What the pills were exactly was to be the subject of heated discussion, but certainly, after she was given them at around one o'clock, Mrs Greenwood sank into a sleep – from which she did not awaken.

The nurse sent for Dr Griffiths again at three in the morning; twenty minutes after he arrived, his patient died. How had Greenwood reacted during this distressing period? 'He did not seem to be put out in any way,' Nurse Jones would say.

Although the death certificate issued by Dr Griffiths attributed death to valvular disease of the heart, suspicion surrounded Mrs Greenwood's death from the start. 'Do you think there was foul play?' were the first words from the vicar when Nurse Jones broke the news to him early that morning that his parishioner, who had seemed in such good spirits two days earlier, was dead. The nurse told him she felt there should at least have been another doctor called in for a second opinion, and, when Mrs Greenwood's remains were buried, she questioned why there had not been a post mortem.

Harold Greenwood, either totally thrown off balance by his wife's death or simply heedless of appearances, at ten that morning drove to the office of the *Llanelly Mercury* and borrowed twenty pounds from Gladys Jones – the thirtyish daughter of the late proprietor of the newspaper, the very woman the telephone operator had heard answer the phone two days earlier – and the two of them went shopping for a funeral outfit for him. Greenwood would have seen nothing unusual about that: there was a remote family connection with Gladys's father, W. B. Jones, and, for years, both before and after the proprietor's death, the solicitor had walked over from his office on Frederick Street to lunch at the *Mercury* offices, where Gladys was employed.

Either the same day or the following day, a woman telephoned Greenwood on Dr Griffiths's line, and, after that, the same person called just about every day. At first Greenwood told Miss Griffiths it was the charwoman at his Llanelly office. No such thing, she chided him, it was Gladys Jones. He admitted she was right.

With Mabel safely buried in the graveyard of St Mary's Church, the rumours might have faded away – if they had not been fanned by Greenwood's behaviour. Nurse Jones, who had shared her suspicions with several others, including the president of the District Nurses' Association, now began visiting Rumsey House, ostensibly on legal business. The business sometimes kept her there late at night. Did she fancy herself as a private detective or, like other women, was she drawn by Greenwood's charms? She did admit to telling his fortune, so, perhaps it was she who put the idea of a honeymoon in the solicitor's head.

If she saw herself going on that honeymoon (there is nothing in the record to show whether Nurse Jones had a husband), her hopes were soon dashed. Mabel Greenwood had died on 16 June; on 12 July, Harold Greenwood proposed to Gladys Jones. On 27 July, after breaking off her engagement to an army officer just returned from India, she accepted a diamond ring, which Greenwood claimed he had originally bought for his daughter Irene, but had kept after giving Irene her mother's engagement ring.

Why the reckless haste? With the death of his wife, her sister, Edith Bowater, who had been living with the Greenwoods earlier, took charge of the household. 'It was not like a home,' Greenwood complained at his trial. Nurse Jones was only one of the women drawn to the affable and now conveniently widowed lawyer, and it's been suggested Greenwood married to get the pack off his heels. Neither of these excuses holds up. Greenwood could easily have asked Miss Bowater to leave and installed Irene to run the house; and if Harold Greenwood had enjoyed the company of women in the past, why should he stop now? It was simple folly that prompted him on 24 September to give official notice of their impending marriage on 1 October, folly that fanned the sparks of suspicion into a roaring blaze. And there was more.

On 26 September, a Friday, Greenwood had a tearful scene with Mary Griffiths, the doctor's sister, who had hoped and expected she would walk down the aisle with him. By Greenwood's account, she was crying and complaining that her friends were laughing at her. Would he, she asked, write her a proposal of marriage that she could then reject to save face with her friends?

Greenwood's explanation has the ring of truth: the letter he wrote on getting home, if it was a proposal of marriage, was certainly a contorted one. 'You are the one I love most in the world,' he wrote, 'and I would be the last one to make you unhappy. Under these circumstances, are you prepared to face the music? I am going to do something quickly, as I must get rid of Miss Bowater at once, as I am simply fed up. Let me hear something from you tonight. Yours as ever, Harold.'

On Sunday, with his marriage to Gladys now only three days off, Greenwood called on Mary Griffiths, 'very frightened that she might accept'. She obliged by refusing him, but, even on the very eve of his wedding, she was sending a message suggesting that the marriage licence he had purchased could easily be torn up. Mary, said Greenwood, 'went to bed howling. I was married the next morning'.

If anything, the shock experienced by Irene Greenwood when her father told her of his plans only two days before the wedding was even greater. She left Rumsey House and went to stay with relations in London and did not return until Christmas.

When Greenwood himself returned from his honeymoon, a police superintendent and an inspector were waiting to interview him. At the end of their talk, the superintendent – whose name, inevitably, was Jones – told Greenwood that, in view of the gossip and rumours, an exhumation order would be sought. 'Just the very thing,' replied the solicitor, whose small talk often sounds as if he'd limited his reading to *Boys' Own Annual*, 'I am quite agreeable.'

The investigation dragged on while the rumours

multiplied, and it was not until 16 April 1920 that the body was finally removed from the grave and a post mortem conducted in Kidwelly Town Hall, where Mrs Greenwood had kept one of her last social engagements. The body was exceptionally well preserved – sometimes an indicator of the presence of arsenic – but there was no sign of valvular disease or any other obvious cause of death.

'I am a victim of village gossip, of village scandal,' Greenwood assured a reporter from the *Daily Mail* at this time, 'and if you know Welsh village life you will know what that means. It all started from the fact that four months after my wife's death [actually three and a half] I married again.'

But an analysis of the organs revealed they contained a little over a quarter of a gram of arsenic. Two grams is generally considered a fatal dose.

'That beats me hollow,' Greenwood, indiscreet as ever, told a reporter from the *South Wales Post* when he was informed of the result. 'I cannot understand how they have found poison.'

'What can I say,' he told the *Daily Mail* rep two days later, 'except that the mystery seems to deepen every day? I should not have been the least surprised to know that they found poison of some kind, for during the last two years of her life my wife took many kinds of medicine.' He added: 'She was wasting away, and she knew it. She used to say, "I am dying on my feet," and to anyone who was associated with her it was quite obvious.'

His wife, he said, 'was so good, so kind.' Tears

sprang to his eyes as he told the reporter, 'We were very happy together ... It was always give and take with us.'

'And isn't that by far the better way!' interposed the second Mrs Greenwood.

Besides, said Greenwood, 'supposing I had bought arsenic anywhere, I should have had to sign the poison book, and that would be traced at once. As a matter of fact, I have not been beyond Kidwelly and Llanelly since October 1918.' The police, in fact, already had some interesting information regarding purchases of arsenic.

An adjourned inquest reopened on 15 June to hear the result of the post mortem. But the police did not wait. Even before the jury returned its verdict the following day, Harold Greenwood was arrested by two plain-clothes officers at Rumsey House and was later charged with murder. It was a year to the day since his wife had died. And when the coroner's jury announced its verdict, that Mrs Greenwood had died from arsenical poisoning 'administered by Harold Greenwood', the Kidwelly crowd cheered.

The trial of Harold Greenwood, which commenced in the Guildhall at nearby Carmarthen on 2 November 1920, had about it the festive air of a country fair, with all the hotel rooms for miles around taken and the streets thronging with people, many of those unable to get into the cramped courtroom remaining outside to boo the prisoner as he arrived and departed. Even Sir Edward

Marshall Hall, England's most famous and flamboyant barrister of that era, retained to defend Greenwood, had difficulty getting a room.

The Crown had taken more than a year building a case against Greenwood, but, as Sir Edward Marlay Samson, a Welsh barrister, rose to outline the facts against the country solicitor, he was aware there were significant gaps in the chain of evidence. The biggest involved motive. When Mabel Greenwood died, her private income of some £20 a week went, under the terms of her father's will, to her children, and, despite gossip to the contrary, Greenwood, to use his own words, had not insured his wife's life 'for a brass farthing'.

If he hadn't killed her for money, then – the classic scenario went – he must have killed her out of hatred or because he wanted to be free to marry another. But, as marriages went, the Greenwoods' seemed fairly benign, and the evidence suggesting Greenwood was having a raging affair with Gladys Jones before his wife's death was weak. His daughter Eileen, at Greenwood's suggestion, had invited Gladys to Rumsey House for the weekend in 1918 while his wife was away, and he travelled back to Llanelly alone with her on the train on the following Monday morning. Greenwood's charwoman in Llanelly testified that he would closet himself with Gladys Jones in the back room, and claimed that, either on the day Mrs Greenwood died or the day after, she found a scrap of burned letter in his fireplace in Gladys's handwriting that said, 'It will be nice when I am your wife', or words to the effect. Considering the tidal wave of gossip that had engulfed Harold Greenwood, these were slim facts to suggest a motive for killing.

Had Mabel, in fact, been poisoned with arsenic? There was a clear difference of opinion, with the Crown's leading expert, Dr William Henry Willcox, stating that the quarter of a gram found in the organs examined indicated there was enough in the rest of the body to have caused death. He estimated the poison had been administered nine hours prior to death and that the immediate cause of death was heart failure caused by prolonged diarrhoea and vomiting brought on by the poison. Dr William Griffiths, for the defence, was equally certain that the quarter-gram did not indicate a fatal dose. Although two grams was generally counted a fatal dose, people, he said, had been known to have five grams of arsenic in their systems without any deleterious effects.

If not arsenic, then what? Marshall Hall, ill throughout the trial, bad-tempered and frequently shouting at the witnesses, and even at the judge, had any number of answers to that question. At the inquest Dr Tom Griffiths had testified that the two pills he had prescribed for his patient shortly before her death each contained half a grain of morphia. Marshall Hall had medical experts standing by, prepared to say that a grain of morphia was sufficient to kill a woman with a weakened heart. But, at the trial, the doctor did a remarkable about-turn. He had made a mistake, he said. The pills were not morphia, but opium, each of them containing only a fortieth of a gram of morphia – nowhere near a fatal dose. Griffiths, who had retired from practice shortly after Mrs Greenwood's death, further undermined his credibility when, after promising to produce his prescription book in court, he arrived to say it had been burned by mistake. Although no morphia had been found in the body, Marshall Hall's experts, on the basis of Griffith's obvious unreliability and Mrs Greenwood's symptoms, were still prepared to say she died as a result of the doctor's mistake in prescribing morphia pills.

And, if the jury didn't buy that, Marshall Hall, following a middle-of-the-night inspiration, bought two bottles at a local drugstore, one of bismuth such as Griffiths said he had sent over for his patient, the other of Fowler's solution of arsenic, which he admitted he also had in his dispensary. The bottles looked alike, and both contained red fluid. Couldn't Griffiths have made a mistake and sent over the wrong bottle? he suggested. And, if that didn't explain it, couldn't the presence of arsenic in the body be explained by arsenic weed-killer getting into the skins of the gooseberries or being blown up from the lawn as Mrs Greenwood walked around the garden?

Because, if one thing was now certain it was that, if Harold Greenwood had wanted to poison his wife, there was more than enough arsenic to hand. On 23 April 1919 Messrs Tomlinson and Haywood, of

Lincoln, had dispatched a one-hundred-pound tin of Eureka weedkiller, a 60 per cent arsenic formulation, to Greenwood at Rumsey House. Marshall Hall asked a chemist from the firm if a seven-pound tin of Eureka would dispose of the whole population of the county of Carmarthen. 'Yes,' he replied to laughter, 'and more – if it was properly administered.' It was not enough: on 7 and 8 June, Greenwood purchased two tins of a liquid weedkiller called Weedicide from a local chemists.

John Webster, an analytical chemist who had examined the organs of the dead woman, gave the jury a dramatic demonstration of just how easy it would have been to put arsenic in the wine. When he handed jury members two small bottles of port wine, one adulterated with Eureka, one pure, visually they could not tell them apart. It would take about half a teaspoon in a bottle of port to ensure a fatal dose in each glass, he said.

Webster had even tasted the poisoned port. 'There is practically no difference to be detected,' he reported. Put into tea, said the chemist, the weedkiller caused a slight but almost imperceptible darkening.

Greenwood's explanation, delivered from the witness box, was that his wife had asked him to get rid of the weeds growing along the garden paths. With the help of the gardener, Ben Williams, he had opened the weedkiller, mixed it in another can, and spread it on the paths, using it all up the same day. Then he swept up all the unsightly worms killed by the arsenic and – we shudder to learn in this environmentally conscious age – threw the tins into the river. Greenwood was never asked, apparently, why he had purchased such large quantities of weedkiller.

In this welter of theories and possibilities, the central issue was: what really happened at lunch the day Mabel Greenwood was taken ill? Apart from family members, only Hannah Williams, the parlour maid, could say, and when she entered the box, a timid and obviously frightened young woman in a top-heavy hat, she only added to the confusion. She still insisted she had put out a bottle of port wine – which she said she never saw again after that day – and that her employer had spent a quarter of an hour in the china pantry before lunch. Irene Greenwood, she said, did not generally drink wine, and did not have a glass on this occasion.

But under Marshall Hall's aggressive questioning – several times the famous barrister was reprimanded by the judge for shouting at and bullying the witness – the girl repeatedly contradicted herself, and would finally answer, 'I cannot remember everything.' Other evidence showed Mrs Greenwood had been suspicious that one of the staff was watering the wine, and just before she died she had given Hannah Williams notice for coming in late. The cook testified to seeing the maid drunk her last day on the job. 'Are you a teetotaller?' Marshall Hall asked Williams. 'Yes, I am,' the girl replied vehemently, 'I am having a name for having drunk it [the wine that was afterwards watered] but I am not drunk today.' One day in the future, Hannah Williams, by then Hannah Edwards, would be mayoress of Kidwelly, but that day in 1920 she did not inspire confidence.

After interviewing Greenwood before the trial began, Marshall Hall had told his clerk, 'I am afraid he will make a bad witness.' Greenwood had been indiscreet and foolish, but the risk was that, if he did not testify, the jury would wonder what he had to hide. Marshall Hall, no doubt with trepidation, put his man in the box, and asked him basically one question, 'Had you anything to do with your wife's death?' It was followed by the inevitable response, 'Nothing whatever.' Greenwood was then turned over to the prosecutor. Speaking in a low voice, gathering confidence as the hours passed, Greenwood acquitted himself well. He admitted the follies leading up to his second marriage, including the foolish letter to Miss Griffiths, while denying he had had any romantic connection with Gladys Jones before his wife's death. He had washed his hands, as usual, in the pantry before that final lunch, and his wife, he said, drank either a glass of burgundy or a whisky and soda with her meal.

When Greenwood stepped out of the box, the jury was faced with a choice between two fairly plausible theories, one that said Mabel Greenwood had been poisoned at her own dinner table and that her husband was the only likely suspect; the other, that she could have died from any number of causes, none of them connected with her husband. But now Marshall Hall had the one witness available who could settle the matter – a witness that the police amazingly had never interviewed: Irene Greenwood.

A handsome young woman now of twenty-two, with fashionably bobbed hair, she spoke in a voice so low she could hardly be heard. Did she remember what they had all had to drink at that luncheon. 'Yes, I can remember everything about it,' she replied. Why was it she could remember so well? 'Because it was the day my mother died.'

There was not even a rustle of notebooks from the press bench. 'At lunch on Sunday,' asked Marshall Hall, 'what did you have to drink?'

Her answer was immediate: 'Daddy drank whisky and soda, Kenneth [her brother] had soda-water, mother and I had burgundy.' There was a collective sigh, an escaping of breath.

'If she also drank from the bottle,' the judge would say in his summing up, 'there is an end to the case.'

Irene also insisted that she drank more wine from the same bottle when she, her father and Miss Phillips had supper later. Florence Phillips, though, said, 'I know there was no wine on the table the night I was there. If there had been, I should have had some.'

Irene admitted under questioning that, after the exhumation, she had talked these matters over with her father, and conceded, too, that her father's second marriage had come as a great shock to her. But, despite any hurt she had felt over his hasty remarriage, she had been willing, as Marshall Hall would put it later, to save her father's life. She may, indeed, have drunk wine from the same bottle. If she didn't, then she must have fought a valiant battle of conscience before agreeing to testify. Perhaps it's significant that, in her testimony, she referred to 'Daddy' and 'Mother'. What were her feelings about her father? 'Daddy was always good to us,' she said. 'We were always together.'

Willing himself to the effort, Marshall Hall, in some pain, spoke for more than three hours on his client's behalf. Whichever way the verdict went, he told the jury with more truth than he knew, Greenwood was already a ruined man. Not waiting for the verdict, Marshall Hall, to Greenwood's disgust, took a private rail car to Cardiff, and was on the platform about to catch the London train when a porter told him the verdict. After deliberating just over an hour, the jury had found Harold Greenwood not guilty.

The Times, next day, editorialized, 'From the outset the prosecution had a weak case . . . When we read the flimsy evidence we marvel that the indictment was ever proceeded with.'

Suddenly it was as if everyone had known all along there was nothing to the gossip and scandal in Kidwelly. The prosecution experts were scorned, and the prosecutor, Marlay Samson, was criticized for a legal gaffe in his summing up when he questioned why the defence had not put the second Mrs Greenwood on the stand to corroborate her husband's story of their romance. Under the Criminal Evidence Act, such comment was forbidden.

In fact, although the public was not told, the Crown case had been rather stronger than most people believed. When the foreman, an industrial chemist named E. Willis Jones, delivered the 'not guilty' verdict, he handed the judge a sheet of paper that clarified the decision. It said: 'We are satisfied on the evidence in this case that a dangerous dose of arsenic was administered to Mabel Greenwood on Sunday, 15 June 1919, but we are not satisfied that this was the immediate cause of death. The evidence before us is insufficient, and does not conclusively satisfy us as to how, and by whom, the arsenic was administered.' The judge chose not to make the jury's detailed findings public.

Somebody in Rumsey House, accidentally or on purpose, gave Mabel Greenwood arsenic. Her husband and the doctor were the most obvious suspects, although a disaffected maid just fired by her mistress cannot be ruled out. Whether the arsenic or some other agent caused her death will never be known. But, one thing is certain – there was more to Mrs Greenwood's death than idle gossip.

The day following Greenwood's acquittal, as the Kidwelly solicitor began the hopeless task of putting his life together again, Herbert Rowse

Armstrong travelled by train to Cheltenham. The Greenwood case was big news in the papers that day, and May Lilwall, journeying from Hay in the same compartment, would remember that the Major talked continually about Greenwood's acquittal, seeming more excited and pleased about the verdict than you'd expect, even considering the fact that Greenwood was a fellow solicitor.

In no sense was the Greenwood verdict on 9 November 1920 the trigger that set off the tragic events at Mayfield. In May 1919, after all, Katharine Armstrong had gone to Dr Hincks with her original disturbing symptoms. On 20 August of the following year, when he next saw her, Dr Hincks was surprised to find her showing signs of mental deterioration. Her speech was affected and she had delusions, blaming herself for being unkind to her children and cheating tradespeople. She was afraid she would be arrested.

Armstrong immediately wired her sister, Bessie Friend, and an old family friend, a solicitor named Arthur Chevalier, who both hurried to Hay. After getting a second medical opinion, it was decided to commit Katharine Armstrong to a private asylum, of which Dr Arthur Townsend was medical superintendent. Doctors at the asylum were puzzled that Mrs Armstrong, in addition to running a high temperature, experienced pain in her arms and legs. Finally they gave her a tonic containing arsenic for a month, and her condition, both mental and physical, steadily improved.

By January 1921 Armstrong was pressing Hincks to have his wife released from the asylum, and sent home. Townsend resisted, arguing that she wasn't well enough yet, and finally suggested she be allowed home on trial, so that she could be returned to the asylum if she had a relapse. Armstrong was insistent: she must be given a full discharge.

When she came back to Mayfield on 22 January 1921 Katharine could not walk very well, although she seemed pleased to be home. A couple of days later she asked the nurse her husband had retained whether a fall from the third-floor attic window would be fatal. On 27 January, Armstrong sent for Eve Allen, an experienced mental nurse, who arrived the same night and remained around the clock with Mrs Armstrong. By 11 February, visitors reported her looking wasted and wan, and Dr Hincks, calling that day, found she had lost some of her coordination and that the peculiar high-stepping walking gait he had noted before she went into the asylum had returned. A few days later, after partaking of a Sunday lunch uncannily like that last lunch taken by Mabel Greenwood – mutton and vegetables with pudding and preserved gooseberries to follow – she vomited and was put to bed.

By 16 February, when Dr Hincks called again, she was in a serious condition, running a high temperature, complaining of abdominal pain, and unable to keep her food down. The morning of 22

February, she lost consciousness, and Dr Hincks, who had been making daily visits, told Armstrong she would not last the day. The Major's only reaction was to ask Hincks if he could give him a lift to his office, as he had a lot of work on hand. Soon after nine that morning, in the large, airy second-floor room that looks across the valley towards Hay, Katharine Armstrong died.

On the death certificate, Dr Hincks listed gastritis, heart disease, and nephritis as the causes of death, and Katharine was duly buried in the grave-yard at Cusop Church, where the Major frequently read the lessons.

It wouldn't be true to say that Mrs Armstrong's death did not arouse comment around town. John F. Davies, the town pharmacist, in particular, was suspicious. Beginning in 1913, he had sold the Major large amounts of arsenic for killing the weeds in Mayfield's extensive grounds. On 11 January 1921 his assistant, John Hird, sold the Major a quarter of a pound of arsenic, to which he thoughtlessly neglected to add the distinctive pink dye required when the poison was sold as a weed-killer. It was mid-winter, an odd time to be buying weedkiller. It was also the day that Armstrong, through Hincks, applied to have Katharine discharged from the asylum.

The suspicions were reported to the authorities, but they decided to take no action. Major Armstrong, after all, was clerk to the local magistrates and former worshipful master of the Hay Freemasons. And, besides, after the recent Greenwood affair, it was only natural that people with overactive imaginations would read something sinister into the sudden death of any solicitor's wife.

Those close to the Armstrongs were puzzled by another curious feature. In 1917, while her husband was away on service, Mrs Armstrong had carefully drawn up a will in which she left £50 each to her sister, Bessie, and to Arthur Chevalier; a small annuity for Emily Pearce, her elderly housekeeper; and the balance to come eventually to her three children. The Major was to receive £50 a year until 1933, and thereafter, £100 a year. At the funeral, Armstrong mentioned to Chevalier that, the previous summer, just at the time she was being committed to the asylum, Katharine had written a new will. Under its terms the Major would receive all her money. The earlier will was in Mrs Armstrong's handwriting. The new one, when it was presented, was in the Major's handwriting and had been witnessed by Emily Pearce and Lily Candy, a maid at the house.

With Katharine's tongue finally stilled, the Major was free to cut loose. The following month he left for Italy and Malta, where engagements with young women figure often in his diary. On his return to Hay, he became a frequent, if embarrassing, presence at local dances, where he often pestered young maids and farm girls. But there was a price to be paid for his new freedom: Dr Hincks was soon treating him for venereal disease.

And if Armstrong thought his worries were at an end with Katharine gone, he was soon beset with real difficulties in his law practice. Shortly before he had returned from war duty, another, younger solicitor, Oswald Martin, had become a partner in the only other law firm in town, that of Robert Griffiths, who practised right across the street from Armstrong. When Griffiths died shortly afterwards, Martin ran the shop, and he and the Major were in head-to-head competition. There were inevitable tensions: Martin, injured during the war, had never risen above private, whereas Armstrong was an officer, even though he had never come under fire. While she was still alive Mrs Armstrong had looked down on Martin as not quite a gentleman, particularly when, in June 1921, he married Constance, the daughter of John Davies, the pharmacist.

What was especially mortifying was that Armstrong's finances were in a mess and, at the same time, young Martin was taking business away from him. Disagreements between the two solicitors came to a head over closing the sale of an estate in the town of Brecon. Armstrong was holding a deposit of £500 but, through delaying tactics, managed to hold up the transaction for over a year, despite appeals from Martin who was acting for the purchaser. Finally, Martin wrote to say the sale would fall through if the deal wasn't completed by 20 October 1921. The Major stalled and won another week's delay.

Then, surprisingly, he asked Martin to tea at Mayfield. After putting him off several times, Martin agreed to go on Wednesday, 26 October, offering that morning to drive Armstrong out to the house in the afternoon. 'No, thank you,' the Major replied, 'I have something to do at the house so must go there before you.'

Considering their professional differences, it could not help but be an awkward occasion. So, Martin was surprised when Armstrong, not mentioning their problems, made a real effort to be cordial. But here's the curious thing: Emily Pearce had put out her homemade currant scones, uncut and unbuttered, along with buttered plain and currant bread. There was no butter or jam on the table. And yet, as twilight fell and the two men made polite conversation, Armstrong handed Martin a buttered scone with the words that stuck in the younger lawyer's mind, 'Excuse fingers.' As Martin was eating it, Armstrong went to turn on the gaslight and broke a globe in the process.

Arriving home at six-thirty, Martin put in forty-five minutes working with his clerk, Alan Preen, before Constance announced supper. 'I feel sick. I don't think I can eat anything,' her husband told her. After picking at his food, Martin was taken violently ill, vomiting repeatedly. Mrs Martin, a nurse, noticed that the vomit was dark and foul-smelling. When Dr Hincks saw him early next morning, Martin was recovering, and the doctor put his illness down to a bilious attack brought on by overwork and lack of exercise.

Curiously, Armstrong called several times at Martin's office that day, asking for him and, when he learned he was ill, enquiring about his health. 'It looks rather bad because he was up at my house to tea last night,' he told Preen in what was taken as a joke. And, meeting Martin on the street after he recovered, the Major said, 'It seems a queer thing to say, but you will be ill again soon.' Queer indeed!

His son-in-law's illness had not escaped the attention of Davies, the pharmacist. To Dr Hincks, he expressed his suspicion that young Martin had been poisoned. The doctor was startled by the suggestion, but after they had gone over Martin's eating pattern they concluded that the only food he had eaten away from home – where no one else had fallen sick – was tea taken with the Major. They should be on their guard, Thomas warned his daughter and son-in-law, against any further possible attempts to poison them. That was when they told Davies about the chocolates.

The previous month, they told him, a box of chocolates had arrived in the mail with no card and no return address. The couple ate a few and then produced them when Martin's two brothers and their wives were visiting. One of the wives, after eating some of the chocolates, suffered a bilious attack, a high temperature and a rapid heartbeat. When she recovered, her illness was put down to a chill.

Examining what remained of the chocolates, Davies discovered that some appeared to have been tampered with. In Davies's mind, that resolved the matter: he had his son-in-law provide a urine sample and gave it, along with the chocolates, to Dr Hincks to have them sent away for analysis. Days and weeks passed with no word of the result. Meanwhile, Martin was in a high state of anxiety: nearly every day Armstrong was pressing him to come to tea again, either at Mayfield or his office, and the younger solicitor was fast running out of excuses.

Dr Hincks, too, was a worried man. If he had been wrong in diagnosing Martin's attack, he thought to himself as he rode one day across the hills to see a distant patient, then perhaps he had been wrong about Mrs Armstrong too. Then, suddenly, it came to him – the high-stepping gait, the vomiting, the discolouration of her skin were all symptoms of arsenic poisoning.

It was on New Year's Eve, in the doldrums between Christmas and New Year's, when little legal work gets done, that Major Armstrong, a tiny soldierly figure (he weighed only seven stones) in riding breeches and an army greatcoat, walked down to his office to put in a couple of hours' work. With his back to the window of his cosy, second-floor office overlooking Broad Street, he did not notice three men enter the front office below. Giving instructions that Major Armstrong was not to be alerted, the three marched up the narrow staircase, knocked and entered Armstrong's office.

They introduced themselves as Superintendent
Albert Weaver, deputy chief constable of Hereford-
shire, and Chief Inspector Alfred Crutchett and
Sergeant Walter Sharp, both of Scotland Yard.
Crutchett, who, since he had been assigned to the
case on 10 December, had been sneaking into town
after dark to interview Davies, Martin, Hincks and
others, swearing them to secrecy, told Armstrong
that arsenic had been found both in Martin's urine
and in the mysterious box of chocolates, and invited
him to make a statement.

'I will make a statement and tell you all I know,'
said Armstrong. After dictating a statement in
which he denied giving poison to Martin or sending
the chocolates, the solicitor was formally charged
with administering arsenic to Martin. He was
asked to empty his pockets, and the contents, which
included several letters, were put on the desk.
Armstrong was asked to sit in the centre of the
room while they examined his desk, but when he
asked if he could sit at his desk and read some
business letters, this was allowed. A few minutes
afterwards, Crutchett noticed Armstrong was
going through the papers taken from his pockets.
He ordered him away from the desk. It would not be
until much later that the police, finally examining
the material taken from Armstrong's pockets,
would discover three love letters from 'Marion' and
a small white envelope containing a potentially
fatal dose of arsenic.

If the Black Mountains, in the lee of which Hay-on-Wye shelters, had disappeared one morning in a puff of green smoke, it could not have caused a bigger shock than the arrest of Major Herbert Rowse Armstrong on suspicion of trying to poison his rival. People refused to believe that the Major, a pillar of the local gentry, was locked up like some common thief in a cell at Hay police station. And then the tongues began to wag. The death of his wife ten months before was the focus of most of the gossip, although soon every suspicious death for miles around was being laid at his door.

The little Hay courtroom was jammed on 2 January, when the Major, just as if it were any old morning and he were coming to perform his customary duties, marched in and gave the magistrates a polite bow. Perhaps forgetting himself, he leaned forward and took part in the discussion of a time for the next hearing. Meanwhile, not far from Mayfield, spades were biting into the chilled ground as the exhumation of Katharine Armstrong got under way. It was dark by the time the coffin, preceded by a sexton carrying a hurricane lamp, was trundled on a trolley to nearby Church Cottage, where the windows had been boarded up in preparation for an autopsy to be conducted by Sir Bernard Spilsbury, the leading forensic scientist of his day. Based on the findings, Armstrong was charged on 19 January with the murder of his wife, and the issue of the tea party became secondary.

As an experienced solicitor, Armstrong realized that his arsenic purchases, his wife's peculiar death, the business of the will, not to mention Martin's illness, could be tied up into a very plausible package by an able prosecutor. But, surely his circumstances were hardly more suspicious than those surrounding the Greenwood case, and if Sir Edward Marshall Hall had been able to win an acquittal for Greenwood, why shouldn't Armstrong go free too?

Armstrong was ignoring a couple of things. Many of the prosecution lawyers, policemen and medical experts who had suffered a bruising loss in the Greenwood case would be on the team opposing him. And they didn't intend to lose again. In addition, instead of a terrier-like Marshall Hall (who was ill and unavailable), Armstrong chose as his leading barrister a much more placid counsel, Sir Henry Curtis Bennett, who was more used to prosecuting than defending. Certain remarks made by Curtis Bennett suggest he did not believe in his client's innocence, and he clearly intended to win by legal manoeuvring rather than a frontal attack on the prosecution.

When the trial opened in Hereford on 3 April 1922 Curtis Bennett was gambling that the judge, Mr Justice Charles Darling, who had tried Sir Roger Casement, Dr Crippen and many notable cases of the Edwardian era, would rule as inadmissible any evidence about the famous tea party as having no bearing on the main charge of murdering Mrs Armstrong. Without the Martin incident, it would be immeasurably easier to defend the

111

Major because no one had seen him administer poison to his wife. And, if she did die of arsenic poisoning, who was to say it wasn't suicide? But Curtis Bennett lost the gamble. Judge Darling, perhaps as determined as the prosecution that another lawyer 'wouldn't get away with murder', was consistently hostile to the defence side, asked mischievous questions of witnesses to put Armstrong in a bad light, and, most damaging, ruled the Martin incident admissible without giving any reasons. The only small bone thrown the defence's way: despite an exhaustive search, the police had not been able to trace the purchase of the chocolates, so these were not mentioned at the trial, although they had already figured in the preliminary hearings, which had been exhaustively reported in the press.

For the prosecution, Sir Ernest Pollock, the attorney-general, built a devastating circumstantial case against Armstrong. Lily Candy, the maid who had signed the second will, said the Major had instructed her to do so in his study, while the housekeeper, Emily Pearce, could not remember the circumstances of signing it.

An analysis of Mrs Armstrong's organs revealed the presence of more than three and a half grains of arsenic, and the indomitable Dr Spilsbury was definite in saying that a dose of five grains must have been taken by Mrs Armstrong in the twenty-four hours before she died. Nurse Allen and Dr Hincks were equally emphatic in saying the woman was incapable of getting out of bed and taking the arsenic herself during the last four days of her life.

The only real surprise was a piece of ambiguous evidence produced by Armstrong's solicitor, Tom Matthews, that still mystifies. After his initial interview with the police, Armstrong announced to Matthews that he had forgotten to tell them that the residue of the white arsenic was in a packet in one of his desk drawers in his study. Matthews went to Mayfield, searched the desk, but did not find it. The arsenic did not appear on a police list of items seized at the house, so Matthews returned several weeks later and, this time, found the arsenic, amounting to about half the amount purchased by the Major, jammed in the back of a drawer. Was it planted by the defence? By the police? Or was it simply, as Matthews suggested, an oversight, indicating that the police had been less than thorough? And what was its meaning? The judge chose to interpret it as an example of Armstrong's deviousness in his dealings with the police. Curtis Bennett said that, in that the discovery showed where the balance of the arsenic went, it might save Armstrong's life.

Armstrong's own explanation on the witness stand of the uses to which he had put the arsenic strained belief. Using one ounce of the white arsenic, he had made up twenty lethal little packages, using nineteen of them to kill nineteen individual dandelions. The one packet remaining was in his pocket when he was arrested. He realized now, he said, that each packet contained a fatal dose for a human being. After a stiff cross-examination from the attorney-general, Armstrong was about to step down when the judge intervened. 'Do you tell the jury that you absolutely forgot about that white arsenic?'

'I do,' replied Armstrong.

'Does it not occur to you it would have been a very, very bad case for you if you had to tell the police that you had got, not only [dyed] weedkilling arsenic but white arsenic in your possession.'

'But I did not remember it,' said the Major, floundering.

'That is not what I asked you,' said the judge, boring in.

'It would have to be explained,' said Armstrong weakly.

'Why make up twenty little packets, each a fatal dose for a human being, and put them in your pocket?'

'At the time it seemed to me the most convenient way of doing it.'

As Armstrong stepped down after six hours in the witness box, it was his final unconvincing replies to the judge's questions that remained with the jury.

Even though Mr Justice Darling's summing up was devastating for the defence, Curtis Bennett, perhaps remembering Harold Greenwood, was so confident of an acquittal that he went for a walk in the country outside Hereford, expecting to meet a freed Armstrong on his return. Stopping at a small post office, he was told by the woman behind the counter that her husband had just phoned the result: guilty.

Asked if he had anything to say before sentence was passed, Armstrong answered quietly, 'Nothing.' Putting on the black cap, the judge said he agreed with the verdict. He described as absurd and unsupported the suggestion that Mrs Armstrong had committed suicide. The little solicitor stood smartly to attention as Mr Justice Darling imposed the death sentence, then, without a word, he wheeled around and marched down the steps to the cells, soldierly to the last.

If Armstrong's thoughts had been with Harold Greenwood at the climax of the Kidwelly solicitor's ordeal, Greenwood was now thinking of Armstrong. In an article in *John Bull* magazine, Greenwood wrote, 'I know what the prisoner felt. Helpless, trapped, overborne.' For him, and probably for Armstrong, the judge's summing up 'is more painful than can be described. For a trained legal mind can appreciate exactly the effect upon the jury. As minute by minute the cultured, measured voice flows on, hope seems to evaporate.'

May 31 – Derby Day with the sun shining out of a cloudless sky – Armstrong, his appeal having failed, walked with erect military bearing to the scaffold set up in the yard at Gloucester Gaol, and declared to the governor, 'I am innocent of the

115

crime for which I have been condemned to die.' He was so light that the hangman had to allow for an unusually long drop of eight feet eight inches to ensure that his neck snapped. He was the only lawyer ever hanged in England.

It was not unusual for men and women to go to their deaths proclaiming their innocence, even in the face of the most damning evidence. (Armstrong, too, might have wanted to provide his children, who were taken into the care of Arthur Chevalier, with a chance to believe in his innocence.) In poisoning cases, the evidence is almost invariably circumstantial – what poisoner invites witnesses? In Armstrong's case there was motive – the apparently forged will, the years of abuse from his wife – opportunity, and a suggestive chain of evidence. But there is another version of the case, developed but never published, by Thomas Kane, who became convinced of Armstrong's innocence as he read the newspaper reports of the trial while still a schoolboy in Leatherhead. He went on to a career as a tea planter in Sri Lanka, then Ceylon, but never forgot the case, and continued to research the background.

Kane, eighty-five when I spoke to him, finds the clue to the mystery in the underlying social currents that were never mentioned in court. Major Armstrong, he says, was gentry, whereas John Davies, the pharmacist, wasn't. Davies had a vested interest in seeing Armstrong arrested: his son-in-law, Martin, would gain a good deal of business. Davies had resigned from the Masons, apparently after a dispute, and may have borne a grudge against Armstrong, a strong lodge man.

Armstrong had another enemy in his sister-in-law, Bessie Friend, who, says Kane, disapproved of her sister's marriage and thought Armstrong 'a horrid little man'. It was under the influence of her sister, he argues, that Katharine wrote her 1917 will, leaving her money to her children, and it was only when her husband returned from the war that she began worrying that she had dealt unfairly with him and had him write a new will.

After extensive reading on the effects of arsenic and a close study of Mrs Armstrong's symptoms, Kane suggests that it is quite possible that the large dose that proved fatal was taken on 17 February, five days before her death. A prying woman, she may have found the Major's packet of arsenic in the cupboard in his study and, mistaking it for bicarbonate of soda, taken it as a remedy for the biliousness she was feeling at that time.

As for the tea party, it was Davies who handled the urine sample, with the chance to tamper with it, and the purchase of the chocolates was never traced. Could it have been, asks Kane, that Davies bought and posted the chocolates, injecting a non-fatal drug, that would cause a bilious attack, into some of them, adding the arsenic only when the chocolates were to be sent away for analysis?

Kanes's thesis is intriguing, if not finally convincing. It's stretching credibility to suggest that Davies would have gone to such elaborate measures to ensnare Armstrong. And two incidents of arsenic poisoning in one small town – well, that's rather hard to stomach.

But, in one regard, both Greenwood and Armstrong received less than justice. Both men were tried on the local gossip mills, and Greenwood was lucky enough to survive. If Armstrong were being tried today, a Hay lawyer, Elizabeth Charles, assured me, he too would likely be found not guilty. The preliminary hearing, especially after the Greenwood fiasco, received such huge publicity that it would have been virtually impossible to find jurors who were not already aware of every detail of the prosecution allegations. Even so, she said, Judge Darling was mistaken in allowing in the tea-party evidence, and that alone should have resulted in a successful appeal. 'I certainly think,' said Charles, as we drank afternoon tea – without scones – 'that if he was being tried now he would be acquitted simply because they were unable to connect him with administering the arsenic.'

But was Armstrong guilty? I asked Charles, who has made an extensive study of the case. She paused before answering: 'I am not convinced either way.'

Rumsey House, in Kidwelly, is today a scene of desolation. After a deal to sell it to the local authorities as a cottage hospital fell through, a religious group called The Independents bought it from Greenwood in 1924 and turned it into a chapel. A gaunt, overbearing building about 150 years old now, it never attracted much of a congregation, and today it's just a mouldering white elephant. The garden where Mabel Greenwood took her daily walks and Harold worked so arduously on the weeds is overgrown now, with brambles filling the flowerbeds and a solitary monkey-puzzle tree brown and dying.

Greenwood himself suffered no better fate. After travelling restlessly for several years, he settled with Gladys on a ninety-acre farm in the village of Walford, near Ross-on-Wye, just a few miles from the scene of the Armstrong drama. They assumed the name of Pilkington, but everyone knew who they really were, and gossip still pursued them. Not even the birth of a little girl to Gladys could lift Greenwood's spirits. He aged rapidly, in 1928, at fifty-four, suffering a stroke that left him paralysed on one side, and died on 17 January 1929, eight years after his trial. 'When we have been out shooting,' a friend, Arthur Morgan, recalled, 'I have known him suddenly burst into tears. Sometimes, when we were walking through the woods, he would talk about his first wife, but it was almost disconnectedly. During later months he seemed like a man in a daze, very sad and worried.'

In Hay-on-Wye you will still find Armstrong's legal offices on Broad Street, his glass-topped desk still in front of the second-floor window, the swivel chair occupied today by a man who wonders about

the meaning of it all. When Martin Beales arrived
in Hay in January 1977 to article with a local solicitor, he had no idea the practice had once
belonged to the notorious Major Armstrong. When
he and his wife Noelle rented an old, renovated
schoolhouse, they only discovered afterwards that
it was here that the inquest was held on Katharine
Armstrong. The coincidences continued: when they
acquired a horse for their children and needed a
house with a paddock, the Beales ended up buying
Church Cottage, where Sir Bernard Spilsbury long
ago conducted the famous autopsy. When Beales
was made a junior partner in the firm, he was not a
bit surprised when he was assigned Armstrong's
old office, with the furniture and even the law
books exactly as the Major had left them when he
was arrested in the room on New Year's Eve in
1921.

There was an inevitability now to the whole
thing. A few years later, a BBC interviewer, doing
a historical item on the Armstrong murder, had a
chat with Beales in Armstrong's office. He had just
come from Mayfield, he said, and he'd learned that
the reclusive couple living there wanted to sell.

'We're bound to live there then,' Beales told the
surprised BBC man. 'It's fate.'

For years Mayfield had been sinking into disre-
pair, dandelions finally conquering the tennis court
where the Major had once dealt out his deadly little
doses. The gates were always closed, the house was
usually in darkness, and most people thought it

was empty. But it had, Beales thought, possibilities. He let the couple know he might be interested.

It was eighteen months later that the wife came to his office one day to say she and her husband wanted a smaller place and would be happy to swap Mayfield for Church Cottage – with a modest cash adjustment. Beales, who had given up smoking, went into the next office and lit a cigarette. Noelle Beales, with three small children – the same number the Armstrongs had – was not excited at the prospect, until she saw the house.

'This house embraced us,' she told me, as I had lunch with the family in the big, bright kitchen at Mayfield. 'I think the spirit of the house has overcome anything that happened here. It was waiting for us to make it into a real family home again. It just seems to enjoy having the kids roller-skating in the hall and sliding down the banisters.'

Guests are sometimes hesitant about sleeping in the big front room where Katharine Armstrong died, but the children refer to it dismissively as 'the dead woman's room', and are not a bit intimidated. Beales recalls only one upsetting incident: 'Our bedroom, you see, was once the day nursery,' he explained. 'And soon after we moved in here, I woke up one night with a start. I could hear a child crying, "Daddy, Daddy!" And my eyes, for some reason, watered.'

The door to the larder, where Armstrong supposedly doctored the scones, was open; the drawing room is much as it was when he offered a scone to

Oswald Martin with the immortal words, 'Excuse fingers.' But with the front of the house cheerfully painted up, rooms sunny and bright, and the sound of children playing in the garden, it takes an effort of the imagination to go back to the sinister events of 1920 and 1921.

To Martin Beales, though, the sequence of events that has brought him and his family to Mayfield seems just too neat. 'What's the purpose of it all?' said Beales, who owns a strongbox filled with documents from the case, and who has even considered writing a book on Armstrong with a local crime writer, Kate Clarke. 'Why has all this happened to us? Why? What are we supposed to do?'

Perhaps nothing at all, I told him. If the spirit of Mayfield is at peace, what more is there to say?

THE DEVIL SAID, TRY CHLOROFORM

You would have liked Dr William Henry King, I'm sure. Everybody did. Tall, charming, energetic, with a sensuous mouth and dark hair, from beneath which he studied his patients with intense brown eyes, he was an overwhelming favourite with the ladies and, in turn, found it difficult to resist their charms. 'Women,' he would write ruefully in his prison cell, 'have been my ruin.'

But, looking back on it all later, it was difficult for people to see how a man who embodied so many of the nineteenth-century virtues could have gone so wrong. At his very first school, when he was only five, his abilities were so pronounced that his teacher would take him to other schools on exhibition days to recite from the stage. When he was eleven years old, his parents homesteaded in the rough country of eastern Ontario, north of what is now Brighton, and a few years later his father became ill.

Young William Henry, in his mid-teens, took

over the farm operation and built up wheat production to a respectable 1,200 bushels. Mature in his manner, he was remembered later by his younger brothers and sisters as more a parent figure than a sibling.

His schooling during this period was restricted to two months in winter, and then often at the hands of incompetent teachers. After the harvest of 1851, when he was eighteen, his parents sent him to Normal School in Toronto, where, in two years, he obtained a first-class teaching certificate.

King was a young man in a hurry. On New Year's Day 1855 he married Sarah Ann Lawson. She was a plain young woman, but she had her uses: her father, John M. Lawson, was a well-to-do farmer who might be expected to provide financial help for King's projected medical studies. The support could not have amounted to much because, when the young couple moved to Hamilton, at the west end of Lake Ontario, where King taught school and studied medicine, Sarah took in boarders to help keep them afloat.

But already there were rumours that King was abusing his wife, and she went home to her parents. It was there, a year after their marriage, that their first and only child, a daughter, was born. King did not take to the baby and, after a month, she died – we hope, of natural causes.

The trouble with Sarah, as far as King was concerned, was that she refused to shake off her country ways. Her conversation was still of the farm kitchen, her manners clumsy, her small talk abysmal. What sort of wife was this for a smart and up-and-coming doctor? From Hamilton he wrote her cruel letters, accusing her of infidelity – letters she showed to her father. Later King apologized, and the letters were returned to him through a friend, but John Lawson was careful to keep copies.

Whatever distress he had caused from afar, in person William Henry was irresistible. He returned to Brighton, was reconciled with Sarah, and even persuaded his father-in-law to give him some money before he set off for two years' study at the Homoeopathy Medical College in Philadelphia, where one of his professors would describe him as his ablest student. He received his diploma in March 1858, returned to Brighton, and went into practice.

From the start, his services were in demand. 'His whole exterior appearance,' said a contemporary report, 'was not only prepossessing, but showed that he was a man of strong, original intellect and determined perseverance.' He was gentlemanly, a regular church-goer, careful in his speech, and well dressed. He was soon pulling in between $100 and $200 a month, a comfortable income for that time. Beneath the genteel exterior, though, King seethed, rueing the day he had married frumpy Sarah.

Now he realized he could have married just about any one of the far more attractive young women flocking to his office. Or was he deluding himself? When he sent one of his Quaker patients, Miss

Dorcas Garrett, a declaration of his affection, adding that his wife was likely to die within a year and suggesting that she should apply herself to learning the skills necessary for a doctor's wife, she was properly shocked. Miss Garrett demanded an apology and declared she would have nothing more to do with him.

Then, on 23 September 1858, only six months after King had gone into practice, Melinda Freeland Vandervoort, a coquettish twenty-year-old, came fluttering into his life like an exotic butterfly. On that day, Melinda took it into her head to pay a visit to Sarah, whom she had known several years before. But, soon, William Henry and Melinda were ignoring Sarah and impressing each other tremendously with their wit and sincerity. Time flew by, and it was nearly evening when Melinda said she really had to be going because she was visiting Sarah's parents too.

'I'll get out the horse and we'll drive you over there,' offered her host. As they drove home later, after leaving Melinda to stay the night at the Lawsons', Sarah said tartly, 'Miss Vandervoort says she has fallen in love with you.' He hunched over the reins and said nothing. 'She loved you before she ever saw you.'

'That would be most singular,' he said.

'Oh yes,' said Sarah, nodding. 'She saw your likeness at my father's while you were away in Philadelphia, and she fell in love with you there and then.' He was grateful that the darkness hid the flush that had come to his face.

Next day, Miss Vandervoort returned to the Kings'. In the evening they gathered around the piano while she sang 'Old Dog Tray', 'Kitty Clyde' and 'Hazel Dell', and William swore that, while he had heard many young ladies sing in Philadelphia, she surpassed them all. 'In fact,' he would write later without a trace of remorse, 'her beautiful voice completely intoxicated me. What a desirable accomplishment in a companion, thought I to myself.'

He added: 'Mrs King had no tune at all, and I never knew her to sing a word. She had no taste for music, the very thing I was particularly fond of. I had urged her very strongly to try and cultivate a taste for and learn music, but it was quite impossible.'

Miss Vandervoort stayed the night, and next morning, as she and William took a lingering farewell, she promised she would send him her likeness. A few days later it arrived at the post office with a note: 'Dr – Please inform me if you receive this. I arrived home safe and quite well. Truly yours, M. F. Van.' 'Sweet little sugar lump of good nature,' he began his reply the same day, 10 October, 'I long looked with prudent anxiety for the arrival of the object of my thoughts, but began to despair. Still I had too much perseverance, and I walked to the P.O. this morning and found the most precious thing (except the original) on earth. Better to me than all California. Could I indulge in the hope that those winning and genial smiles would ever be found in my possession, all troubles would then cease. It is a perfect infatuation to me. Can you keep from sacrificing yourself on the hymeneal altar for the next year? I wish so.'

And why should Miss Vandervoort hold back from marrying anyone for the next year? Almost as an afterthought, William Henry added, ' — [meaning Sarah] is very sick. Last night we thought she would die.' At that point Sarah King was quite well. It was not until four days later that she fell ill.

In her reply of 18 October, Miss Vandervoort pronounced herself overwhelmed and a little confused. 'I hardly know in what manner to address you,' she wrote. 'As circumstances are with you, it appears almost in vain for me to think of you only as a friend. Yet something seems to whisper, "Still hope." Since I first had the pleasure of an introduction, my heart is constantly with you and I am not contented for a moment. O! could I for ever be with you, I think I should be happy.'

Then she added playfully, 'Well now, Dr, don't you consider it very wrong of me to correspond with you? I'm afraid if known it would destroy Annie's [Sarah was known by her middle name] happiness and if I were in her position I would much rather be in my grave than suffer the idea of your intimacy with another.'

At that point Sarah King had other worries. She was gravely ill, and her husband was assuring her she was not likely to recover.

Arriving at the young couple's door on the morning of 14 October in response to a summons, Mrs Lawson found her daughter declaring herself a little better than she had been earlier. But, after William gave her a spoonful of a white medicine, she began vomiting. 'Keep it down, Annie,' he told her.

'She tried to do so, but she could not,' Mrs Lawson would say. 'The vomiting continued fifteen or twenty minutes.' Two hours later he gave her another dose of the medicine, which Sarah complained was fiery-tasting, with the same results.

What was the matter with her? William Henry spoke vaguely of a fall she had taken getting down from the buggy a few weeks before. She was also two months pregnant, and he announced that her womb was 'cankered right through'.

In the weeks that followed, Mrs Lawson was never away from her daughter for more than an hour. One day she found black spots on a nightdress of Sarah's and showed it to her son-in-law. 'Burn it,' he said, but, when she didn't, he cut out the spots with scissors. As Sarah failed to improve, her father wanted to know why another physician was not called in. His suggestion only angered his son-in-law. Finally, on the father's insistence, Dr A. E. Fife made several visits but, perhaps out of feelings of delicacy where a fellow-physician's wife was concerned, he did not examine Sarah and simply prescribed ipecacuanha and camphor, a mild remedy, for the vomiting, which, he thought, was caused by her pregnancy.

On his last visit, on 3 November, Sarah told him, 'I feel much better than at any time since my illness began.' Dr Fife would say, 'She did not look like a dying woman.'

That evening she was worse, and her husband brought her a mixture in a teacup. 'Here's Dr Fife's good medicine, Annie,' he said. When she said it burned and refused to drink any more, John Lawson was ready for a showdown. 'William Henry, if God spares my life, I will have a jury of doctors in the morning,' he declared.

'Who would you have?' asked King.

'Dr Gross for one,' said Lawson.

'Gross is the greatest enemy I have. I know very well what he would prescribe.' And what would that be? 'Calomel and opium,' replied William Henry. Would it ease her, Lawson wanted to know. It might. 'Would you take it, Annie?' William asked his wife. 'If it will do me any good,' she replied weakly.

King returned from his office a few moments later with something in a spoon. A moment later Sarah vomited. 'Keep it down, Annie,' he ordered, holding her down by her shoulders. 'Oh, oh, I cannot. I'm dying,' she gasped.

'Now, she's thrown it up!' said her husband, exasperated. 'She must have some more.'

'Give her very little,' pleaded Lawson.

'I won't give her a quarter of what Dr Gross would give her,' said King grimly.

After a second dose Sarah went to sleep. The following day, at Lawson's insistence, Dr Gross was called in, but there was little to do. By evening she died.

Her husband was prostrate with grief, sobbing and throwing himself about. Finally, he had to be given a sedative. But when the Lawsons suggested an autopsy, he declared Sarah had been firmly against it.

On 7 November, following Sarah's instruction, the body of her baby was disinterred from the cemetery, and together, mother and daughter, they were buried on the Lawson farm. At the funeral, King was again overcome with grief. The Lawsons were not convinced. Several days before her daughter's death, Mrs Lawson, who had heard rumours about her son-in-law, took advantage of William's temporary absence from the sickroom to go through his jacket pockets. She found the likeness of Melinda Vandervoort, kept it, and said nothing.

A pattern of suspicion was forming. A friend of Sarah's reported that Dr King had told her that, while Sarah was a good wife from a financial viewpoint, he would like her improved in many ways. The letter from Miss Vandervoort had been discovered, and now Miss Garrett came forward with the indiscreet letter King had sent her. The day after the funeral, Clinton Lawson, Sarah's brother, took the evidence to Simon Davidson, the county coroner. When it also emerged that Dr King had purchased half an ounce of arsenic a few days before his wife fell ill and later a quantity of morphine, the coroner did not hesitate: he ordered an inquest, empanelled a jury, and had Sarah's body exhumed.

The body was placed on a door and carried to the schoolhouse where, in the presence of the jury, a post mortem was conducted by candlelight by Drs Gross, P. R. Proctor, and James Gilchrist.

The findings: body and organs were in healthy condition except for the lungs, which presented a congested appearance, but not sufficient to cause death. The womb contained a healthy foetus three or four months old. The doctors were particularly interested in the stomach, which appeared congested and contained a dark fluid, and the bowels, which showed signs of inflammation.

The stomach, obviously the key to the mystery, was removed and placed on an earthenware dish in the sight of the jury so that no one could tamper with it. When the inquest adjourned for the night, the coroner washed it, put it in a pickle jar, and took it with him to Brighton, where it was locked in a closet at Mr DeLong's tavern, the coroner's lodging for the night. 'I kept the key in my pantaloons, which I did not take off that night as I sat up writing out papers relative to the inquest,' Coroner Davidson would testify.

Next day, as the inquest resumed, the stomach again took pride of place on the table in front of the coroner so that the doctors could better study it by daylight. Eventually Davidson put it back in the jar, sealed it, and dispatched it to Kingston, where a professor at Queen's University refused to examine it and sent it, in turn, to the University of Toronto. There the much-travelled organ was finally examined by Henry Croft, a professor of chemistry. He found it contained eleven grains of arsenic. Two grains can kill.

King would claim that the arsenic could have been added after death; to preclude such a defence, Croft immediately sent for the liver and kidneys. He found some arsenic in the liver, which, he said, could not have been added after death.

Meanwhile, King, returning from his rounds the day the inquest was called, got word of it and left home straightaway, saying he had to contact the authorities.

At ten o'clock that night, John Vandervoort and his wife, Elizabeth, had already gone to bed when there was a banging on their door. A man they had never seen before, who introduced himself as Dr King, said he had an urgent message for their daughter. Melinda was called, and the two went into a room on their own.

After an hour, Vandervoort knocked on the door and asked, as any prudent father might, if the message was delivered yet. The answer was in the negative. Presently, the couple emerged. 'My wife has unfortunately died,' King explained. 'They have got her body up and, in consequence of a likeness of your daughter being found in my pocket, a warrant has been issued for my apprehension as well as your daughter's.' They were accusing him of poisoning his wife, he said. It wasn't true, but he felt it would be wise if he took Melinda to her aunt's across the American border until things were straightened out.

Showing a surprising lack of discretion – and a vote of confidence in King's persuasive powers – the couple entrusted their daughter to this stranger they had just met, and saw the two ride off into the night.

Sarah's brother, Clinton, was enraged at the news. He had himself sworn in as a deputy and, with a revolver and a warrant for King's arrest in his pocket, he too rode southward. Picking up the couple's trail, he crossed the St Lawrence River and, at St Vincent, on the American side, he learned of their whereabouts.

Accompanied by a US marshal, he approached an isolated farmhouse, telling the marshal to knock at the front door while he hung back. In a couple of minutes, Lawson saw King leap out of a back window and run towards the woods. Seeing his brother-in-law in pursuit, the doctor dashed into the barn.

'We went in,' Lawson would report, 'and found him under the straw in a hogs' nest.' Brandishing his gun, Lawson told him he would be shot if he ran. Did King come willingly? Lawson was asked later at the trial. 'No, sir,' he told the judge. And then he shook his head: 'No, siree!'

King's flight to the United States had provided

the prosecution with undeniable proof of *mens rea*, or guilty mind. But poisoning is notoriously hard to prove, and when on 4 April 1859 large crowds converged on the town of Cobourg for King's trial, the presence of a dozen top-hatted and frock-coated pillars of the medical establishment engaged to testify either for or against the accused, clearly indicated this would be a hard-fought legal battle. The medical faculty of Victoria University, in fact, gave their students time off to attend the trial, believing no doubt that they'd learn more of a practical – and perhaps moral – nature in the courtroom than in the classroom.

King, according to a contemporary account, entered the courtroom 'with a light, airy step, dressed in gentlemanly manner in a suit of black broadcloth, with a gold chain across his vest'. But most of the ladies who had arrived in their carriages to see the handsome young doctor had turned back at the sight of the crush.

Melinda Vandervoort was an early sensation in the witness box, claiming that it was Sarah and not William who had asked for her likeness. 'I never had any improper intercourse with Dr King,' she insisted. 'I sent him [the] letter for amusement.'

'Go down,' said the prosecutor, Thomas Galt, severely. 'I must read these letters, but not in your presence.' King made no good impression when he joined in the general laughter as the letters between himself and Miss Vandervoort were read.

With his first witness, King's counsel, the Hon. John Hillyard Cameron, established the defence line. Professor Charles J. Hempel of the Homoeopathy College in Philadelphia, who had taught King, testified that, in homoeopathic medicine, 'for the cure of disease we administer medicines, which, if taken by a healthy person, would produce a like disease.' For cholera morbus, for example, he would prescribe arsenic, which, if taken by a healthy person, would produce symptoms similar to the disease itself.

It was a defence more easily believed in the nineteenth century, when people commonly dosed themselves with small amounts of poison. For Asiatic cholera, Professor Hempel said, he had prescribed a fifth of a grain of arsenic, the dose to be repeated twelve to fifteen times in the course of twenty-four hours. 'The patients have done well and recovered,' he reported.

Sarah's death, he suggested, was the result of either nervous exhaustion or the cumulative effects of arsenic. Prosecution witnesses had testified that arsenic is not a cumulative poison, but, on that point, Hempel, who argued that it is, has been vindicated by modern knowledge.

A. H. Flanders, a Philadelphia professor of chemistry, testified that he would himself have prescribed arsenic for a pregnant patient experiencing pain and vomiting, and ascribed her death, not to the poison, but to her earlier fall from the buggy. He was hissed from the public galleries when he suggested the arsenic found in Sarah's stomach was introduced after death.

Dr Thomas Nichol, a Canadian in practice for three years, offered himself as living proof of Hempel's and Flanders' theories. In 1855, he testified, he had given himself a third of a grain of arsenic three times a day for twenty-one days to gauge its effect. He had no symptoms until the eighth day, when he experienced fever, vomiting, thirst and violent purging. The symptoms persisted for three weeks after he stopped taking the arsenic. He had also experimented with another poison, belladonna, and found it produced paralysis in his legs, said the rash young physician.

It was an ingenious defence, and apparently an effective one because, after an afternoon of deliberation, the jury was still unable to agree and – an unusual move for that day – adjourned until the next day. But by ten the next morning, the foreman was able to announce a verdict: guilty with a recommendation for mercy. There could be no more socially dangerous crime than a doctor using his medical skills to commit murder. The mercy recommendation in that light was ludicrous and can have resulted only from some sort of compromise in the jury room to arrive at a verdict.

The decision struck King like a thunderbolt. It was obvious that, in spite of everything, he had expected to go free, and he was struggling to control his emotions as he was led away. Two days later, brought back for sentencing, he looked 'ashy pale' as Chief Justice Robert Easton Burns told him, 'I cannot see that yours is a case in which such a recommendation [for mercy] is justifiable,' before passing the death sentence.

According to a diary kept by an anonymous constable who guarded King during the two months while he awaited execution, the prisoner initially felt very sorry for himself, repeating over and over, 'O, what an unfortunate man I have been! Is it possible I must be executed?' His death, he said, would finish his poor mother.

He was visited by a steady succession of ministers with whom he prayed, and, on 20 May, the constable, who frequently joined in the prayers, could report, 'Dr happy now in the love of God.' Dr Norman Bethune, who had been a witness against him, now called on him regularly and laid down a programme of exercises to keep his colleague fit.

Finally, sighing, 'O, how I wish I had never married,' King sat down to write his confession for publication in the newspapers. If his confession was intended as a warning to others, it must be counted a failure. It starts well enough: 'Having sinned against society as well as God, I feel it my duty to confess my guilt with deep humiliation and sincere repentance.'

But humility quickly turned to callous self-justification. He had been cruelly disillusioned when he discovered after his marriage that Sarah was not a virgin, he wrote. 'The law may compel man and wife to life together, but I defy it to compel them to live together.'

And then – and you can sense his spirits lifting – King turned to contemplate Melinda Vandervoort. 'She was both lovely and loving. I looked upon her with all her personal charms and attracting graces and virtues, her attainments and literary acquirements, her mild and affectionate disposition . . . and it was as impossible for me not to love her as it would be to fly to the moon.'

He still insisted that Sarah's illness stemmed from her fall from the buggy and from her pregnancy, and solemnly denied giving her arsenic until she showed symptoms of cholera morbus. 'Here I may observe that the whole scientific world are [sic] deceived in reference to the cause of death . . . for I must assert that arsenic had nothing whatever to do in causing death.' It was as if, in murdering his wife, King had been indulging in a stupendous schoolboy joke at the expense of the experts.

On her last evening, he wrote, Sarah had asked him if he planned to marry Melinda. 'No,' he replied. 'You are engaged to her,' his wife insisted. 'You're crazy,' he answered.

Then Sarah King finally emerges to us as a living and properly resentful woman. 'Oh, that bitch! That bitch!' King reports her as saying. And a few minutes later: 'O, Lord, take me out of this world. I don't want to live. Can't you give me something?'

'Now here was a temptation I could not resist,'

wrote King, expecting his readers to sympathize. For the previous three weeks, he said, he had been thinking of ways to shorten her life, 'yet I would never have killed her by violent means. But here was (something whispered to me) just what you want and you will not be guilty yourself. I said, "Will you take anything yourself?" "O, yes," responded she. The Devil said, try chloroform.'

Just before daybreak, related King, as Sarah's parents slept, he fetched a half-ounce vial containing about a drachm of chloroform, 'which I gave her'. In the morning she was half-conscious as they got her out of bed and into a chair while the bed was made, but later she sank into a coma from which she did not recover.

King's 'confession' was greeted with derision and anger. His talk of Sarah taking chloroform, in any case, does not have the ring of truth. Taken internally, it sears the throat and is difficult to swallow, and, suggests Douglas Lucas, director of the Centre of Forensic Sciences in Toronto, if it had been administered in the normal fashion, dripped on to gauze or cotton wool held over the mouth and nose, it is not likely Sarah would have been semiconscious the following morning, sinking into a coma later. And wouldn't her parents have smelt chloroform in the room? The fact was that, whether by arsenic or chloroform, Sarah King was dead, and her husband was responsible.

Snow coated the countryside as I walked up the hill

outside the old Cobourg courthouse (now part of a senior citizens' home), where the scaffold was set up on 9 June 1859. Thousands had been trailing into town since the previous day, bringing picnics and making a holiday of it. As King mounted the steps, they formed a sea of faces beneath him.

'It is very hard,' began King, reading from a prepared text, 'to be deprived of life in comparative youth.'

'What about your wife?' shouted a voice.

As King urged them to take warning from his example, people began shouting to the hangman, 'Get on with it!' The doctor brought his speech to an abrupt end, wiped his perspiring hands on his trousers, and shouted, 'I bid you farewell – a long farewell.' He shook hands with his friends and kissed his brothers, then, after a mask was put over his head and his hands were tied behind his back, he kneeled on the trapdoor for the rope to be placed around his neck.

A long sigh escaped from the crowd at the thud of the rope. Suddenly the bright summer day seemed not as festive after all, and people began drifting away without speaking.

And Melinda Vandervoort? She took up first with an American and then with a man in Montreal, finally returning to Brighton, where she lived under the scornful eyes of her neighbours. Reportedly she died in a Toronto asylum in the late 1890s after taking to drink.

King, whose likeness can be seen in the carved

face that crowns the front doorway of Victoria Hall – the Cobourg courthouse and municipal offices officially opened by the Prince of Wales, Queen Victoria's eldest son, the summer after King was hanged – was buried at his parents' farm in the hamlet of Codrington, north of Brighton.

It was there I met Lloyd Ames, eighty-seven, who told me King was his mother's uncle. He was born in the King family home, and remembered Dr King's gravestone well. He and his brother had stripped away the undergrowth long ago to note down the dates on the stone. But, a few years ago, said Ames, his son, who had moved into the homestead, called him to say that while ploughing up a field to put in strawberries, he had hit the gravestone, breaking it clean in half.

'Well,' said Ames, 'I went up there and I dug a hole somewhere else and I buried the pieces. I put 'em good and deep. Thing that happened so long ago, I reckon it's better to let bygones be bygones.'

HANDYMAN
SPECIAL

'This is your first officer speaking. We're just commencing our descent into New York – La Guardia, ladies and gentlemen. Conditions are clear, visibility eight miles, and the temperature in New York this afternoon, fifty-two. We expect to have you on the ground on schedule at four-fifteen. It's been real nice having you along with us, and thank you for flying Eastern.'

Airline pilots are people we trust. We trust their competence, their training, and most of all the unflappability we detect in those drawling, reassuring public announcements from the flight deck. The voice tells us that here is someone capable of dealing with any crisis – calmly, coolly and with an almost superhuman degree of self-control. And we don't stop to think that if, by some chance, an airline pilot turned to murder, those same qualities of discipline, self-reliance and coolness in the face of danger might equip him to be a killer of impressive competence.

Murder was exactly what Richard Crafts, a forty-nine-year-old first officer with Eastern Airlines, had in mind one day in October 1986, as he pulled out of the Eastern parking lot at La Guardia in his lumbering Ford Crown Victoria and headed north towards his suburban home in Connecticut. The mission target would be Helle, his thirty-nine-year-old Danish-born wife, who worked as a flight attendant with Pan American Airlines, and as Crafts reviewed his plans he must have taken a certain wry satisfaction in ticking off the assets that would be working in his favour.

The car alone tells us something about Richard Bunel Crafts. The identical model to that used by the police, it had antennas front and back, a red flashing light behind the grille, and another flashing light that could be put on the dashboard. Crafts was, in fact, without the airline knowing, a part-time cop with the Southbury police force not far from his Newtown home. As a policeman, he knew the procedures, knew too that cops weren't likely to push hard in an investigation involving a fellow officer. But that was only part of the story.

The son of a well-to-do New York certified public accountant, Crafts had a mediocre academic record, and only really found himself when he joined the Marines. He headed a Marine drill team, learned to fly planes and helicopters, and, in 1960, while still in the military, began flying combat and training missions with the Laos army for Air America, an arm of the CIA. A dour individual who turned on the charm only when he had to, Crafts talked little about his CIA days, but it's certain his training would have included hand-to-hand combat and instruction on how to withstand interrogation – including how to beat the polygraph.

In his basement, despite Helle's fears that one of their three children – Andrew, ten; Thomas, eight; and Kristina, five – might be shot accidentally, Crafts kept a whole armoury of weapons, some of them loaded, in addition to a loaded revolver in a drawer in their bedroom. But shooting Helle Crafts would be too obvious. Too many husbands had tried the old ruse of inventing an intruder to account for the presence of their dead wives on the family-room rug. A guy with Crafts's experience could surely come up with something smarter than that.

Crafts was a machinery buff, but he rarely got around to fixing things around the house; their dilapidated home at 5 Newfield Lane, in Newtown, was the despair of their neighbours, as it was always cluttered with vehicles and equipment, including a huge backhoe for which he started to build a shed that he never finished, a pickup truck, a tractor, two riding mowers, a snowblower, a cement mixer, a log splitter, a generator, and thousands of dollars' worth of tools.

As a cop, Crafts knew it was no big deal when a person went missing. Hundreds of missing-person reports are filed with every police department every year, and the people usually turn up later unharmed. It would not be unusual for a flight attendant – with the possibility of boyfriends in far-off places – to skip out, and Crafts figured his wife's disappearance, even if it was reported, would give the local police no great concern. The real challenge was disposing of the body. And Richard Crafts believed he'd discovered a way, using his handyman-equipment savvy, to make Helle disappear without a trace. He'd just need to do some shopping – heavy-equipment shopping.

Crafts congratulated himself that, by lucky chance, one element of the plan was already in place: he owned a plot of building land just a few minutes' drive from his home, land overgrown with brush and ideal for concealment. Now, he told himself as he drove along, unaware of the autumn reds and golds along the suburban streets, he would just have to put himself out to be cordial to his wife in the coming weeks to prevent any hint of suspicion.

Helle Crafts, everyone agreed, was a nice person. Fluent in English and French, as well as Danish, she had been one of eight Danish women hired in Copenhagen by Pan Am as flight attendants in 1967, and it was while Helle, tall, slim and, inevitably, blonde, was training in Miami that she met Crafts. Until the day of her death, people would wonder why she put up with him. Handsome in a rugged bulldoggish sort of way, with a mop of unruly dark hair always falling into his eyes, Crafts's giveaway feature was his mouth – small, tight and, apart from the rare occasions when he smiled, mean.

146

Fidelity was not a notion Crafts was familiar with. Even when, later, he and Helle were living together, Crafts always insisted on keeping up affairs with other women. As a pilot, he would explain, opportunities came his way, and why should he reject them? They had a stormy, on-again-off-again romance, Helle at one point getting an abortion after Crafts beat her up. They were married finally on 29 November 1975, when Helle was four months pregnant, and the following year bought the house in Newtown.

It would be truer to call it the exurbs rather than the suburbs, the large lots tending to isolate people rather than bring them together in any sense of community. The Crafts's neighbours hardly knew them – except as the owners of that unsightly mess of machinery – and Helle found her friends mostly among other flight-crew families dotted around the Connecticut countryside. With both Richard and Helle on flying schedules that took them away up to a week at a time, they didn't even see that much of each other, and a succession of nannies were more of a constant in the children's lives than their parents.

Helle made the effort, conscientiously attending PTA meetings, and making a big thing of family festivities like Thanksgiving and Christmas. To be fair, Richard Crafts did his bit in the Cubs as a father and, with his welding equipment and tools, he was Mr Fixit when neighbourhood kids' toys broke. Other than that, he was an aloof father, leaving the parenting to Helle. He also had a violent streak, knocking Helle to the floor once when they were having dinner with friends. She made no public complaint and when she'd appear with black eyes, she'd make the excuse that she had just banged into something.

Then, in the summer of 1984, Crafts was diagnosed with cancer of the colon. In August, he had an extensive operation, and it would be sixteen months before he was able to return to flying. During that time, as Helle nursed him, she thought they had become closer and that their marital troubles were behind them. But, soon after Crafts started flying again, she became suspicious of charges on their phone bill to a New Jersey number. Crafts seemed to be away flying more than usual, and when she had a friend at Eastern check his flying schedule, she discovered he was slotting in extra time away from home, presumably to spend with another woman.

In September 1986, Helle went to see Dianne Andersen, a lawyer who handled the divorces of many air-crew couples in the area. At her suggestion, and in order to put Crafts at a disadvantage in the coming divorce action, Helle hired a private investigator, Keith Mayo, who quickly identified the owner of the New Jersey number as Nancy Dodd, an Eastern flight attendant. Shortly afterwards, Mayo and an assistant photographed Crafts emerging one morning from her apartment and being very affectionate before climbing into his

Crown Victoria and heading for home.

Mayo had warned Helle to be extra nice to her husband so as not to arouse suspicion that he was being tailed. Instead, she couldn't hide her hurt, and let him know she knew he was seeing the other woman. Worse, she told him his girlfriend's name would certainly be dragged into the divorce. Crafts too may have said more than he intended: Helle told several of her friends, as well as the lawyer, Andersen, something rather odd. 'If something happens to me,' she told them all, 'don't believe it was an accident.' But she wouldn't explain. Starting 12 November, the sheriff made several attempts to serve divorce papers on her husband. Crafts eluded him without much difficulty.

On Tuesday 18 November three women driving from Kennedy Airport towards Newtown were full of talk about their preparations for Thanksgiving, just over a week away, and Christmas. She had bought two turkeys for Thanksgiving because everyone in the family liked drumsticks, said Helle Crafts, casting her eyes up. Helle and her friends, Trudy Horvath and Rita Buonanno, both also Pan Am attendants, had been an hour late arriving home on their flight from Frankfurt, Germany, due to headwinds. But they counted themselves lucky: they had just missed an early winter snowstorm fast approaching the East Coast and due to dump at any moment. At the Crafts home, the live-in nanny, Marie Thomas, was out at her part-time job, working at McDonald's, but after a quick glance at the vehicles in the driveway, Helle announced, 'Richard's home.' Reversing out of the driveway, Trudy could see Helle heading for the door with her flight bags. It was the last time anyone outside the Crafts house saw Helle – alive or dead.

It was snowing heavily by the time Marie, the nanny, arrived home at 2:00 a.m., and the house was quiet. By 6:00 a.m. Crafts was waking her. The heavy snowfall had brought down powerlines, he told her. The electricity was off, the house would soon be ice-cold, and he was taking her and the children to the home of his sister and brother-in-law, Karen and David Rodgers. The haste to get the children up and fed seemed unwarranted: the house had fireplaces, Crafts had prided himself on being self-sufficient in using wood heat, and, besides, there was an emergency generator in the garage. Where was Helle? 'She left before us. She'll meet us at my sister's,' explained Crafts, looking tired, his hair wet and clinging to his head as they climbed into the pickup. Why, Marie wondered vaguely, even if the move to the Rodgers' was necessary, would Helle leave others to get her kids ready and bring them? Their mother wasn't, in any case, at the Rodgers' when they got there. Where was she? 'I don't know,' Crafts told Marie irritably.

That evening Rita Buonanno tried to reach Helle at home and was told by Crafts, 'She's not here.' When she called the following morning, Marie said her flight bags were gone so she must be working. Marie did not share with Rita a second discovery she had made: a large dark stain on Helle's favourite rug in her bedroom, a stain that Crafts said had been caused when he spilled some kerosene. A couple of days later he threw the rug and several others out, and a man called to measure for new broadloom.

Later, Crafts called Rita to say Helle had phoned him from London and was on her way to visit her mother in Denmark, who was sick in hospital. That was strange, considering Helle had phoned her mother, with whom she was very close, while they were in Frankfurt that week and hadn't said anything about her being ill. Helle did not turn up for a Pan Am training class she was supposed to attend with Rita the following day, but when Rita reported for the Frankfurt flight the two women were scheduled for on 22 November – four days now since Helle had been seen – she noticed her friend's Toyota Tercel in the Pan Am parking lot. Helle did not report for the flight.

When she returned from Europe two days later, Rita again contacted Crafts, who this time gave her a number for Helle's parents in Denmark. Only after calling a second time with the assistance of an operator who spoke Danish did she discover it was the wrong number.

As the week went on, and Helle failed to show for another flight, Rita and her other friends at Pan Am were becoming increasingly worried. It was so out of character for the almost compulsively conscientious Helle to disappear in the middle of a snowstorm, leaving her children behind without an explanation, and if she missed one more flight she stood to lose her job – something she couldn't afford to do with divorce looming.

Rita had hesitated to call the Newtown police because Crafts had once worked there, and she didn't feel they would take her concerns seriously. But, by 1 December, something had to be done, and Rita and two friends of Helle's called the lawyer, Dianne Andersen, who in turn called Keith Mayo. Scenting publicity for himself and his fledgling agency, Mayo pestered the Newtown police, who showed little interest in the case. The private detective's abrasive ways would even have turned Helle's friends against him, but it was Mayo who, on a tip that the stained rug had been taken to a landfill, persuaded the landfill site crew, for a price, to sift through tons of rubbish, searching for the item. On 16 December they thought they'd found it. In fact, it would turn out to be the wrong carpet, but its discovery did eventually help spur the authorities to action.

The following day, Patrick O'Neil, a young reporter with the *Danbury News–Times*, had a story in the paper headlined, 'Police Seek Missing Newtown Woman'. Crafts's reaction when O'Neil had called him was: 'I have no comment.' To others Crafts had been telling a different story – that Helle had taken off with an Oriental boyfriend with whom she had been having an affair.

Still, the Newtown police showed little interest –

and for what they thought was a very good reason. They had interviewed Crafts and, with no trouble, had persuaded him to take a state police polygraph test. The pilot passed the test, even giving a negative answer to the question, 'Did you kill Helle?' without registering any giveaway reaction. How could he be lying? To beat the machine, Crafts could have inflicted pain on himself while answering unimportant questions, by, for example, having a tack in his boot, so that his reaction would be no different when he responded to the key questions. Or, drawing on his military training, he could simply have blanked his mind from any feeling while he answered.

So, Helle's car remained unclaimed and unexamined in the Pan Am lot, and no tests were done on the carpet. Finally, after a good deal of pushing from Mayo, Andersen and Helle's friends, state attorney Walter Flanagan intervened and demanded a proper investigation of the mounting accusations against Crafts. And, right away, the cops hit pay dirt.

Checking Crafts's credit-cards purchases, they discovered he had bought bedding worth $257.96 on 19 November – perhaps to replace bloodstained bedding he had disposed of after the murder. Even more interesting, on 18 November, the day Helle disappeared, her husband had rented a woodchipper, a heavy machine for disposing of tree limbs and logs. And then a Southbury cop remembered something that had seemed curious, but not

significant at the time. A highways employee, Joey
Hine, snow-ploughing along River Road the night
of 20 November, had told him of seeing a man
operating a woodchipper.

Yes, Hine confirmed when detectives found him,
it was around 3:30 a.m. when he'd spotted the
woodchipper, which was attached to a truck, and –
the darnedest thing – a man in an orange poncho
had stepped out and directed him and a car coming
the opposite way around the truck, just as if he
was a cop directing traffic. A couple of hours later,
heading back towards the garage, he'd seen the
woodchipper again near a bridge, and had noticed
several piles of woodchips along the river bank at
that point. Two other people would report seeing
the woodchipper in operation beside the bridge that
night, and a Southbury constable, Richard Wild-
man, at 4:00 a.m. on 21 November, saw Crafts, still
in uniform at the end of a police shift, putting his
police equipment into a truck attached to a woodchipper. What was he doing with a woodchipper?
Clearing tree limbs brought down around his house
by the storm, Crafts claimed.

The woodchips were still there beside the river,
spread about an inch thick on the ground. And, just
as if Helle Crafts was trying to tell them something, the attention of the two officers accompany-
ing Hine to the spot was immediately caught by an
envelope on the bank. 'American Cancer Society' it
said on the front. It was rain-sodden, but the
officers could still make out the addressee through

Pam and Greg Smart on
their wedding day. Greg
was shot dead just a week
before their first
anniversary (*AP/Canapress*)

Abbé Adélard Délorme

Mrs Isabella Ruxton. More than thirty parcels containing her dismembered body were discovered in and around a ravine in Moffat, Dumfriesshire (*Popperfoto*)

Dr Buck Ruxton, who was hanged for the murder of his wife, Isabella, and his maid, Mary Rogerson (*Hulton Picture Company*)

Harold Greenwood (*Syndication International*)

Mr and Mrs Oswald Martin. Herbert
Armstrong's attempts to poison
Oswald Martin eventually led to the
exhumation of Katharine Armstrong's
body and his being charged with her
murder (*Syndication International*)

Herbert Rowse Armstrong
(*Syndication International*)

The reburial of Mrs Katharine Armstrong on 6 January 1922, following
the autopsy by Sir Bernard Spilsbury (*Syndication International*)

Dr John Baksh and Dr Madhu Baksh after their wedding at Bromley Register Office (*Photonews Service*)

Richard Crafts being brought to Danbury courthouse on the morning of his arrest for the murder of his wife, Helle (*The News-Times, Danbury, Connecticut*)

Jeanette and Pat Kelly. On 29 March 1981, he threw her to her death from the balcony of their seventeenth-floor apartment

Dr William Palmer
(*Hulton Picture Company*)

Mrs Edith Morrell. On being charged with her murder, Dr Adams made the potentially damning statement 'Can you prove it was murder?' (*Popperfoto*)

Dr John Bodkin Adams. It took the jury only forty-six minutes to find him not guilty (*Topham*)

Dr Arthur Warren Waite

Dr Marcel Petiot
(*Topham*)

The many suitcases
visible here contain the
clothes and belongings
of the victims who
believed that Petiot
would help them to
escape to safety
(*Topham*)

the plastic window: 'Helle L. Crafts.'

Convinced the chips would tell the story, the police gathered up more than thirty bags of them, took them back to the station, and spread them out on tables in a garage for the grisly search to begin. Embedded in the chips, officers found clumps of blonde hair, bits of bone, and a metal dental crown. More fragments of flesh and hair were discovered among wood chips found in the trunk of the Crown Victoria, and a further search of the bank produced another pathetic piece of evidence – a pink-painted fingernail, some flesh still attached to it.

The pattern was becoming clear. The police suspected they would find another piece of equipment that had played a part in Helle's murder. A few hours later, divers scouring the bottom of the river found it: an orange chainsaw of a type owned by Richard Crafts. The serial number had been filed off.

Still the search went on, and on 14 January Dr Constantine Karazulas, a forensic dentist, standing up to his boot-tops in the flowing water, saw something gleam. It was a tooth cap, with part of the tooth still attached, and it would play an important part in identifying the remains as belonging to Helle Crafts. Another search, this time of the Crafts house, produced little – except some blood spatters on a mattress that, from the angle they fell at, suggested Helle had been bending or kneeling down – making the bed perhaps? – when she had been struck. Obviously expecting the search, Crafts had left a note on the fridge that began, 'Helle, I'm at mother's with the children. Please come.' It was dated 23 December, although Crafts had left for Florida with the children on 22 December.

Reporter Pat O'Neil, tipped off, was hiding behind bushes in Newfield Lane the night of 13 January as state police surrounded Crafts's house. Ordered with a loud-hailer to come out with his hands up, Crafts's only answer was to switch lights off and on, appearing in front of windows, then disappearing. 'Leave me alone,' he shouted once, opening the door briefly. When an officer phoned, he said, 'I want to say goodnight to the kids. I'll be out in five minutes.' Shortly after, Crafts gave himself up. A neighbour entering the house found the children in their nightclothes and asleep in bed.

The detailed story of what happened the night of 18 November will likely never be known. It can only be pieced together from charge slips and clues here and there. Richard Crafts may have first conceived his scheme for disposing of his wife after hearing about a case the summer before, when a man was charged after putting a German shepherd dog, whose barking annoyed him, through a woodchipper. Crafts would have realized that to put a body through a chipper would produce a grisly mess. We can deduce his answer from his purchase on 13 November of a $375 home freezer. The same day he purchased a shovel and a pair of fire-proof gloves – useful for burning incriminating evidence.

Crafts's first suspicious purchase had occurred back on 29 October, when, without telling his wife, he had bought a 1980 Volkswagen Rabbit. If Helle's car was to be left at the Pan Am lot, Marie would need another car to get around. On 22 November, in fact, the Rabbit was in the driveway, and Crafts, without explanation, handed Marie the keys.

The woodchipper Crafts planned to rent weighed more than four tons – not something that could be towed by a car or light pickup. So on 10 November Crafts, for $15,000, bought a dump truck, which he said he needed for spreading gravel on his driveway. The truck, in fact, was not ready by the 18th, and Crafts was forced to rent a truck to go to pick up the woodchipper.

How did Crafts carry out the crime? Arthur Herzog, in his book *The Woodchipper Murder*, conjectures that, judging by the droplets of blood, Crafts may have come up behind his wife in the bedroom and struck her with a heavy object, quite possibly the police rechargeable flashlight he kept in the bathroom. It had the advantage that, if she turned and saw it in his hand, she would not see it as a weapon. With a few hours before Marie was expected home from her job at McDonald's, Crafts would have wrapped the body in bedding, carried it out to the freezer, which he had already running and lined with plastic sheeting in the back of his Toyota pickup, linked with an extension cord to the garage. He would have had to lower the freezer to the ground to open the top, and then lift the loaded freezer back into the truck before heading indoors for the big clean-up.

During the night he would have moved Helle's Tercel to his secluded vacant lot – planning to drive it to the Pan Am lot later. The unexpected snow so far had helped his plans, keeping people indoors, but on his return he found the storm had caused a power cut. Would Helle's body still freeze? If the worst happened, and the power stayed off, he could still use his emergency generator. While everyone slept, he gingerly lowered the freezer from the truck, dragged it into the garage, and jammed the garage door shut. (When he hustled Marie and the children out of the house in the morning, they were surprised that he made them walk down the treacherous front path instead of going out the usual way through the garage.)

Herzog believes Crafts now backed the truck to the rear of the house, loaded up a bloodstained boxspring and bedding as well as Helle's travel bags and belongings, and took them to the vacant lot for burning. Later that day, after taking Marie and the children to his sister's, Crafts would have loaded the freezer back on the truck, along with the generator, and driven them to the vacant lot, where, starting up the generator from time to time, he could keep the body frozen.

With the dump truck unavailable, Crafts must have been in a sweat until he finally procured a rental truck on the 20th. Only then, and with some trepidation at having to use the conspicuous rental truck, would he have returned to the vacant lot and, using a chainsaw, sliced the limbs and head from the frozen body, putting them into plastic bags. Because none of the fragments found among the woodchips relates to the torso, some experts conjecture that he disposed of that elsewhere. Herzog suggests that Crafts used his pickup to tow his wife's Tercel to the Pan Am lot, unhitching it some way away, then driving it the last short distance.

The murder was carried out with imagination and resourcefulness. Had it been an exercise in strategy, Crafts would have scored high points for the originality of his plan and the flexibility he showed in responding to surprise factors like the snowstorm. The major flaws in his scheme were his reliance on credit cards – with their tell-tale slips – and his plain, dumb ignorance about human motivation. He apparently didn't realize people would not believe a dedicated mother would leave her children right before Thanksgiving, and the various stories he told to explain her absence only served to point the finger of suspicion at him.

Why did he do it? A divorce would cost him plenty and he'd lose his house. But there was more to it than that – revenge. Richard Crafts wasn't going to have some detective snooping in his life, was not going to have his girlfriend's name dragged into this. Not when he knew how to handle it.

At his trial, which began in New London on 14

March 1988, prosecutor Flanagan had to prove two things: that Helle Crafts was, in fact, dead, and that her husband had killed her. Through no fault of his own, he failed.

People have been successfully prosecuted for murder in the past where no body was found. In this case, all the forensic scientists had to go on was seventy-five fragments of bone, five droplets of blood, 2,660 strands of hair, three ounces of flesh, two fingernails, a portion of a finger, and two tooth caps, the whole amounting to no more than a handful. Who could say if this was Helle Crafts?

The blood type – O – matched Helle's. Dr Karazulas, who had found a crown and part of a tooth in the river, was prepared to say on the basis of Helle's dental X-rays that it and the other cap matched hers, and the hair strands were blonde. But the links in the chain of identification were loose enough that the prosecution basically had to depend on the evidence of Crafts' suspicious behaviour to secure a conviction. Early on in the trial, although Flanagan didn't know it, the case was doomed when a juror, Warren Maskell, a Vietnam vet, catching what he thought was a smile between Helle's mother, who had come from Denmark to testify, and Crafts, formed the fixed opinion that Helle was still alive somewhere. With Maskell the only holdout on the jury, the judge called a mistrial.

In November 1989, at the end of his second trial, Richard Crafts was found guilty of murder. The trial was a replay of the first one with the exception of the evidence of his brother-in-law, David Rodgers, an ex-Navy commander. At the first trial, Rodgers, who sided with his brother-in-law during the investigation, was defensive on the stand. By the second trial, he had made up his mind. Crafts, he testified, had told him there was no body left for the police to find, and that he had disposed of the evidence.

Karen Rodgers, Crafts' sister, who had custody of the three Crafts children, urged Judge Martin L. Nigro to impose the maximum sentence on her brother. 'I am concerned that Mr Crafts has not publicly nor privately demonstrated any remorse for the murder of his wife,' she said. 'I believe he has paid lip service only to the concerns of his children.' Judge Nigro obliged by sentencing Crafts to fifty years in prison. At the time of writing, he spends his days in the library at the state maximum-security prison at Somers, Connecticut, preparing grounds for appeal.

Patrick O'Neil tells me that these days he feels 'kind of spooky' listening to those calm detached voices from the flight deck when he flies. Of course, most pilots are decent ordinary folk, good fathers and faithful husbands. But, says O'Neil, in his part of Connecticut, the hinterland of several major airports, 'you get to know a lot of pilots, and a lot of them are not unlike Richard Crafts. They have this ego trouble, they're on a macho trip. They seem to have been married and divorced three times; they seem to function in a whole other world.' O'Neil has spoken to men who flew with Crafts: 'They say he was a very good pilot.'

DR BAKSH'S SACRIFICE

Thank heavens for the intrepid British naturalist. Neither rain nor dark nor muddy swamp can turn him from his quest. In Keith Corbett's case, it was toads. Corbett, a professional ecologist specializing in reptiles and amphibians, was doing field-work on the night of 4 January 1986, on Hayes Common on the outskirts of London, when he heard the unmistakable sound of frogs croaking and splashing in a pond.

Now, Corbett has a special warm spot for toads and, in particular, the toads that live around Keston Ponds, in South London, and breed against all odds. The trouble is that, during the mating season in March and April, the toads foolishly sit in the middle of the road, waiting for a mate. What they frequently encounter instead is a car. The result: splat! No more toad.

Corbett was campaigning at the time to have Fishponds Road, as it is called, closed to traffic during the toad mating season, but Bromley

163

Council, within whose jurisdiction the picturesque ponds lie, wanted more proof of toad activity. And that's how Corbett, who describes himself as 'a naturalist with nocturnal habits', became mixed up in murder.

If the frogs were active on Hayes Common, thought Corbett, then likely the toads would be up and about in their hibernation spot, called Caesar's Bank, at Keston Ponds. So, instead of going home, he drove to the ponds, switched off the motor and, walking soundlessly and with his ears attuned for any sound in the darkness, he made his way to the bank. 'I heard a wheezing noise,' he would say later. 'At first I thought it was an injured fox.' As he came closer he was able to make out a pair of legs – women's legs – sticking out from under a holly bush.

'My initial reaction was that she was drunk. For a moment I didn't want to get involved. Then I touched her and she was wet and sticky.' By the light of his flashlight he saw blood everywhere. Running to the nearest house up the road, where a party was taking place, Corbett cried, 'Help me! There's a woman in the park and someone's tried to cut her head off!'

Melodramatic – yes – but it certainly got attention, and within a few minutes the woman of the house had brought a blanket and was rubbing the chilled hands of the terribly injured woman in the park. When the ambulance had departed with her and the police asked their inevitable questions,

Corbett offered an interesting scientific obser-
vation: as a biologist used to dissecting, he had
noticed the cut in the woman's throat had been
made neatly – as if by a professional. The detectives nodded and thanked him. 'Stick to your toads'
was the message he got.

In hospital, the woman was identified as a doctor,
forty-three-year-old Madhu Baksh, and a colleague
performed an emergency operation that narrowly
saved her life. That evening, at around 9:30 p.m.,
her husband, fifty-three-year-old John Baksh, who
was also a doctor, had reported to the police that his
wife was missing. She had left their £400,000 house
at about 5:00 p.m. to do some shopping before the
shops in Bromley closed, and he feared she had
been abducted. Sure enough, the police found her
grey Ford Orion car abandoned in the town centre
and next morning issued an appeal for anyone who
might have seen the abduction to come forward.

That morning, Madhu Baksh opened her eyes in
hospital to see her husband's face close to hers. He
was smiling and holding a bunch of flowers. But it
was a smile of desperation. Speaking in Hindi so
that police and nurses nearby would not understand, he told her she must say that masked men
surrounded her and kidnapped her. Unable to
speak, she shook her head. How many men were
there? he asked, getting her to rehearse her story.
And then, in what surely must be one of the most
dramatic murder accusations of recent times, she
held up one finger to indicate there was only one

165

attacker. Mutely she pointed her finger at him.

Baksh pleaded, 'Save me, save me, or I will go to gaol.' She began to be afraid. She worried about the safety of her two children from a previous marriage. And, finally, she agreed to tell the false story.

Baksh, enormously relieved, returned to his two general medical practices in nearby Eltham and Chislehurst (a stone's throw from Winston Churchill's home, Chartwell), and sent her a note: 'My darling Madhu, I am very sorry for what happened – that I put a knife to your throat. I did not know what I was doing and hope you soon recover. Children are fine. Love, ever, John.'

But as she mended, his wife was more and more troubled by the lie. Finally, still unable to speak, she wrote on a blackboard, 'My husband is a killer. Tell the judge he killed his first wife.' This time, when the police came to see her, she told them the real story, a bizarre story that had its beginnings in 1970 when her first husband brought the leonine and very charming Dr Baksh home one day. Ten years later, the petite and dazzlingly pretty, and by then separated, Dr Madhu Kumar joined the practice run by John Baksh and his wife of twenty-one years, Dr Ruby Baksh.

Madhu was surprised one night to find John Baksh at the door of her Bromley apartment, holding out a bottle of champagne. 'Why are you alone?' he asked. 'This is the permissive society.' She made him dinner, they drank the champagne, and kissed for the first time. 'I liked it as a woman,' she would say, 'but I was afraid what I was getting into.' By October 1982, she was saying that she would marry him if he divorced Ruby.

That could be expensive. Baksh had a better idea, which he kept to himself. On 23 December 1983 he took Ruby and their two children to stay at a villa near Almería, in southern Spain. The couple went out to a party New Year's Eve, and by next morning Ruby was dead. 'She suffered from a heart condition,' Baksh told the elderly doctor who attended. The doctor put down heart attack as the cause of death.

Ruby's relatives wanted the body flown back to England, but Baksh insisted she had loved Spain and would have wanted to be buried there. That didn't stop him complaining about the large funeral bill when it was presented, and Paul Polanski, film director Roman Polanski's brother, helped get the bill knocked down.

On New Year's Day, Baksh phoned Madhu and broke the sad news. It had been so sudden, he said. They had gone to bed, and when he woke the next morning she was dead. 'He seemed very upset and depressed,' she said.

Sorry for him, Madhu agreed to care for him and his two children, and, two weeks later, although her divorce was not final, he arrived at her home with two rings, one of them his dead wife's wedding ring, so they could go through an informal Hindu ceremony.

'I always had statues of Hindu gods on my chest of drawers,' said Madhu afterwards. 'We stood in front of them. He put the rings on my finger, and I bent down and kissed his feet. I got up, we embraced, and he said, "From now on you are mine." From that moment on I considered I was his wife.' A year later, when Madhu's divorce came through, they were married officially.

By then, Madhu was in possession of a terrible secret. In May 1983 they were staying at a hotel in Montparnasse in Paris. He was lying on the bed while she got changed, when he asked her to come closer. 'John started to cry,' she would say. 'I was surprised. I stroked his head to comfort him and asked what was troubling him.' The courtroom would be absolutely still as she repeated his words: 'He told me that he had sacrificed Ruby for me.' What did he mean? She asked him to repeat it. Ruby always had a glass of milk before going to sleep, he said. That New Year's Eve, he had spiked it with sleeping pills. When she was soundly asleep, he had given her a massive injection of morphine in her thigh. Ruby hadn't suffered a bit, he reassured her.

'I felt as though I had fallen from heaven to earth,' said Madhu. 'I felt a mixture of disbelief, fury, and depression. I was in absolute turmoil. The man who I loved and I thought was so wonderful was actually a murderer. I was lying next to him.' Baksh's reaction after creating this turmoil: he wept a little more, turned over, went to sleep and began snoring.

The questions that Madhu Baksh will be answering for the rest of her life are: why on earth didn't she report her husband to the police? Why, at the very least,' didn't she leave him? And why, eight months later, did she actually marry him?

Her first reaction, she said, was to run out of that hotel room, screaming to the world what he had done. Baksh told her what was done was done. But even flying home to London she was determined she would tell the police at the first opportunity. As soon as he left their apartment, she locked the doors and went to the phone, intending to call the police. Why didn't she?

'I thought, supposing the phone is bugged. Supposing John finds out.' This was only the first of many excuses Madhu made to herself in the coming weeks as she talked with her husband again and again about the events in Spain. How could she go to the police, she thought. Her husband was so respected in the community and so obviously a gentleman, no one would believe her.

She told him, 'If you did that to Ruby, you could do it to me as well.' He laughed at her fears. How could she be so cruel? Didn't she see – he had made the greatest sacrifice anyone could make for love. Why had she continued to live with a man she knew to be a murderer? 'I did not think of him as a murderer after a time. I think he was a human being who had made a big mistake for which he was ashamed,' she would say.

When I spoke to Dr Madhu Baksh I too couldn't resist asking the inevitable question about why she

169

hadn't turned him in. 'He was so regretful about the whole thing,' she explained. She thought he had seen the error of his ways. 'That was my big mistake,' she said wryly.

The ultimate reason, of course, as she said in court, was: 'I thought he loved me. I certainly by now loved him.' And, as he told her one night when she asked him yet again why he had done it, 'If I had not done it, I would not have got you.' The doctor obviously did not believe in anything as troublesome as divorce.

Doubtless Madhu would have been safe enough – if her husband had not run into financial difficulties. He had collected £90,000 life insurance on Ruby's death, but that was long gone. By the beginning of 1986 he owed £6,000 on his income taxes, had a bank overdraft of £2,000, and had to find £2,000 for his children's fees at private school. Where was a chap to turn! John Baksh knew.

He began taking out life-insurance policies on Madhu, some of which she knew about, others she didn't, until he had her insured for £215,000. One policy was taken out so close to the Keston Ponds affair that it didn't arrive in the mail until Madhu was in hospital, and by the end the premiums amounted to around £1,000 a month (out of their joint income of £80,000 a year).

On 4 January – only three days before their wedding anniversary – Baksh announced he had 'a big surprise' for her. There was a bottle of champagne, tickets to a play – ironically a production of *Dr*

Jekyll and Mr Hyde – and, he promised, he would buy her 'a very nice present'. She never got to see the present. The champagne was drugged. Once she was comatose, he injected her with morphine, loaded her into the trunk of his BMW, and drove her to Keston Ponds. His medical training would have made it easy for him to cut her throat to cause her to die almost instantly. Instead, he cut it so she would bleed slowly to death, giving him time, apparently, to return home, establish his alibi, and call the police to report his wife missing.

Driving away from the ponds, Baksh suddenly realized he had left his glove at the scene. He turned around and went back. 'I found her still breathing,' he would say. 'But something stopped me from stabbing her again.' In fact Madhu, according to medical evidence, was only thirty minutes from death. She survived because of three factors: the near-lethal dose of morphine, which reduced the degree of shock; the sub-zero temperature that night, which slowed the bleeding; and the lucky inspiration of Keith Corbett to go toad-watching that night. Her recovery was slow: she was sedated for days, and it was three weeks before she recovered her speech.

On 10 January, six days after he had left Madhu for dead, Baksh was arrested and charged with her attempted murder. He still thought he could get out of the scrape. He wrote Madhu, urging her to withdraw her accusation. 'We are both alive,' he wrote. 'It is a storm in a teacup. Worse could have happened. I need psychiatric help.' In a letter to her brother, he wrote: 'I think we all have split personalities, good and bad in us. Sometimes one prevails, sometimes the other. I did not want to kill her.' Even Ruby's sister, under the impression Baksh's first wife had committed suicide, wrote Madhu: 'Take back the case, it will be good for all of you. Life will be back to normal soon.' She would say in court that she had asked Madhu to forgive Baksh, whom she found 'a very nice gentleman', because in every family from time to time there is 'trouble and tension'.

But events were moving too fast for any last-minute reconciliation. When Bromley restaurateur Barry Willmott saw a wedding photograph of John and Madhu Baksh in his local newspaper after she was found with her throat slashed, his mind immediately flashed back to the day three years earlier when, on holiday in Spain, a man had come walking into his villa and said without any sign of emotion, 'My wife is dead'.

'You don't forget a face like that. It's so unusual the way the cheeks sag,' he said. Willmott phoned the police with his suspicions. At first they were sceptical, but eventually Madhu told them of her husband's Paris hotel-room confession. In Spain, his first wife's remains were disinterred from beneath the gravestone inscribed 'To my beloved Ruby'. Traces of morphine were found in parts of the body flown back to Britain.

Suspicion surrounded the deaths of others closely

connected with Baksh. Two partners in his practice had both died suddenly, one of them on a golf course in Spain. His elderly mother had died in a Kent nursing home shortly after he had visited her. Baksh, the son of a minister, had always been an advocate of euthanasia. It was simply a matter, he told police, of killing people who no longer served any purpose.

In the end, though, the only murder Baksh was charged with was that of Ruby. In the witness box at the Old Bailey, Baksh, who described himself as 'a good Christian', claimed that, on the day he slit Madhu's throat, a day that had promised well but that turned into 'sheer hell', they had quarrelled and she threatened him with a kitchen knife. Afterwards she complained of pain in the chest, and he had given her an injection of morphine. Then, according to his story, they had gone to see some friends to get their advice on their marital problems, and he had taken along the knife, just to show them how serious matters were.

'When we got to Keston Ponds, I wanted to stop. I thought if we both got some fresh air, we would be better.' Then, as they sat near the bushes, he said, 'I thought I would demonstrate to her what it was like – how it felt – to have someone point a knife at someone's neck and threaten them. I told her, "There's your knife." She pushed it with her left hand. It all happened in a split second.' He did not think she was dying. He thought she might walk home, he said.

His first wife's death? Suicide, he claimed, because she was depressed about his affair with Madhu. And the confession in Paris? He had said that only to impress Madhu.

Surprisingly, it took the jury of nine men and three women more than two hours to find Baksh guilty of murder and attempted murder. As Baksh stood hunched, with eyes watering, the London Recorder, Sir James Miskin, told him: 'You intentionally killed your first wife when you knew she was both unwell and utterly miserable because of her suspicions – which were well founded – that you were carrying on with Madhu. You killed her skilfully so as to gratify your lust for Madhu.' And of the attempted murder: 'Your plan was not lacking in skill.' He had told a tissue of lies to relatives, friends and police about his wife's alleged abduction, said the judge in sentencing him to serve a minimum of twenty years in prison.

On hearing the sentence, Madhu Baksh said, 'The memory of these events may fade, but, like the mark on my neck, I will carry the scars for ever.' It was nearly five years later when I spoke to her at her office, where, although long since divorced from Baksh, she still practises under her former husband's name. She has continued to care for her own two children by her former marriage as well as Baksh's two adopted children. 'We have been very supportive of each other,' she said. Three of the children have done well, although the fourth has had difficulties.

Incredibly, she still occasionally visits Baksh in prison – simply to talk about matters involving his children. 'At first I felt very frightened seeing him,' she said. 'I never go alone.' At the start he showed no remorse, but, as time has gone on, he seems to feel regret, she said.

Will she ever marry again? The question shocked her. 'No way!' she exclaimed. 'I just can't even think about it. I have got no faith any more in men.'

THE COP WHO
CRIED AND CRIED

In the early 1980s there was only one Lakeshore
address in Toronto that set you apart and established you immediately as one of the toney people.
It was the Palace Pier, a glittering, forty-six-storey
finger pointing insolently skyward at the west end
of the Toronto Bay, establishing once and for all
that it was again fashionable to live at the edge of
the slate-grey lake on which the city had so long
turned its back.

The Palace Pier, where doormen in nautical navy
gold-trimmed uniforms kept the unwashed at a distance; the Pier, whose windows picked up the bur-
nished sun rising out of Lake Ontario at dawn and
saw it sink beyond Oakville in the evening; the
Pier, for which some of the wealthiest old names in
Toronto traded in their old Rosedale mahogany for
Italian chic and, on a clear day, a glimpse of the
spray from Niagara Falls.

So it seemed all the more disturbing and,
well . . . unseemly when, on 29 March 1981, a

cloudy but not especially cold late-winter's day, a thirty-three-year-old woman named Jeanette Kelly fell from the balcony of suite 1705. Her husband, an ex-narcotics officer with the Royal Canadian Mounted Police, said, in between great gulping sobs, that Jeanette, Scottish-born, had been annoyed by a piece of metal flashing that rattled in the wind; had carried a stool from the kitchen out to the balcony; and, in climbing up, had toppled backwards over the edge.

He was in the kitchen making a pot of tea when he heard her scream, he said. A squash player of some ability, he dashed out to the balcony just in time to grab her by the thighs as she fell. For one terrible instant she stared terrified into his face, but then he was unable to hold her and she slipped from his grasp.

Kelly said he immediately phoned the doorman to call an ambulance, then took the elevator to the ground floor, pushing the emergency button all the way down to give the alarm. Jeanette's smashed body lay near the building's loading dock. She had landed in a sitting position, pulping her body from the waist down. He felt her pulse, then closed her eyes, took off his shirt, and covered her face. Kelly, people would say, was sobbing and hyperventilating. Someone asked if there was a doctor around, and a distinguished, grey-haired man hurried forward, put his arm around Kelly, took him to a second ambulance that had been called, and, to the surprise of the ambulance attendants, hugged and kissed Kelly to console him.

Staff Sergeant Ed Stewart, one of the Metropolitan Toronto Police homicide squad's duty team that weekend, was having supper when he was called in, as he would be for any suspicious death. Suspicious? Well, yes. The first officers to arrive at the tastefully furnished suite had noticed immediately that the overturned stool on the balcony from which Jeanette had supposedly fallen was too high to have been placed up against the forty-two-inch-high balustrade in the way Kelly had described. And some things didn't feel right. How did a guy who had never earned more than $30,000 a year before he'd quit the RCMP only a year ago afford a place like this, manage to run a late-model Porsche, and, as they quickly discovered, lead a highly extravagant lifestyle involving eating in expensive restaurants and frequently travelling abroad? Of course, that had nothing to do with the question of whether Jeanette Kelly's death was accidental, but still, those other questions were there. 'Background music', the judge would call them.

At St Joseph's Health Centre, still accompanied by the solicitous 'doctor', Kelly had his blood pressure tested and was found to be normal, and he was given tranquillizers. Talking to a police officer afterwards, he seemed completely composed, asking the man, one cop to another, what his work conditions were like and telling him if he needed a job any time to come and see him.

It wasn't until the next day that Stewart and his partner rode up to the seventeenth floor of the

Palace Pier to hear Kelly's account. The man who met them at the door was athletic-looking and well built, the biceps and shoulders those of a weight-lifter. The features were boyish and open, the eyes humorous, and the wide mouth, at less serious moments, quick to spread in an engaging grin.

Pat Kelly, like a good cop wanting to help his buddies, couldn't have been more cooperative. He told them how it was while he was vacationing in Acapulco with his best Mountie friend, Wayne Humby, that he met Jeanette Hanlon, the daughter of a Glasgow car dealer. Jeanette, with fragile Scottish features reminiscent of a medieval portrait, worked in fact for Avianca, the Colombian national airline. Right there they had something in common because Pat had just completed a Spanish immersion course at the University of Javeriana in Bogotá, where he'd been sent by his bosses on the drug squad.

Jeanette returned to Scotland to visit her family, but the lovers, as they now were, kept in touch by phone. After a preliminary visit to Toronto to visit Pat, Jeanette emigrated to Canada and moved in with the Mountie; on 20 September 1975, ten months later, they were married. The following year Pat and Jeanette bought their first home, in Cookstown, an hour's drive north of Toronto. These were their glory days as they renovated and redecorated the house, and Jeanette, enraptured by the small-town rustic atmosphere, opened a little business, The Quilt Shop, where she sold quilts sewn by local farmers' wives.

But Pat had no taste for small-town life; his fancy was caught by ritzy ads for the proposed Palace Pier. If they got in quick, he told Jeanette, they could still get an apartment at a price they could just afford – $87,000 – and it would be a sure-fire investment later (for once Pat's business judgement was sound: in the real-estate boom that followed, the apartment would have sold for half a million dollars or more). Well, at least, Jeanette admitted, Pat, whose comings and goings in connection with his drug undercover work were highly unpredictable, would probably be home more if they weren't so far out of town. They put down an initial $3,000, put their Cookstown home up for sale, and Jeanette sold her quilt business at a modest profit. But, for ten long months the 'for sale' sign stood on the lawn. With the Palace Pier people demanding another $5,700 to close the deal, Pat was getting desperate.

Then, in August 1978, while Jeanette was away visiting her parents in Scotland, Pat took a short break at a lodge owned by some friends in Algonquin Provincial Park, two hours's drive north of Cookstown. The first night he went to bed early – only to be awakened the following morning with the news that their home had burned to the ground. Pat broke into tears, phoned Jeanette, and told her to come home right away.

Arson was immediately suspected, and Pat told

the Ontario Provincial Police officers investigating he had a good idea who was responsible. He'd got on the inside of a big drug ring, he told them, and this was their warning to him.

A young OPP man investigating didn't buy that. A new plastic gasoline can had been found at the scene. 'We've got a new way of raising fingerprints using lasers,' he bluffed Kelly. 'We're going to check that plastic gas can.' Next day Kelly called him. 'I was just driving along Kipling Avenue, and it came to me like that,' he said. 'I did buy a new gas can. I just forgot about it.' Kelly was charged with arson and suspended from duty, though the case was eventually thrown out of court for lack of evidence. Kelly collected $60,000 insurance on the house plus $55,000 on the contents.

But the Mounties had been investigating irregularities in the way Kelly had handled funds on drug investigations. Money given him for buying drugs seemed to have ended up in his own bank accounts. Kelly, once regarded as one of the force's brightest and ablest drug officers, ended his nine-year career with the force in 1980 with a parting gift: an honourable discharge.

How did he support his handsome lifestyle? With the contacts he'd made in the drug trade, he confided, he was able to smuggle funds across the Mexican border for investment in the United States, charging a 20 per cent commission. In the five previous years, including the time he was in the RCMP, he would claim, he had made $400,000 in unreported income.

When the questioning turned inevitably to Jeanette's death, Kelly stuck to his story that he had run from the kitchen to try to save her, and once again he broke down. 'He cried real tears,' said Stewart. 'Mucus was coming out of his nose. I have never seen such a scene. You have to have some compassion.' But, at the back of his mind, Stewart had a doubt. A cop, of all people, learns to control his emotions. Even considering the traumatic death of his wife, Kelly's reaction seemed excessive, and when he signed the statement, his hand was trembling so badly he could hardly form the letters. Stewart was not surprised to discover later that Kelly had been taking acting lessons. You could say he was overacting, but he may have had his reasons: it's hard to ask harsh questions of a man who is blubbing his heart out.

As Stewart and his partner were leaving the apartment, a curious incident occurred. Outside the door, they ran into the distinguished-looking 'doctor' who had been caring for Kelly since Jeanette's death. He introduced himself as a lieutenant-commander in the US army attached to the Pentagon. A pathologist by training, he was in Toronto on special assignment, he told them mysteriously. Paul Stewart, it would later emerge, was an employee of a Toronto funeral parlour, and was living at the time in the Palace Pier apartment of the sister of a former governor general of Canada.

Curiously, for all his emotion, Kelly did not show up for Jeanette's burial and, at a dinner afterwards, he spent more time talking on the phone than talking to guests. Two days later, confident, perhaps, that everything was going according to plan, Kelly was in ebullient spirits as he talked at dinner to auto dealer Roger Davidson about his Rolls-Royce servicing franchise in Los Angeles, his $100,000 Ferrari, and his homes in France and Switzerland. He also let drop that, at the age of sixteen, he had been called in to teach judo to the armed forces and, as a matter of fact, had once 'wrapped up' seven or eight attackers in 3.5 seconds. The only person who seemed to believe him, Davidson would say, was Kelly's girlfriend, a librarian named Janet Bradley who seemed enthralled as she held his hand during dinner. 'A real fun evening' was how Davidson's wife, Jill, described it.

Sergeant Stewart would be surprised to discover just how many women there were in Pat Kelly's life. One was Dawn Bragg, a close friend of both Jeanette and Pat. She told the homicide officers that, when she had split up with her Mountie husband, the Kellys had considerately invited her to stay at their apartment. While Jeanette was away in Europe, Pat had come home unexpectedly on the red-eye overnight flight from Vancouver and, finding her sleeping on the pullout couch, had had sex with her. Dawn, who had once done undercover police work herself, continued to live with the Kellys and to enjoy Jeanette's friendship. She did not even show alarm when Pat, swearing he loved her, started talking about how easy it would be for him to fake his own death so they could slip away to France to live on the proceeds of his life insurance. He even showed her a fake passport he owned in the name of Patrick Ryan. Other times he talked about how easy it would be to get rid of someone over the balcony. Dawn still remembered the word he'd used to describe how the body would look: 'Jelly.'

Kelly was wrong there. While the lower part of Jeanette's body was a mess, her face did not come in contact with the ground. And the pathologist found bruises and cuts consistent with her having been hit. Witnesses noticed that Kelly also seemed to be bloody and scratched, and it didn't take long to discover that Jeanette had, some time before, visited her family physician, complaining that Kelly had hit her.

There were other inconsistencies. A woman prepared to scramble up on to a kitchen stool on the edge of a seventeenth-floor balcony would have to be fearless. But Abigaile Latter, a friend, said that, when they had dinner on the balcony, Jeanette would shrink away from the edge and sit well back in her lounge chair. Besides, at the time of her death, she was just packing to leave for the airport to fly to Italy – hardly the time to worry about a noise on the balcony roof. Besides, Jeanette was not the sort to fix things herself. Checks with the building management showed she was a bit of a nuisance, always calling the desk when the least thing needed fixing. As to Kelly's story of not being able to hold on to his wife, even though he had his arms around her thighs, friends had seen him lift tiny Jeanette with one hand by the neck as a rather heavy-handed feat of strength.

The homicide squad had only the bare bones of a circumstantial case of murder against Pat Kelly when, eight days after the death, Stewart got a call from an old associate with the Mounties at Pearson International Airport. Kelly, he said, had just gone through customs and was boarding a flight for Hawaii. The reservation had been made in the names of P. Kelly and V. Simpson. Victor Simpson was, in fact, an old school chum from Victoria, British Columbia, a lawyer now, with whom Kelly had gone into the investment business. At the check-in desk, Kelly changed the name from Simpson to that of Jan Bradley, who was with him. 'Have you changed girlfriends?' Valerie White, the woman behind the desk, joked. Kelly did not seem amused.

If Kelly thought that, in Hawaii, he and Bradley would be unobserved, he was mistaken. An old friend of Jeanette's, Sheree Brown, spotted them there and was taken aback, in view of Jeanette's recent death, to see them hugging and kissing. And the mysterious Paul Stewart, the funeral-parlour employee with whom Kelly had been staying, although he had no previous connection with Kelly, called the police to say his new friend had departed suddenly, leaving him a most surprising letter.

'Thank you for all last week,' wrote Kelly. 'Without you it would have been impossible. We've become very close very quickly. When you speak of your brother, I'm proud to be spoken of in the same sentence. We have something most people only read about between two people and it can never be taken away, it will only grow. I know she [Jeanette] will rest well knowing I am with a good friend.' And, added Kelly, would Stewart mind putting Jeanette's jewellery in a safe; check on how their sheepdog, also named Kelly, was doing at the boarding kennel; and water the plants. Kelly had also advanced Stewart a $50,000 loan to buy a boat and given him a $10,000 china set. Stewart, reading Kelly's letter aloud in court years later, would burst into tears.

A postcard he sent from Hawaii at this time to a woman named Brenda Rodine was worded in similarly extravagant emotional terms. 'The evenings are rough (too much time to think). The nights are terribly still. I love you dearly and hope that soon we can be together again to laugh and play as before.' Surprising sentiments, considering his contact with Rodine had been brief and then concerned only with business.

On the return trip, Kelly parted company with Jan Bradley, flying north to Victoria while she returned to Toronto. His old friend, Victor Simpson, and Simpson's wife were there to take him into their home, console him, and help the sorrowing Kelly put his life together again. A decade earlier Victor had applied to join the RCMP, and Pat, whose father had been for a while a policeman, had followed his friend's example. Simpson had failed the height requirement by a quarter of an inch, and went to law school, whereas Pat had been accepted.

When Pat was suspended from the force following the arson episode, he had come west and worked for Victor's investment firm, K and V Enterprises, looking into such schemes as ballooning and marketing greeting cards. Now, Pat was about to collect $271,000 on Jeanette's life-insurance policies, so he had his Porsche shipped west to him, and began serious wheeling and dealing. There was the scheme involving the King of Tonga, a small Pacific island to which Pat flew with one of Victor's clients to set up an import-export business.

And there was the scheme to import gold from Kenya. Simpson told me he and Kelly had their shots and reservations, and were all set to leave for Africa in late 1981 when a telegram arrived at Victor's office, delivering another devastating blow for Pat. The telegram, ostensibly from a mutual friend, asked Victor to break the news gently that Pat's oldest RCMP buddy, Wayne Humby, and his wife and child, had been wiped out in a car accident. Kelly broke down once again at the terrible news. Going to Africa was out of the question, Victor said. Pat anyway seemed happier staying in Victoria, where Jan Bradley, having thrown over her librarian's job, had recently joined him.

Two and a half years later Victor Simpson would be sitting in a Toronto courtroom, waiting to testify against Pat Kelly. 'You look familiar,' he said to the guy sitting beside him. 'Do I know you?'

'I'm Wayne Humby,' said the very-much-alive officer.

'But you're supposed to be dead!' said Simpson. By then Simpson thought nothing could surprise him about his old friend. Kelly had proved him wrong again. Simpson can think only that Kelly arranged the elaborate deception because he wanted to remain in Victoria with Bradley.

Mostly, though, Kelly seemed to spend his time in Victoria, practising his fabulous technique with women. 'You look great!' he called as a woman named Leslie walked down the street. 'Thanks,' she said. 'You still look great,' he told her in the bank where they both seemed to be heading. 'Can I take you out?' When she turned him down, he tracked her down to the boutique where she worked, and next day she received a dozen roses and a note inviting her to 'coffee, drinks or dinner or a weekend in San Francisco'. There were always roses, sometimes delivered in big bunches; on one occasion, a single rose dropped on the squash court where the woman he was chasing had just finished a game.

The aura of tragedy hanging over Pat Kelly only engaged their sympathies all the more. Hearing that Pat's best friend, Wayne, had been killed with his family, Tracy Charlish, a bank teller whom Pat was romancing, bought a sympathy card and dropped by unannounced at the elegant little house he

189

was renting in classy Oak Bay. She found him in his bathrobe, sipping wine with Jan Bradley.

The curious thing, said Victor Simpson, who was well aware of the cost of all this entertaining because Kelly's credit-card bills were routinely mailed to his office, was that as soon as a woman showed a real interest in Kelly, he would back out of the affair.

Bradley seemed to be the exception. Their marriage, he assured her, would be a never-to-be-forgotten event. And he was right. There was a civil ceremony in Victoria, in May 1982, and a week later Jan and her mother boarded a plane at Montreal's Mirabel Airport and flew with Pat to the south of France, where he had a rented villa with a swimming pool near Cannes. Victor Simpson, flown to France with a dozen of Kelly's friends, remembers that the Anglican church in Cannes was filled with flowers for the wedding, while a Los Angeles musician friend of Kelly's, Robert Rapson, played the flute (Rapson would recall later that Kelly told him, as he told a number of people, that his wife had fallen while watering the plants on the balcony – 'He had tears come to his eyes'). After the ceremony Pat took them all out to a sumptuous dinner before he and Jan left for a month-long honeymoon in Ireland.

Back in Victoria, with the bills piling up – the villa in France alone was costing $25,000 a month – and some of his clients' investment funds on the line, Simpson phoned Kelly to tell him he must come up with some of the money he owed. 'A man came to my door shortly after with $15,000,' said Simpson. The lawyer was supposed to fly to Los Angeles, where Pat would have the rest for him. In LA, Kelly's story was that he had been unable to fly into the United States with the funds. If Victor would pop over to London, getting the money would be no problem. Simpson cooled his heels in London, Cannes, Venice and Miami, waiting for the money that never arrived. Adding to his problems, Princess Grace had just died in a car accident, and it was almost impossible to get through to Pat on the jammed telephone lines to the south of France.

Flying home from Miami, Simpson knew it was all over. The following months, though, he made one last attempt to save things. He told Kelly, 'Like, we've got to sit down and we can work it out.'

'Speak to my lawyer,' said Kelly abruptly. 'As a lawyer myself, I knew what that meant,' says Simpson. He reckons he lost $300,000 of his own money through Kelly and almost lost his law practice too. 'I put my family's well-being in his hands, and that was destroyed,' he says today, with undiminished bitterness.

In December 1982, Kelly felt it was finally safe for him to return to Toronto. He was wrong. Fraud-squad officers arrived at the suite in the Harbour Castle Hotel he was sharing with Jan Kelly, as she now was, and arrested him for signing cheques on Paris banks for which there were no funds. A con artist of the first order, Kelly got bail, had a woman friend fly in from Los Angeles to swear it was all a misunderstanding and that Kelly had lent her $100,000, of which she was now returning $25,000. Later, she admitted there was no $100,000 debt. She had raised the $25,000 by mortgaging her cottage as a favour to Kelly, who had once advanced her a small sum to treat her sick horses. It was to be Kelly's last con.

Ed Stewart, who had spent much of his two years on the homicide squad investigating the Kelly case, had been increasingly impressed by the fact that just about everything Kelly had told Dawn Bragg – about dropping Jeanette from the balcony, about going to France and living on the proceeds of the life insurance – had come true. The police had even found a fake passport in the name of Patrick Ryan and bearing Kelly's picture in his safety deposit box. Bragg had moved back to the United States, where she originally came from, but she was finally tracked down by Latter, the friend who had never believed Jeanette's death was an accident.

Stewart had just come in from a court hearing one day when he heard Dawn had called. 'I told her that Kelly was in town and that we were still investigating. I told her just about everything she'd told us had come true.' He could feel the emotion in her voice, says Stewart, and sensed that she was holding something back. 'I think I know what you are going to say,' he said.

Her voice came, small and unsure: 'I don't think you do.' She hesitated, then: 'I was there that day. I saw it. I was scared and shook up.'

It was the kind of break you could expect only once in a career. And, with judges making it tougher all the time for an honest cop to clear all the legal hurdles, it was the sort of break that could turn to dust in your hands. The danger here was that maybe Dawn Bragg was involved in the murder. But, even if she was, Stewart had to have Kelly. It was Kelly, he was sure, who was the main actor here.

Stewart thrashed it out with the Crown attorney. What they'd do, they decided, was give Bragg an assurance that whatever she said, even if it amounted to a confession, couldn't be used against her if she was charged in the future.

On a cold January day, Stewart flew to Boston, then drove on to New Hampshire. Then, with a local officer in attendance, he spent eleven hours over two days questioning Dawn Bragg. The first thing she set him straight about was the fire. Kelly, she said, had told her how he had climbed out of the back window of the cabin that night, driven to his home, spread gasoline throughout the house, set it alight, and driven back to his cabin. Kelly had, in any case, been cleared of that charge and couldn't be charged again. It was Jeanette's death Stewart wanted to hear about.

The day of the murder, she said, she had driven to the Palace Pier to see Jeanette off and to offer to drive her to the airport. Pat and Jeanette were arguing. As usual, the subject was divorce. They

asked Dawn to have a seat in the den. Dawn heard
Jeanette threaten to squeal to the cops about Pat
burning down the house. It was a threat that she
had heard her friend make before. This time,
though, it was followed by the sound of blows. She
heard Jeanette scream. When she came out of the
den, Jeanette was lying unconscious on the floor,
Pat stooping over her. He stood up, cradling her
in his arms. He seemed unaware that Dawn was
watching as he walked out through the sliding
doors on to the balcony and dropped her over – as if
he were putting out the garbage.

'Oh, my god, what have I done?' he said, turning
to Dawn. She walked to the edge of the balcony,
looked down, then collapsed. Things would be okay,
she shouldn't worry, she must keep calm, he told
her. 'I love you,' he assured her. His arm around her
shoulders, he led her out to the elevator, took her
up a few floors, and told her to go home without
speaking to anyone. Telling the story, even after
two years, made her feel faint. Stewart broke off
and opened the window to give her air.

Why had she waited two years before telling her
story? Bragg would be asked at the trail. 'I was
afraid of what I had seen. I was afraid of Pat. I was
afraid I knew too much,' she replied.

Was Dawn Bragg involved in a conspiracy with
Kelly to kill his wife? That question still intrigues
Stewart. She admitted that, when she worked in an
insurance office, she drew up a proposal to increase
Kelly's insurance on his wife, although he did not

go through with it. She was plainly infatuated with him, and one thing Stewart still wonders about is: who opened the sliding doors to the balcony, one of which was off its tracks?

Bragg's evidence was his ace, but as he flew home from New England, Stewart knew he would need other cards. Just in case anything went wrong, the circumstantial evidence had to be strong enough on its own to convict Kelly. And there was still a lot of 'homework' to be done on that. Kelly's story of how Jeanette died, for a start, had to be checked. An exact scale model of the apartment was set up at the Metro Police College, and Constable Paul Malbeuf was assigned temporarily to homicide. Malbeuf, who was five foot nine and 170 pounds – the same height and weight as Kelly – held the record for the obstacle race in the annual police games between the Toronto and Detroit forces. If Malbeuf couldn't get to that balcony in time, no one could.

A policewoman would scream as if she were falling, and Malbeuf, poised in the kitchen, would dash out to the balcony, dodging furniture on the way. His best time was 4.5 seconds. But an engineer, Eric Krueger, had calculated that it would take Jeanette only three seconds to fall. Even if Kelly had superhuman reflexes and realized instantly what her screams meant, she would be on the ground before he ever got to the balcony. Another interesting finding: when Stewart had an officer tumble over the balcony a few feet into padding, the man always fell head first. In other words, if

Kelly had grabbed Jeanette, as he claimed, he would have been looking at her feet, not her face.

In March 1983, Kelly was charged with the first-degree murder of his wife; if he had killed her as a result of an uncontrollable impulse in the course of a row, it would only be second degree. Stewart was confident he could show Kelly plotted his wife's death. One small incident that occurred during the year Kelly was in custody awaiting trial supported that image of the cold-blooded killer. A prisoner testified at the preliminary hearing – although not at the trial – that Kelly told him it was his 'dearest wish' to have witnesses in the trial murdered, and Dawn Bragg's and Victor Simpson's names were mentioned. Kelly wanted to know how much a motorcycle gang would need in the form of a drug payment to carry out the contracts.

In April 1984, in a courtroom dominated by a mock-up of the fatal balcony, Kelly confronted the woman who said she had seen him kill. He showed no emotion as Dawn Bragg said of her former feelings towards him: 'He was just the whole world . . . I thought that Pat was the most perfect person in the whole world . . . He walked on water.' One night, at the Palace Pier Club, she testified, 'he said he loved me and wanted to spend the rest of his life with me.' That was when he talked about them going to France and starting a new life. 'Jeanette will be taken care of,' he told her. She would be unconscious just before she fell. 'There were no emotions. He was just explaining it to me, what was going to happen. He still claimed that he loved her.'

It was the burning of the house in Cooksville, said Bragg, that had effectively ended the Kelly's marriage, and Pat had told her Jeanette was close to a nervous breakdown. The fact that the charges against him were dismissed did nothing to restore her faith in him. Kelly persuaded her to take a trip to Europe, lending Dawn $4,000 so she could go along with Jeanette. In Rome, though, Jeanette left Dawn, and went on a trip to Austria with an Italian friend, Marchello Rodacachi. Jeanette told her she was undecided whether to stay on in Italy with Rodacachi, or return to Pat in Toronto. Dawn returned to Toronto a few days ahead of Jeanette. If she thought Pat would be waiting for her with open arms, she was mistaken. His interest had waned. Shortly afterwards, she moved out of the Kelly apartment.

Did Dawn Bragg believe that, after witnessing Jeanette's murder, she would again become number one in Pat's affections? The man she was living with at the time of Jeanette's death had testified at the preliminary hearing that Bragg was 'very jealous . . . [She] thought if something happened [to Jeanette] that Pat would come and live with her.'

Like so many women in Pat Kelly's life, she was to be disappointed. A few days after the murder, he called to say he was going away on his own and would call her if he needed her. She had no inkling that Kelly was going away with Jan Bradley, the librarian he had met during the course of a police investigation in 1975, and with whom he had been spending expensive weekends at the Algonquin and the Plaza hotels in New York prior to Jeanette's death.

How could Kelly afford all that high living? Stewart laughs at Kelly's claim that he made $400,000 smuggling funds for the drug barons. 'It was a total fabrication,' he says. Donald Holmes, an accountant who specializes in white-collar crime, explained to the jury that Kelly's method was far more mundane: he simply lived beyond his means. He juggled money between six bank accounts and four brokerage accounts, and held twenty credit cards. Believing in sharing bank as well as bed, he had joint bank accounts with Jeanette, Dawn and Jan. In the twenty-one months prior to September 1981, he spent $151,000 while taking in less than $45,000. The gap, said Holmes blandly, 'must be financed by other money coming in.' The 'other money' was the $271,000 insurance proceeds he received from the death of his wife.

Judge John O'Driscoll properly warned jury members they were not there to pass judgment on Kelly's morals, sex habits, or lifestyle, nor to try Dawn Bragg. They had only to decide if Jeanette's death was an accident, the result of an impulse, or 'a planned and deliberate killing', in which case Kelly would be guilty of first-degree murder. It took the jury, eight men and four women, nearly fifteen hours over two days before they chose the third option. Kelly and his second wife, Jan, who had attended court daily, closed their eyes as the verdict was announced. She blew him a kiss as he was led from the courtroom after being sentenced to life imprisonment with no possibility of parole for twenty-five years. An appeal to the Supreme Court of Canada was later rejected.

But the trial and verdict leave some questions unanswered. Why did Kelly choose to kill his wife with a witness present? And what turned Kelly, whom Victor Simpson describes as 'a happy-go-lucky, friendly, outgoing guy' in his younger days and whom his RCMP superiors regarded as 'a likeable and very successful officer', into a callous killer?

Simpson still doubts whether the murder was planned deliberately. 'Why did he do it himself?' he says. 'It would have been comparatively easy for him to have it done in Italy.' Perhaps, he says, it was, after all, a crime of passion, a spur-of-the-moment impulse that led him to kill her because she threatened to expose him.

And Sergeant Stewart says that, despite his police training, Kelly 'was certainly not very intelligent' in the way he carried out his crime. 'I don't know why in hell he had her [Dawn Bragg] there,' he says. 'And when he skipped town right after – how clever is that!'

I believe it's not so hard to explain the inconsistencies. Jeanette wanted a divorce; she was leaving for Italy; when would he see her again? When would he get another chance? Alive and threatening to expose him, she could be very expensive indeed in any divorce action. Dead she was worth $271,000. And Kelly, with his debts catching up with him, needed that money fast.

And what difference did it make whether Bragg was there? He had told her already he planned to throw his wife off the balcony. Even if she only read about it in the newspaper she would know immediately what had happened. As a witness, though, she would be frightened to tell what she knew for fear of being charged as a co-conspirator.

What turned a good cop bad? Stewart and Simpson are in agreement there. 'He has a sociopathic personality,' says Simpson. 'He will do what he has to get what he wants. I think it was developed in the RCMP. I think his training helped him to see the goal was to capture someone, and it didn't matter what you did to achieve that goal.' As an undercover man for several years, says Simpson, his former friend learned to play a role, learned to mix fact with fiction.

'There are always inherent dangers in putting people in these undercover jobs for too long,' says Stewart. 'They are trained to lie and manipulate people in order to gather the evidence in narcotics cases. After a while, depending on the maturity of the individual, there is always a danger they might start to live the lies. He was driving Mercedeses and Cadillacs and playing different roles. When he left the force, he couldn't give that up.'

It was with women, of course, that Pat Kelly played his roles to the full. And they were, for the most part, only roles. Once he'd won over a woman with his roses and talk of romantic weekends, as Simpson says, he'd back off. He didn't even have sex with some of the women he ensnared, says Stewart. It was as if sex was secondary. At the preliminary hearing, Dawn Bragg was quoted as saying Kelly was homosexual. Why then did women put their faith in him, even, in some cases, ignoring the plain evidence that he was the most cowardly sort of murderer? Charm is the only explanation, charm and flattery that inspire a willing blindness.

It was Judy Seres, a friend of Jeanette's from airline days who wrote and told me of the final act in the drama. 'Several days after Pat's conviction,' she wrote, 'Jeanette's friends and I had a "celebration". I bought a bottle of Dom Perignon and we toasted Jeanette and saved a few drops. The following day, I went to Mount Pleasant Cemetery and sprinkled the remainder on her grave. Jeanette loved champagne, and she loved the best. I think she would have been pleased. Then I took some mud and covered the part of her flat tombstone that read, "beloved wife of Patrick Kelly", leaving only, "Jeanette Kelly – January 20, 1948–March 29, 1981".'

SAINTLY
BILLY

We are standing on Market Street in Rugeley, Staffordshire, in front of the hideous video shop that now occupies Dr William Palmer's Tudor house, while two history buffs argue fiercely over whether, 135 years ago, the good doctor did in fact poison all those people.

'Of course,' says historian John Godwin, darkly. 'There were all those illegitimate babies of his. He was alleged to have done away with all of them.'

'Fooey!' exclaims Edwina Morgan, a retired teacher who is chairman of the Landor Society, the local history society. 'Everything was put on Palmer, but I rather like him. It's dreadful, but I do.'

That was always the way with Billy Palmer: he was a scamp, a rascal, a cheat, and quite possibly one of the most prolific murderers in British history. But you couldn't help liking him. While a sinister aura surrounds Dr Neill Cream and other medical poisoners of the nineteenth century, Dr

Palmer, to whom sixteen murders are commonly ascribed, went about his deadly business with such cheerful élan that it was hard for some even in his own day to take him seriously. Part of the explanation, I suspect, is that Billy Palmer was a sport, a follower of the turf. His crimes, for the most part, were committed, not in gloomy gas-lit rented rooms or dark back streets, but at the racetrack and in the boisterous taverns favoured by touts, bookies and nobblers who followed the race meets.

Only a sport like Billy, on hearing the death sentence passed on him, could say, 'When the jury returned to court and I saw the cocked-up nose of the perky little foreman, I knew it was a gooser for me!' And the ladies, they could never resist Billy. Fourteen bastards born to various young women during the five years he was doing his medical training. As to what happened to all those babes, better not to ask, but some thought it more than coincidence that, whenever Billy gave them a cuddle, they went into convulsions.

Even Billy's old mother couldn't resist his charm, not even after he'd forged her name and defrauded her of thousands of pounds. 'I'm Dr Palmer's mother, and not ashamed of it neither,' she told an artist she came across sitting beside the canal, painting scenes of Rugeley to feed the insatiable public appetite for books and pictures detailing the life of the notorious doctor. 'Yes,' she added with a regretful sigh, 'they hanged my saintly Billy.'

So, on a chill, foggy day in early summer, I've

come to Rugeley, a market town not far from the famous Staffordshire potteries, to learn more about Saintly Billy and the passions he still arouses. Here on Market Street, as Edwina, John and I stand chatting, I can almost hear his loud laugh off in the mist. Behind the windows of the video shop where they're advertising Hollywood's cheap thrills, Billy served the finest port to his racing cronies – sixty-seven dozen bottles were left to auction when they took him off. And where we're standing, Billy, a chubby, bland-faced little fellow, came fussing back and forth to the Talbot Arms Hotel – now renamed the Shrewsbury Arms, or 'The Shrew' to locals – where his friend, John Parsons Cooks, lay ill in room ten. It was his death on 20 November 1855 that wrote finis to Billy's sporting career.

'This is where his garden was,' Edwina is telling me. 'He was very fond of his garden.' Odd, I can't imagine Billy bending down to sniff the pinks and wallflowers. 'But it's a shame what's been done,' says Edwina. Like many another town linked with some notorious murderer whose misdeeds have long since become the stuff of legend, Rugeley has tried to obliterate every reminder. Palmer's house has been gutted and destroyed visually, and not the teeniest plaque informs visitors of what is Rugeley's main claim to fame.

'The dislike for him, it's still there,' says Edwina. When we get to St Augustine's Church, where Billy sang in the choir, she points out the tombstone on

Cook's grave that helps keep the resentment alive. Sacred, it says, to the memory of John Parsons Cook, 'whose life was taken away from him on the night of 20 November 1855 in the 29th year of his age. Amiable and affectionate in his disposition and generous in his conduct, he was sincerely beloved and will long be lamented by his kindred and friends.' Edwina says that, when she was a girl, there was a very old lady who actually remembered Palmer, 'and she said he was a very nice man.'

Nice? I don't suppose even Billy would have made that claim. He was born across the road from St Augustine's in that fine, old Georgian house once known as The Yard in consequence of the timberyard out back where his father, old Joe Palmer, was said to have grown rich on timber stolen from the estate of a local nobleman. A mixed bag, the six Palmer children were: Tom became a clergyman; Walter, a hopeless drunk. When old Joe keeled over with a heart attack, leaving an unsigned will, the eldest boy, Joseph, allowed his mother the use of the property providing she didn't remarry. It was a mean thing to do, but easily got around: she simply took as her lover a lawyer, Jeremiah Smith, many years her junior.

So, Mrs Palmer was, you might say, broadminded, and she didn't seem a bit surprised when Billy, who, on leaving the Rugeley Free Grammar School at seventeen, had been apprenticed to a Liverpool pharmacist, was caught stealing money from the mails. Especially when he explained to her that he needed the money to pay off his landlord's daughter, who was pregnant by him and demanding money for an abortion. Mrs Palmer simply made good the money stolen and set him up in a new career, apprenticing him to a surgeon.

It was while he was furthering his medical studies at the Stafford Infirmary that Billy first came under suspicion of wrongdoing more serious than drugging his mates' drinks to make them throw up or pee green. He challenged a shoemaker named Abley to a brandy-drinking contest. After downing the second tumbler, Abley, feeling ill, went out to the inn yard, where he was found groaning in pain an hour later. He died that night. His widow, an attractive young woman who had caught Palmer's eye at the Infirmary, was said to be quite consolable.

By October 1847, Palmer, his student scrapes behind him, came home from London's St Bartholomew's Hospital a fully qualified surgeon, married (over her guardian's serious reservations) Annie Brookes, his long-time sweetheart, and set up in practice in the old house on Market Street. He was popular and able, and quickly made his mark. But Rugeley was a horse town (its horse fair is still one of the annual highlights) and just before the birth of their first child, a boy they named William, the doctor, using money he had inherited from his father's estate, leased stables and a paddock, and became a horse breeder.

It was his downfall. Billy was a great judge of horseflesh, but a mug when it came to business. After his first, Goldfinder, won the Tradesmen's Plate at the Chester meeting and netted him nearly £3,000 Palmer, who had by then abandoned medicine, thought breeding winners was as easy as tumbling a girl in the hay. Instead, he got deeper and deeper into debt, finally resorting to having his wife, Annie, forge his mother's name on loan guarantees.

And then occurred a most unfortunate series of deaths, each taking place while Billy Palmer was close at hand. Annie's mother, an alcoholic, came to stay, and died within two weeks. Dr Bamford, an elderly physician friend of Billy's, put down apoplexy as the cause of death. A punter named Leonard Bladon, to whom Palmer reportedly owed £600, stayed the night at the Palmers' with several hundred pounds in his moneybelt, and left feet first and with no sign of his money. Bamford, on the death certificate, put it all down to a stable accident of a few weeks before.

And then Annie herself caught a chill and, despite having survived five pregnancies (although four of the children died), succumbed soon after. Others in the family had committed suicide, and there was talk of her having taken mysterious powders. For once the doctor was distraught. 'Saw the last of my beloved wife for ever. How desolate life is,' he wrote in his diary. Nevertheless, there was a policy worth £13,000 on her life that enabled Billy to pay off some of his debts.

The coincidences continued. To improve his stock and, it was hoped, his income, Palmer bought two top-ranked horses, The Chicken and Nettle, for several thousand pounds. As a result, the loan sharks were quickly at his door again, in particular one Thomas Pratt, a London solicitor with a pug nose and billowing mutton-chop whiskers who charged eager clients 60 per cent interest per annum. Palmer's eye this time settled on his own brother Walter, who, having separated from his wife and being in the later stages of alcoholism, seemed a likely bet to die quite soon – a better bet, anyway, than some of the horses Billy was putting his money on. Billy's plan, eagerly embraced by Walter, was to insure Walter's life for a substantial amount and give him a cash advance of £400 against future profits when he died. The £400, of course, would be spent by Walter on booze, which would be likely to hasten his death. Although several insurance companies wisely turned down applications made in the name of Pratt, the Prince of Wales fund, which had already been stung in the Annie Palmer episode, amazingly went for a policy for £14,000. On Wednesday, 14 August 1855 Billy spent the day in Stafford with Walter, who was drinking hard. Receiving a solid tip on a race just as his brother was expiring, the doctor fired off a telegram, placing £50 on the horse. It lost, Walter died, and the insurance company, suspicious this time, refused to pay.

Rumours were getting about, but Billy met them with a laugh. 'Here comes the poisoner,' he would announce, entering a bar, and then, with a wink, 'What's your poison, boys?' It's a cry still heard in the pubs of Staffordshire.

Then why, we must ask ourselves, didn't young John Parsons Cook avoid Billy Palmer like the plague? Why did Cook, three years Palmer's junior, a solicitor who, like his friend, had given up his profession for the pleasures of the racetrack after inheriting £12,000, carouse with Billy, bet with him, and get into no end of drunken scrapes with this man who everyone said was as dangerous as a viper? The answer, as with the girls who believed Billy's stories about marrying them, was that Billy was an awfully plausible scoundrel – and a desperate one at that.

By 6 November Palmer's house of cards, built largely on fraud, was about to collapse. On that day, two writs for £4,000 were issued, one against Palmer and one against his mother, who was unaware her name had been forged on promises to pay. Pratt was delaying service of the writs, but with another £1,500 due in three days' time was fast running out. Then, on 14 November, a new opportunity opened up to Palmer when Cook's horse, Polestar, won the Shrewsbury Handicap, netting his young friend, with bets he had with others, a total of about £2,000. Palmer had bet heavily on his own horse, The Chicken, at the Shrewsbury meet, and was in an even worse financial position when it lost.

At the Raven Hotel in Shrewsbury that night,

Palmer issued a familiar challenge. When Cook asked him if he'd take a glass of brandy, he replied, 'Not until you down yours. You must play fair, old cock – drink for drink.' Cook downed his glass at a gulp, then complained that it tasted strange and that his throat was burning. Palmer sipped the little remaining in the bottom of the glass, and declared there was nothing wrong with it. By midnight a doctor was in attendance on Cook, who complained of violent stomach pains and a burning throat. By the following day, though, Cook was well enough to return with Palmer to Rugeley, where he put up at the Talbot Arms, across the road from Billy Palmer's house. The doctor insisted that Cook must take his meals at his place, and when Cook, not feeling well, was unable to leave his room, Palmer, on two occasions, sent him over bowls of reviving broth.

With the bills coming due, Palmer now left his friend in Rugeley and made a dash for London, where, pretending to be Cook's partner, he collected £1,000 of Cook's winnings at Tattersall's, the betting house, and then forged a cheque in Cook's name, using the money to pay down some of his debts.

Cook had been well enough to go for walks, but following Palmer's return to Rugeley he took a turn for the worse and, with Palmer and another physician, Dr Jones, in attendance, he went into violent convulsions, his back arching like a bow, and died.

The helpful Dr Bamford, in his eighties and

doddery, suggested apoplexy when called in for the customary death certificate. Dr Jones first thought tetanus might be the cause of death, but later put it down to convulsions caused by the over-excitement of having his horse win. A housemaid at the Talbot Arms would report seeing Palmer going through Cook's belongings; afterwards no sign was found of £600 in banknotes Cook had with him. When William Stevens, an irascible elderly relative of Cook's, arrived, demanding to see Cook's betting book, in which he recorded all his transactions, no trace could be found of that either. How much had been owed to Cook? He was sorry to tell him, said Palmer, straightfaced, that Cook actually owed him £4,000, which he'd be pleased to receive out of the dead man's estate. Stevens's response was to demand an autopsy.

As a physician and friend of the deceased, Palmer insisted on being present as Cook's body was opened up. We should not be surprised to learn that the doctor performing the job had his arm mysteriously jogged, causing him to spill some of the stomach contents, that the sealed jar containing the contents had a slash in the top after Palmer handled it, and that the messenger assigned to deliver the jar to an analyst in London was bribed by Palmer to shake the bottle along the way. Even so, Billy Palmer was in a state of anxiety as he waited for the autopsy result, and got another of his cronies, Francis Cheshire, the postmaster at Rugeley, to promise he would steam open the report to the authorities when it arrived so that, if the results were not encouraging, Billy could make his escape. A few days later, Cheshire contacted Palmer with the best news possible: neither strychnine, nor prussic acid, the two suspected poisons, had been found. To be on the safe side, Palmer dispatched a gift hamper containing a twenty-pound turkey, a brace of pheasants, a cod, and a barrel of oysters to the Stafford Coroner, William Webb Ward, along with a note mentioning the autopsy finding (which he wasn't supposed to know about) and ending, 'I hope the verdict tomorrow [at the inquest] will be that Cook died of natural causes.'

Ward handed the note to the police; Cheshire was afterwards jailed for tampering with the mails, and two police officers arrived at the Palmer house to arrest the good doctor for forgery, pending more serious charges. When Jeremiah Smith, his friend and sometime collaborator, and his mother's lover, saw the fix he was in, he cried, 'William, oh William, how is this?' Billy didn't answer, but his cheeks glistened with tears. But such hostility, such booing, such spitting greeted Billy Palmer's every appearance while in custody that a special act of Parliament was quickly passed, allowing him to be tried at the Old Bailey in London rather than in the atmosphere of hatred that, for the time being, prevailed in Staffordshire.

Immediately, the moneylenders closed in, and, Mrs Palmer stoutly refusing to yield to their demands for the sound reason that her signature had been forged on their orders, Palmer's effects as well as his horses were auctioned, Prince Albert, the Queen's husband, buying one of the horses, Trickstress, for 230 guineas. The final indignity: a photographer offered to take photographs of 'ladies, gentry and inhabitants', posed at the rear of the notorious Palmer house, something guaranteed to thrill and chill their loved ones.

Mrs Palmer might repudiate his debts, but only the best lawyer would do for 'my roguish Billy', and when his trial opened on 14 May 1856, on a charge of murdering Cook with strychnine, he was represented by Mr Serjeant Shee, a brilliant Irish attorney, while the prosecution was in the hands of the attorney-general, Sir Alexander Cockburn. This was the first of the great Victorian poison trials involving medical men, and it was attended by vast public interest, the *Illustrated London Times*, for example, publishing a special Rugeley number that sold an unprecedented 400,000 copies. Readers got their money's worth. As Cockburn paraded no fewer than sixty-six witnesses into the box, such a tale of fraud and deceit was uncovered as had rarely been heard, even at the Old Bailey.

But Palmer, who sat bland and unmoved for the whole twelve days of the trial, confident that he would be acquitted, was not being tried for fraud, but for murder. And on the question of whether John Parsons Cook had been poisoned with strychnine, twenty-four scientists and doctors called by both sides were totally and irreconcilably divided.

It was the first case in which strychnine poisoning had been alleged, and John Glaister, professor of forensic medicine at the University of Glasgow, in his book, *The Power of Poison*, suggests knowledge and testing were simply not advanced enough at the time for anyone to be sure of the cause of Cook's death. So, when the jury, after an absence of only one hour and seventeen minutes, returned with a guilty verdict, it was not so much a case of deciding how Cook had died as delivering the final judgment on the doctor's whole scandalous course of conduct. The fact that Palmer's proven purchases of strychnine and prussic acid may have been intended for poisoning rivals' horses made him an even greater villain in the eyes of the racing public than if, as the prosecution contended, the poisons were intended for humans. And perhaps for Billy it was just as well to get the thing over with: the authorities, after exhuming the bodies of his wife and his brother, Walter, stood ready with two more murder charges if the first failed.

Billy Palmer, at thirty-one a rotund and balding junior Mr Pickwick, paled for only an instant when the verdict was announced, then recovered his composure. His only comment, a racing man's tribute to the attorney-general's masterful performance, was: 'It was the riding that did it.'

The three judges who tried Palmer ordered that he should be hanged at Stafford in his own county as a terrible example to local people, and when he arrived home he was greeted by a jeering mob. But

215

within a few days, opinions began to change. Doctors and scientists disputed the verdict in letters to *The Times*, and in London a crowd packed a hall in Long Acre to protest the verdict. Instead of inferring the criminal from the crime, declared the motion passed at the meeting, the jury and the judges had inferred the crime from the criminal.

There was, at that time, no criminal appeal procedure. It was, as Palmer so aptly observed, the gooser for him. On 14 June 1856, after a sleep of only a couple of hours, Palmer was awakened by the prison chaplain, and the preparations began. Shaved, washed, breakfasted, he emerged at eight o'clock to face a vast throng that had been gathering in Stafford for days prior to the execution. 'Murderer! Poisoner!' they shouted. The common expectation at public executions was for a confession, at the very least a speech. Palmer made as if to speak, and the crowd went silent. Then he turned, and a moment later he was dangling from the end of the rope with hardly a twitch.

Did Palmer poison Cook? We had completed our walk around Rugeley and were sitting opposite the Penny Bank, a building Billy would have known. 'Well, you know what he said while he was in prison,' said Edwina Morgan. 'He said, "I never gave Cook strychnine." I think he just doped him up to keep Cook out of the way long enough to get his money, and things got out of hand. But the joke is' – I could see Mrs Morgan was enjoying herself –

'the town council of Rugeley was so upset with the town's name being associated with Palmer that they actually went to London and petitioned the prime minister of the day to change its name. He told them they could change it only if they named it after him. And you know what his name was?' I shook my head. 'Palmerston!' Several people looked around in surprise as we sat laughing on the bench.

SISTER GODFRIDA'S
FATAL HABIT

Nothing much could happen to you in Wetteren. A Belgian town of some 20,000 souls, located about ten miles east of Ghent, Wetteren conveyed an air of peace and security – in this world and the next – as the bells from its seven Roman Catholic churches summoned the faithful to mass on Sunday mornings. The education of most of the children in this Flemish town was safely in the hands of the nuns, and, at life's end, the elderly of Wetteren had the serenity of knowing that their needs would once again be met by the sisters of the Apostolic Order of the Holy Joseph, who operated the old people's home adjoining their cloister. No homicide had been reported to Wetteren's sleepy police station in thirty years.

The atmosphere of good order and efficiency at the convent owed not a little to the Mother Superior, Sister Godfrida, a stern-looking woman with a prominent nose and hawkish blue eyes whose intense gaze novitiates found intimidating.

The daughter of a Flemish farmer from the nearby village of Overmere, Cecile Blombeck, as she was christened, was fifteen when her parents pressured her into joining the order. Sister Godfrida, as she became, to all appearances overcame her early distaste for the cloistered life, and her quick intelligence and self-assurance marked her early for promotion. By her late thirties she was Mother Superior, grown a little plump, but with the reputation for being a strict disciplinarian.

So, surprise would be an inadequate word to describe the reaction of a young nun, Sister Ursule, who had recently joined the order, to the scene she witnessed when she entered the room of a man in his sixties at the old people's home at ten o'clock one night in the summer of 1972 or 1973, and found Sister Godfrida standing beside his bed. Shock or horror might be better words.

'I thought that I had gone insane or was having a vision sent by the Devil,' she said later. Sister Ursule returned immediately to the sisters' duty room, sensibly downed a small glass of brandy to steady her nerves, and prayed devoutly for the restoration of her sanity.

Five years passed, years during which the shadow over the Order of the Holy Joseph deepened, years during which the nuns watched and prayed, and, then, finally, one by one, found the courage to discuss with each other their horrible fears. But when a brave few dared to inform the priest who was their director, they discovered how ultimately powerless they were as nuns: he ordered them to remain silent. Three of them nevertheless expressed their fears to a physician who worked at their clinic, Dr Jean-Paul De Corte, and, in 1977, after carefully checking their reports, the doctor informed the home's administration that he believed Sister Godfrida was a drug addict and warned of dangers to which the patients were, as a result, exposed.

Perhaps his warning caused Sister Godfrida to be discreetly spirited away on 'a retreat' – in fact, for treatment at a drug rehabilitation centre. The nuns breathed a collective sigh of relief. The atmosphere at the convent visibly lightened. Then, at Christmas, a card came from Sister Godfrida. After offering a seasonal greeting, the Mother Superior informed the sisters cheerfully, 'I shall soon be with you.'

Her arrival in the New Year was awaited with apprehension. She might, after all, be cured, and that would be an end to the matter. There was strain in the greetings the sisters offered their returned superior. And if they had hoped the treatment had worked, their hopes were quickly dashed. Almost immediately, Sister Godfrida went back to her old ways.

On Sunday 15 January 1978 three nuns, Sisters Franziska, Pieta and Godlive, agreed among themselves that the time had passed for complaints to their superiors. The civil authorities must be brought in. Murder, after all, was more than simply a little matter of internal discipline.

We have seen, in the case of Abbé Adélard Délorme, how reluctant the authorities – and juries – are in Catholic societies to even contemplate murder committed by a man of the cloth. Imagine, then, the fright that was in store for the law-enforcement authorities in quiet Wetteren as the three sisters filed into the police station that over-cast and rainy Monday morning, fully prepared to accuse their own Mother Superior of, not one murder, but ultimately dozens.

Consider for a moment, too, the immense com-munications barrier that had to be overcome in order that this impossible idea could be conveyed – the nuns fidgeting, unsure where to begin; the desk sergeant wondering idly what had brought no fewer than three nuns to the station. 'Yes, Sisters?' he said, with a deference harking back to his own schooldays. But the authority was all on his side now, and the young nuns stammered and looked at each other.

'We think we want to report a murder,' one said finally.

There was silence while the sergeant pondered these unlikely words. Did they mean they weren't sure whether or not to report it? he asked cau-tiously. No, not that, replied one of the three. They just weren't sure that what had happened was a murder.

It was not a good start to his week. The sergeant wondered again how three very innocent-looking nuns had found themselves caught up in a murder. As accidental witnesses to a Saturday-night brawl perhaps? As the trusted confidantes in some domestic tragedy?

'Who has been murdered?' he asked finally.

The name, they told him, was Mrs Maria van der Gunst, an eighty-seven-year-old resident of the old people's home who had died the previous summer, on 5 July. And who had done away with her? The three young women looked at one another, 'Our Mother Superior,' one answered. 'Sister Godfrida.'

The sergeant knew it was time to call in help, and shortly afterwards the three sisters, growing a little more confident now, were telling their story to Inspector Dyke Van Horne in the criminal investigation department. But, why on earth, asked the perplexed inspector, would the Mother Superior murder an elderly patient? What was there to gain?

'Her money and jewellery,' replied one of the nuns. It would have been easy to smile. What use would a Mother Superior have for money and jewellery?

To pay for the fine wines and brandies and expensive meals she ate at restaurants in Ghent, replied one. To buy her dirty magazines and sex gadgets, answered another. And for drugs – morphine, cocaine, heroin – replied the third.

That's when the world as he had known it cracked for Inspector Van Horne. Sex, drugs, murder – in the familiar convent and old folks' home down the street! At that point the inspector would not have been surprised to learn that flying saucers had landed in the police-station parking lot and that little green people were racing around town on police motorcycles. He would have to go carefully until he could establish whether the three nuns were completely mad – infected, perhaps, by some communal hysteria – or whether there was some grain of truth in what they were telling him.

If Mrs van der Gunst had been murdered six months before, and all those remarkable goings-on had been, well, going on, for so long, how was it that they were telling the police only now? he wanted to know. They had been ordered to remain silent, said one of the nuns. And, said another, they would likely have continued to hold their tongues if, on her return from the addiction treatment programme, Sister Godfrida had not fallen into her old ways. They had to do something, even if it meant going against their superiors and the church, before other patients were murdered.

Was Mrs van der Gunst not the only one, then? The nuns shook their heads. There had been others. Over a period of seven years. Who knew how many! And how had the old woman been killed? The sisters were quite definite: a diabetic, she had been given an overdose of insulin.

Inspector Van Horne nodded. There was at least a hint of plausibility in the method allegedly chosen by the Mother Superior. In Holland only the year before, Frans Hooijmaijers, a forty-one-year-old former monk, had been jailed for eighteen years for using insulin overdoses to kill five elderly patients on an old people's ward.

(In fact, the untimely extermination of hospital patients, young and old, by members of the 'helping professions' would become a not-uncommon phenomenon in the 1980s. Among the cases: the unaccounted-for deaths of a number of babies at the Hospital for Sick Children in Toronto, and the conviction in Vienna, in March 1991, of four assistant nurses in the deaths of forty-two elderly and 'bothersome' patients, some of them killed with overdoses of insulin.)

However, there was no more difficult allegation to prove than murder, or attempted murder, by insulin – as the several trials in the United States of Claus von Bülow for the attempted murder of his wife, Sunny, demonstrated in the 1980s. When the patient is already taking insulin, establishing that an overdose has been administered is almost impossible. Add to that the political problems Inspector Van Horne faced in conducting a discreet investigation into one of the most prominent church figures in Wetteren, and you have the perfect policeman's nightmare.

After ushering the nuns from his office with assurances that they had certainly done the right thing and had no reason to reproach themselves, the inspector turned to Detective-Sergeant Franz Gropa, who had listened open-mouthed in the inspector's office to the nuns' revelations. He hardly needed to explain to the detective-sergeant that, in this investigation, he would need the tact of a master diplomat.

Gropa was not long discovering that the severe Mother Superior had another life altogether away from Wetteren and away from the convent. She had been seen in restaurants in Ghent and Brussels, wearing smart pant-suits and ordering lavish meals, drinking to excess and publicly fondling her companion, a teaching sister of the order by the name of Sister Mathieu. On other occasions, calling herself Madame Cecilia and wearing low-cut dresses, she was seen at strip clubs and porn shows. At no point had she shown any inclination to bring home to the girls and their clients the error of their ways; on the contrary, she seemed to be enjoying herself hugely.

Sister Godfrida's behaviour might be unconventional, but that did not make her a murderer. Inspector Van Horne knew that, whatever the risks, other sisters at the convent must be questioned. Would they observe the ban of silence that had been imposed upon them? To his immense relief the sisters gladly cooperated, relieving themselves of the terrible secrets they had harboured for so long.

The troubles had apparently begun with the scene between Sister Godfrida and the patient in his sixties, 'and still vigorous', that Sister Ursule had witnessed about five years earlier. Sister Godfrida was standing beside the bed as the other sister entered. 'She lifted the skirts of her habit, and was showing him her body,' Sister Ursule told the police. 'I heard her say, "If you pay me well, I will make you happy." She then asked him for three thousand francs, and he agreed. He was lying on the bed in his dressing gown and she put her hand inside it. He also began touching her body.'

At the time, said Sister Ursule, she had not long been in the order, and was reluctant to tell anyone what she had seen. But soon it was hard to ignore Sister Godfrida's activities. By day, she was the pious, authoritarian figure; by night, a common wanton. 'I was in my room when Sister Godfrida opened the door with a master key,' testified one sister. 'She took off her habit. She was naked under it, and she stood in the brazen posture of a street-walker. She wanted to make love to me, but, when I threatened to shout for help, she left hurriedly.'

Several novices told Detective-Sergeant Gropa that, when they came on duty, Sister Godfrida would have them kneel and kiss her feet. Then she would lift her habit and invite them to kiss higher. And if they seemed reluctant, she would pull up their habits, and jab them in the buttocks or private parts with a hypodermic syringe. If they still refused to comply, she would beat them with a whip.

While nearly all the nuns resisted Sister Godfrida's approaches, one nun, Sister Mathieu, plainly enjoyed them. She and the Mother Superior made a show of their physical relationship and, while the other sisters lived on a spartan diet, these two enjoyed sumptuous meals accompanied by the best wines.

By their vows, by their training, the sisters were conditioned to accept a harsh life and hard treatment, and Sister Godfrida's scandalous behaviour might have continued unchecked if a number of patients had not died under mysterious circumstances. One old man had just sold his house; the money from the transaction disappeared when he died following a midnight visit from Sister Godfrida. An old woman would show her jewellery, worth about £1,250, to friends and to the nursing sisters. But, when she died one night for no apparent reason, the jewellery had disappeared. And then, the previous summer, Sister Godfrida had been seen emerging from Mrs van der Gunst's room, carrying a large syringe. By next morning, the old lady was dead. In each case, the deceased had no close relatives to create a fuss.

Amidst mounting gossip and excitement, shovels dug into the graveyard in Wetteren, and bodies were exhumed. But when the results of autopsies landed on his desk, Inspector Van Horne was no farther ahead. Clearly, there were traces of insulin, but no one could say for certain that the deaths had resulted from overdoses.

Without that evidence, the inspector knew he had no case to bring to court. Sister Godfrida had been well aware of the investigation, but had carried on normally. Normally in her case meaning that she continued to abuse the sisters and the patients. The only sign she might be cracking: she and Sister Mathieu had to be torn apart by the horrified nuns when they indulged in a donnybrook, ripping, scratching, throwing punches and damaging furniture.

Inspector Van Horne felt no confidence at all when, finally, he called on the Mother Superior to confront her with his suspicions. He expected outrage, denial, anger. But when he got the words out, when he asked Sister Godfrida if she had had anything to do with the death of Mrs van der Gunst, she answered matter-of-factly, 'Yes, indeed. I sent her to Heaven because she was too noisy. She disturbed my sleep.' Yes, she confirmed, she had given the old woman an overdose of insulin. Besides that, she had also sent two others, Peter Diggmann, eighty-two, and Leonie Maihofer, seventy-eight, to Heaven.

The inspector had never listened to a confession with a greater sense of relief. Suddenly the weight lifted from his shoulders. There would be no need for an embarrassing confrontation with the church and a trial that might well end in acquittal. The woman was obviously as mad as a hatter.

The explanation for why a woman of such steely demeanour and such self-discipline had experienced such a radical personality change gradually emerged. Several years earlier, Sister Godfrida had been operated on for a brain tumour. The operation had been an apparent success – except that the nun became addicted to the morphine prescribed for her as a painkiller after the operation. The combination of the fatal habit – for which Sister Godfrida would forge prescriptions, steal drugs and ultimately commit murder to get money for drugs – plus the subtle changes in her brain that had unleashed her long-suppressed libido set this train of tragedy in motion.

Beyond the three homicides Sister Godfrida could distinctly remember being responsible for, her memory was hazy. But after a medical commission made a study of death certificates and medical records, Dr De Corte told the press, 'She might well have killed thirty people.' Sister Godfrida was found unfit to stand trial, and today is a patient in a mental institution, where she is likely to remain for the rest of her life.

MURDER? CAN YOU PROVE IT WAS MURDER?

A certain kind of Englishman always dreams of dying and going to Eastbourne. The South Coast resort, with its creamy Edwardian architecture, its immaculate flower beds, the Palm Court Orchestra forever in the memory playing selections from *The Chocolate Soldier*, is a particularly British notion of what Heaven must be like. In practice, of course, the elderly rich, instead of dying and going to Eastbourne, go to Eastbourne and, eventually, die, their path into the hereafter eased by the ministrations of physicians, many of whom are noted for their bedside manner as much as their medical abilities.

In 1922, there arrived in Eastbourne a recently qualified twenty-three-year-old physician from Northern Ireland named John Bodkin Adams whose chatty Irish loquaciousness and comfortable, old-shoe manner suited him ideally for the hard slogging among the Rolls-Royces and lapdogs of Grand Parade. Who then could have foreseen that thirty-five years later the genial doctor would go on trial at the Old Bailey, charged with murdering one of his rich, elderly patients.

Adams was always a man of contradictions. Coming from a strong Protestant background, his father a jeweller, he bagged his first job in Eastbourne by answering an ad in an evangelical newspaper for 'a Christian young doctor-assistant'. Yet, his ruthless legacy-hunting as the years went by was anything but Christian. In Eastbourne today you will still find former patients of his who swear they never met a finer physician; others, probably the majority, believe he was the worst sort of murderer.

Even the professionals who observed him during the time of his trial in 1957 have widely differing opinions. Dr Tony Norton, the first psychologist appointed at Brixton Prison, where Adams was held in the prison hospital, no doubt in tribute to his professional status, tells me he had numerous discussions with the Eastbourne doctor about psychology and psychiatry. 'He impressed me as really quite bright,' says Norton. In contrast, Lord Devlin, the judge who presided at his trial, describes Adams as 'a stupid, obstinate and self-righteous man'.

At any rate, Adams was smart enough to gain a doctorate at Queen's University, Belfast, in 1926, and his diploma in anaesthetics in 1941. By 1930, he was installed in a large house called Kent Lodge, just behind Grand Parade, in the most

fashionable part of town. By the time of his arrest,
Adams, who never married, had four expensive
cars in his garage and about £62,500 in his bank
account, and enjoyed grouse-shooting holidays in
Scotland. By then, too, Adams was in the 'supertax'
bracket, and he made no bones about telling his
patients he would appreciate a legacy, a form of
payment on which, happily, the estate rather than
he paid the taxes. As early as 1935, we find the
family of one of his deceased patients unsuccess-
fully contesting a £7,500 bequest to Dr Adams, and
in a nine-year period prior to his arrest he received
fourteen bequests worth an average of £7,500. His
lucky touch with the dying netted him no fortunes,
but provided a handy hedge against the tax-man.

That the doctor should have a pecuniary interest
in his patients' early demise was bad enough; that
he also made a practice of writing prescriptions for
large amounts of heroin and morphine made his
behaviour even more suspect. But, to accord Adams
his due, he gave his patients freely of his time, the
poor as well as the rich, and, having no family himself, he made himself part of their social lives. In
the early 1950s, for example, he introduced one of
his patients, a Mrs Tomlinson, who was depressed
and suicidal after the death of her husband, to Jack
Hullett, a wealthy man in his sixties whom Adams
visited regularly on Sunday mornings. The happy
outcome was that the couple married and found
consolation together.

In 1955, though, Hullett, at home following an

operation, experienced a 'breathless attack'. Adams was sent for and, after receiving a morphia injection from the doctor, the man died in his sleep. From his estate, amounting to nearly £250,000, Hullett left the doctor £1,250. Adams, ignoring the law, stated on the form ordering cremation that he had no financial interest. No one seems to have given much thought to the circumstances of Hullett's death.

Immediately afterwards, his wife, widowed a second time in only a few years, was again depressed and suicidal, talking of throwing herself from Beachy Head, the chalk headland to the west of Eastbourne. Dr Adams was in regular attendance, and on 17 or 18 July, honouring a promise made by her husband that Dr Adams should have a new car, she gave the doctor a cheque for £2,500. An unnecessary piece of generosity this, you would think, considering she had made a will on 12 July leaving him her Rolls-Royce. Adams hurried down to his bank and, on being told it would take two days to clear the cheque, asked if it couldn't be done sooner. At his special request, it was cleared on the 19th.

The same evening, Mrs Hullett, complaining of a headache, went to bed early, and the next morning did not wake up. With Adams away at a meeting, his partner, Dr R. V. Harris, called at 3:30 p.m. and found her comatose. Harris thought the cause might be an overdose of barbiturates. Adams rejected the idea, but ordered an antidote to barbiturates anyway, and slept for several nights at the house, getting up in the night to give Mrs Hullett injections. She died on the 23rd.

Prior to Mrs Hullett's death, Adams had phoned the coroner to ask about the possibility of a private post mortem – a very unusual request, considering the patient was still alive, and one that might, when she did in fact die, have helped to precipitate the calling of an inquest.

And that was enough to unleash the maelstrom of publicity that has ever since swirled around the chubby, myopic Eastbourne doctor. Fleet Street was out in force when the adjourned inquest resumed on 21 August to hear the results of the post mortem. On the face of it, the facts uncovered seemed rather tame. Mrs Hullett had taken a fatal dose of barbiturates on the evening of the 19th. Adams testified that, knowing her suicidal tendencies, he had given her only two tablets a day of sodium barbiturate, although he had to admit there might still have been supplies he had prescribed for Jack Hullett in the house, and that, when he went on holiday in June, he had ordered thirty-six tablets for Mrs Hullett. The verdict was suicide, and apart from a mild suggestion of negligence, there was little that reflected badly on Adams. But, at the end of the inquest, a fateful encounter occurred when the coroner introduced Adams to a middle-aged man of military bearing, Detective-Superintendent Herbert Hannam of Scotland Yard.

Fuelled, it turned out, by the most reckless and damaging leaks from the police, the newspapers went to town. 'Yard Probing Mass Poisoning: 25 Deaths in the Great Mystery of Eastbourne', headlined the *Daily Mail*. And again: 'Inquiry into 400 Wills: Rich Women Believed to Have Been the Victims.'

Only one journalist held back from the pack. Percy Hoskins, the roly-poly veteran crime reporter with Lord Beaverbrook's *Daily Express*, was appalled at what he saw as a witch-hunt. The inquest had revealed nothing to justify the headlines. When he travelled up to London the following day with Dr Adams, though, he found the doctor naively ignorant of the danger in which he now stood. After ignoring Hoskin's warnings, the gabby doctor would have only himself to blame for providing the police with some of the most damaging evidence against him.

Detective-Superintendent Hannam, known to some as 'The Count' for his elegant gear and expensive cigars, and to his colleagues as 'The Sorcerer' for the miraculous way he produced confessions from suspected persons following intimate conversations alone with them behind closed doors, saw police work very much as a battle of wits. He believed in the one-to-one approach, which is why, arriving home in his car at 9:00 p.m. one October evening, Adams encountered Hannam standing beside his garage. 'I was just passing by,' Hannam would claim in court with a straight face.

The exchange began innocuously enough: 'Good evening, doctor,' said the policeman. 'Did you have a good holiday in Scotland?'

They talked in the early-winter dark about shooting in the Highlands and then, skilfully, the detective-superintendent got Adams talking about himself. He talked of his early days, his Christian upbringing. 'I gave a vow to God that I would look after my poor patients, day and night I will turn out for them . . . I think that makes people jealous of me.'

Then, a hint of steel, Hannam asked about the legacies. 'A lot of those were instead of fees,' Adams babbled on. 'I don't want money. What use is it?' And the chest of silver Mrs Edith Morrell, a patient who had died in 1950, had left him? 'Mrs Morrell was a very dear patient. She insisted long before she died that I should have it in her memory, and I didn't want it. I am a bachelor – I have never used it. I knew she was going to leave it to me, and her Rolls-Royce car.'

But – the stiletto clearly visible now – Dr Adams had signed the cremation forms for Mrs Morrell and Mr Hullett, declaring he was not aware he was a beneficiary under their wills.

'Oh, that wasn't done wickedly,' replied the talkative doctor, 'God knows it wasn't. We always want cremations to go off smoothly for the dear relatives . . . It wasn't deceitful.' A few minutes later the detective-superintendent took his leave. 'Good night, and thank you very much for your kindness,' said Adams, completely unaware of the fact that all the help and kindness had come from his side.

Cracking Dr Adams, as Lord Devlin has said in his remarkable memoir of the case, *Easing the Passing*, 'turned out to be like cracking a soft-boiled egg – one tap and the yolk was over the brim and away.' And when Hannam, accompanied by two other officers and half the world's press, arrived at Kent Lodge the following month with a search warrant, he must have been confident that, like the spider, he only had to sit still for the fly to enmesh itself in the web. 'There is no question of a statement,' said Adams, meeting them in the hall in evening dress on his way to a YMCA dinner, 'for I have been told not to make one.' Hannam, smiling inwardly no doubt, invited him into the office, while an inspector, acting on a dangerous-drug warrant, searched the house.

What drugs were they talking about? asked Adams. Morphine, heroin, that sort of thing. 'Oh, that group. You will find none here. I haven't any. I very, very seldom ever use them.' Could Hannam see the register he was required by law to keep? 'I keep no register,' replied Adams.

Hannam had come prepared for such stonewall answers. He invited Adams to examine a list of the drugs he had prescribed for Mrs Morrell. 'Who administered the drugs?' he asked. 'I did,' replied the doctor. 'Nearly all. Perhaps the nurses gave some, but mostly me.' Were any left when she died? 'No, none. All was given to the patient.' But, said

Hannam, seventy-five heroin tablets were prescribed the day before she died. 'Poor soul,' said Adams, stuck with his story now, 'she was in terrible agony. It was all used. I used them myself.'

While the police searched his office Adams, according to Hannam, held his head and appeared to be crying. Then he got up, took out a key, unlocked one of the two cupboards in the room, and appeared to slip something into his pocket. 'What did you take from that cupboard, doctor?' asked Hannam. 'Nothing,' he replied. 'I only opened it for you.' The policeman persisted. 'You put something in your pocket,' and finally Adams produced two bottles of hyperduric morphine.

'Doctor, please don't do silly things like that. It's against your own interests,' said the detective-superintendent.

'I know it was silly,' he replied. 'I didn't want you to find it in there.' The bottles were left over after two patients died, he explained. Two days later, Hannam returned with a warrant for Adam's arrest on a number of minor drug offences. 'Easing the passing of a dying person is not all that wicked,' Adams told the detective-superintendent this time. 'She [Mrs Morrell] wanted to die. That cannot be murder. It is impossible to accuse a doctor.' A decade or two later other doctors would be making similar statements in the great debate over euthanasia. But, of course, in Adam's case, there was the small matter of the Rolls-Royce and the chest of silver.

From the four hundred possible murders hinted

at at the start, the police had narrowed their investigations down to a dozen cases, and Hannam himself presented these to the attorney-general, a large
and florid gentleman named Sir Reginald Manningham-Buller (and referred to behind his back by
legal colleagues as 'Bullying-Manner') at the
House of Commons for decision. Manningham-
Buller selected the Morrell case as the strongest
and, on 19 December, Hannam arrested Adams at
Kent Lodge and charged him with murder. Again,
Adams did not disappoint his nemesis. 'Murder?' he
said, looking puzzled. 'Murder. Can you prove it
was murder?'

'You are now charged with murdering her.'

'I did not think you could prove murder. She was
dying in any event.' It is hard to imagine a more
damaging response, short of an actual confession.

A substantial group of Adams's patients still
believed in his innocence. In the public realm only
Percy Hoskins still stood behind him – even though
he was under severe pressure. The gnomic Canadi-
an-born Lord Beaverbrook, chafing at the sensational stories the rival *Daily Mail* was running,
would demand day after day of the *Daily Express*
editor, Ted Pickering, 'Are you sure?' Hoskins
knew he'd be out of a job if Adams was found guilty.
Chafing for a different reason was Geoffrey Lawrence, QC, the brilliant civil-court lawyer who
would defend Adams and for whom this case would
be a rare venture into the criminal courts. At a
terse meeting with Lord Devlin before the start of

the trial, a bitter Lawrence said that, in spite of the judge's intention to sequester the jury, so much harm had been done to his client through publicity that he saw no hope at all of him receiving a fair trial.

The one issue settled at the preliminary hearing, apart from the committal of Dr Adams for trial, was that evidence on the Hullett deaths would not be presented at trail to bolster the Morrell charge, although Manningham-Buller assured Devlin that if Adams was found not guilty on the first charge, he would be tried later in connection with the Hullett deaths.

The stage was set and on 18 March 1957 John Bodkin Adams, looking like an absent-minded dormouse suddenly exposed blinking to the daylight, pleaded not guilty in number-one court at the Old Bailey and the attorney-general rose to his feet and delivered what was seen as an unusually aggressive two-hour opening statement. Mrs Morrell, he said, was eighty-one and worth £392,500 when she died in November 1950 in her house on Beachy Head Road. She had suffered a stroke in 1948, and was attended by Dr Adams and four nurses. It was unusual for such a condition to result in pain, and yet, said the attorney-general, Dr Adams had prescribed large amounts of heroin and morphia for her.

Through all this, Adams, according to Sybille Bedford, who wrote an account of the trial, *The Best We Can Do*, sat slowly shaking his head from side

241

to side, as he would do through much of the evidence in a way that was 'oddly convincing'.

In April 1949, Adams had called in Mrs Morrell's solicitor because she wanted to write a new will in which she bequeathed him the chest of silver. A year later, Adams called the solicitor again and instructed him to prepare a codicil to the will. Mrs Morrell had forgotten to put him down for her Rolls-Royce and a locked box of jewellery, he said. Could it wait until the weekend, when Mrs Morrell's son, Claud Morrell, would be in town? the solicitor asked. But Adams insisted the codicil should be prepared right away. 'It showed, did it not,' said Manningham-Buller, lingering over the word, 'a certain keenness?'

Mrs Morrell signed the codicil but – and here the first tiny unravelling in the Crown case occurred – Adams went away on one of his Scottish holidays, and Mrs Morrell was so miffed she wrote him out of her will. In what were the final weeks of his elderly patient's life, Adams was increasing the dosage. 'The submission of the Crown,' said the attorney-general, 'is that he did so because he had decided the time had come for her to die.'

The jury, he said, would hear that, on the night of her death, Dr Adams himself came at 10:00 p.m. and filled – Manningham-Buller held up a large syringe for the jury to see – a 5 cc syringe, gave it to the night nurse, and told her to administer it. She did so, and the doctor refilled the syringe and told the nurse to give that too if the patient did not settle down. The nurse, reluctant to give such a large amount, later phoned the doctor, but was told to go ahead. She gave the second injection, and Mrs Morrell died at 2:00 a.m. And then there was Adam's peculiar statement: 'Can you prove it was murder?'

'Is that what you would expect an innocent man to say?' boomed the attorney-general, 'or is it what a man might say if he had committed a murder but thought he had done it so cleverly that his guilt could not be proved?'

The effect, in spite of Manningham-Buller's strong words, was one of anticlimax. After the talk of four hundred victims, was this all there was – one old lady being nudged down the road she was already headed on? Did Adams even know he'd been cut out of the will? And, if he didn't, would a doctor really murder for a car and some silver he thought he would be getting anyway when the patient died, inevitably, in a matter of days? The jury and the press of the world waited for better than this.

The second day was to see what Percy Hoskins calls 'one of the most vivid scenes that ever happened in the Old Bailey'. The prelude was a note handed to Hoskins from the defence team: 'Don't leave the courtroom. Fireworks in half an hour.' On cue, a man tiptoed in, carrying a suitcase, and, in a way guaranteed to rivet the attention of the whole court, stooped as he passed in front of the bench and put it down beside Lawrence. The first of Mrs

Morrell's four nurses, Nurse Stronach, was on the stand, answering questions from the defence counsel that seemed to be going nowhere.

She had, she confirmed, given Mrs Morrell a daily injection of a quarter-grain of morphia, while the doctor had given a further daily injection, with the nurses, on Mrs Morrell's orders, out of the room. Another of the nurses, said Lawrence, with deceptive vagueness, had said something at the preliminary hearing about everything being written down by the nurses in a book.

'Yes,' said Stronach, 'that is quite correct. We noted down every injection we gave.'

'All experienced nurses do it?'

'They should do.'

More serious: 'Everything that happened of significance in the patient's illness would have to go in the book – everything that was of any importance?'

'We reported everything. A proper report is written day and night.'

And now, a certain wistfulness crept into Lawrence's voice: 'So that if only we had these reports now we could see the truth of exactly what happened?'

'Yes,' said Stronach, adding reassuringly, 'but you have our word for it.'

Then, the bombshell: 'I want you to have a look at that book please.'

Claud Morrell had found the complete run of nurses' books covering his mother's illness in the house after her death. He'd sent them around with

the chauffeur to Kent Lodge, where they'd lan-
guished, first in a filing cabinet and later on a back
shelf, until discovered by a junior on the defence
team. They would transform the trial, providing
day-to-day evidence of what happened in the sickroom in place of the uncertain recollections of the
nurses of events that took place six years earlier.
And, by holding them back from the prosecution,
Lawrence had given himself the advantage of being
familiar with them, chapter and verse, while his
opponents had to scramble during recesses to try to
get a grip on this large and complicated body of
evidence.

Lawrence began to mop up right away. The books
showed that, for most of the period Stronach was
nursing Mrs Morrell, Dr Adams had not, as she
had said earlier, visited her daily and given her
injections. And where the nurse had earlier
described Mrs Morrell on the last day of her life
as 'semi-conscious or rambling', the book recorded:
'seemed bright this a.m. and not confused', while
for lunch she had partridge, pudding, and brandy
and soda.

Lawrence said, eyebrows raised, 'Consumed by a
semi-conscious woman? Miss Stronach, let us face
this: it is another complete trick of your memory to
say that on the last day Mrs Morrell was either
semi-conscious or rambling, isn't it now?'

'I have nothing to say,' replied the nurse. Rarely
in a courtroom can professional smugness have
been so quickly reduced to sullen silence.

The following morning, all the nurses were in hot water when Lawrence rose to say that, following strict instructions from the judge not to discuss their evidence outside the courtroom, the four women had been seen reading newspaper reports of the case and freely discussing it among themselves on the train to Eastbourne and back again that morning. Even more damaging, one nurse was heard saying to another, 'Don't you say that or you'll get me in trouble.' The 'that' concerned a locked cupboard in which Stronach had testified drugs were kept at all times. It turned out the drugs were never kept under lock and key.

As Lawrence took each of the nurses, entry by entry, through the books, the pattern became clear; the prosecution had been relying on the total amounts of morphine and heroin prescribed to show that Mrs Morrell had been progressively poisoned. But the record showed that, of the 41 grains of morphia for which prescriptions had been written, only 10.5 were administered, while of the 37.75 grains of heroin ordered, only 16 were given to Mrs Morrell. What happened to the residue is another question. The notebooks indicated that the two final injections, on which Manningham-Buller laid such emphasis as having finally caused Mrs Morrell's death, were neither morphia nor heroin, but paraldehyde, a harmless soporific, and of these two injections, only one was administered.

As to that suggestive reaction of Dr Adams: 'Can you prove it was murder?' – Detective-Superintendent Hannam, while betraying a characteristic arrogance towards defence counsel when he took his place in the box, at least offered the defence this: 'I think it is only fair to say this: Dr Adams was a very, very shaken man indeed [when he made that response]. I think he was very distressed.'

With so much of the Crown case in tatters, Judge Devlin had expected at the beginning of the second week that Manningham-Buller would drop the case. Instead, the judge found on his desk a new statement from the Crown's chief medical expert, Dr Arthur Douthwaite, saying that, in his opinion, even the lesser amounts of heroin and morphia actually administered to Mrs Morrell would have been sufficient to cause death. Manningham-Buller was pressing on.

If the prosecution thought that Dr Douthwaite, senior physician at Guy's Hospital and Britain's leading expert on opiates, a handsome man who towered six foot six and breathed decency and common sense, was the rock to which its foundering ship could attach itself, they were mistaken. At the very end of Douthwaite's testimony, after the doctor had conceded generously to Lawrence that other doctors might well disagree with his conclusion that Dr Adams had an intent to kill, the judge asked, in the mildest way, for some clarification regarding exactly when Adams, in the doctor's opinion, set out to kill his patient. And then, to the court's astonishment, the doctor announced an entirely new theory that had Adams beginning the fatal round of injections on 1 November rather than on 8 November, the date he had selected previously. Manningham-Buller, in the face of the nurses' notebooks, had already had to abandon the original theory put forward in his opening address. Due to poor prosecution preparation of the witnesses or simply to Douthwaite's inexperience in the witness box, the rug had again been pulled out from under him.

The evidence of the Crown's number-two medical witness, Dr Michael Ashby, who pointedly did not subscribe to Douthwaite's new theory, and the defence's only medical witness, Dr J. B. Harman, a stroke specialist who found the treatment given Mrs Morrell reasonable, must have confirmed for the jury the feeling that medicine is a very inexact science indeed.

The one decision remaining for Geoffrey Lawrence was whether to call Dr Adams to testify in his own defence. Can there really have been any doubt? An accused person who refrains from testifying runs the risk of the jury saying, 'What does he have to hide?' But Dr Adams had shown time and again that he was his own worst enemy. There was no telling what he might say in the witness box, undoing all the hard work and lucky chances that had clearly given the defence team the upper hand. Dr Adams, for once, would remain mute.

Lawrence had done his work. All that remained for him to do was to lay out the facts in his summing up. For a doctor to murder a patient 'whose life is limited to terms of hours or days or weeks for the sake of getting a bit of silver in a cabinet,' he said, 'is too ludicrous, isn't it?' The injections, the notebooks showed, had usually been given by the nurses, contradicting Adams's original statement to the police that he had given them; the nurses, present at nearly all times, had entertained no suspicions of foul play, and all the doctor had done was to ease the final sufferings of his dying patient. Confirmation of that had come from one of the nurses, Miss Randall.

'Mrs Morrell,' she said, 'told me that Dr Adams had promised her he wouldn't let her suffer at the end.'

Although the jury had been told to ignore the remark as hearsay, undoubtedly the words were remembered.

It took the jury only forty-six minutes to find the doctor not guilty. Manningham-Buller's discomfiture was complete when he announced that the Crown would not proceed with two further counts charging Dr Adams with the murder of the Hullett couple.

What had Adams done with all those dangerous drugs he had overprescribed, not only for Mrs Morrell, but for other patients? Logic would suggest the mercenary doctor was selling them on the side to the illicit drug trade. If so, he was never caught, and when he was again brought into court it was for a series of relatively minor misdemeanours in the handling of drugs, as well as making false statements on cremation forms. He was fined a total of £6,250 and was struck off the medical register, and his authority to prescribe dangerous drugs was withdrawn. He was restored to the register four years later, in 1961, though his regular patients had been coming to him anyway. He also had the satisfaction of collecting several libel settlements against his former tormentors.

In his summing up, Lord Devlin, going well beyond what is customary in judicial comment, had told the jury, 'I do not think that I ought to hesitate to tell you . . . the case for the defence seems to me to be a manifestly strong one.' But a strong defence is not the same as simon-pure innocence, and in his memoir, published after the doctor's death, Devlin writes, 'The mercenary mercy-killer fits best the picture of [Adams] I have in my mind.' The judge speculates that Adams may only have told the nurses those final injections were paraldehyde, when they were, in fact, heroin. Paraldehyde has an obnoxious and pervasive odour, and such was not noticed by the nurses. In his own mind, suggests Devlin, Adams would not have considered himself a murderer, but nevertheless, by the law as it stood then and stands as of the time of writing, the doctor, by terminating a life, even one that was hastening towards its close, was committing murder.

Adams was eighty-four when he died in Eastbourne in 1983, and, true to his philosophy of life, he rewarded forty-seven of the friends who had

stood by him during his troubles with legacies.
Among the recipients was Percy Hoskins. But, on
the very day the trial ended, Hoskins had earned
an exoneration he would never forget. He had only
just arrived back at the *Daily Express* office after
helping to smuggle Dr Adams out of the Old Bailey,
when the phone on his desk rang. He would recall:
'The rasping Canadian accents of Lord Beaverbrook declared, "Percy, two men have been acquitted today – Adams and Hoskins." '

MURDER ON THE
DENTAL PLAN

Alfred Hitchcock had a special affection for New York's Grand Central Station. In *Spellbound* (1945) and again in *North by Northwest* (1959), he had his heroes, played, respectively, by Gregory Peck and Cary Grant, pursued by police through the station's magnificent great hall and labyrinthine corridors. Our drama, too, begins in the great monument at the age of steam travel – to be precise, on 18 March 1915, with a young man, handsome and dashing enough to be played by Cary Grant, leaning out of the window of one of the first-class cars of The Wolverine, a crack express, as it drew sighing into the station from the wintry cold of Detroit and Grand Rapids.

Not even waiting for the train to stop, he leapt down, a newspaper clutched under his arm, and hit the ground running. Bounding up the stairs three at a time, he dashed to a pay phone on the upper concourse. The number he dialled was that of the Plaza Hotel. 'Mrs Walters, room 1105, please,' he told the operator. 'Margaret,' he said when the phone was answered, 'Arthur. Pay your bills and pack your bags and get out. I'll explain later.' Without waiting for her reply, he put down the phone. On the hotel switchboard, a private detective made a careful note of the one-sided conversation and, with a satisfied smile, put down his earpiece.

This scene too had its genesis in Grand Central Station, where, several days earlier, a young New Jersey schoolteacher, looking visibly agitated, got off a suburban train and made her way to the telegraph office. The message she wrote on the telegraph form consisted of only five words: 'Suspicions aroused. Demand an autopsy.' Then, flustered for a moment how to sign it, she remembered the name of a girlfriend, an ordinary enough name, and signed it, 'K. Adams.' 'Yes,' she told the clerk, 'it's to go to Mr Percy F. Peck in Grand Rapids.'

The arrival in Grand Rapids some twelve months earlier of Dr Arthur Warren Waite had not gone unnoticed by the mothers of that city with daughters of a marriageable age. Indeed, Waite, who was twenty-eight, made sure he was not overlooked by arranging an interview with the local newspaper in which he described his exploits and accomplishments. The mothers would have been impressed by the fact that he was not only a dentist, trained at the University of Michigan and the University of Glasgow, but that he was the son of a respected local merchant and his wife and had just returned from several years of dental practice in South

Africa. Their daughters were more struck by Dr Waite's matinee-idol good looks, a mane of dark brown hair that he would throw back as he spoke, and the fact that, with his sun-bronzed complexion and boundless vitality, he indeed put in the shade his winter-pallid Michigan rivals. And no one thought to mention that, when Arthur was growing up in Grand Rapids, he was known as a nasty little boy who enjoyed drowning kittens.

After his travels abroad, Waite showed no immediate enthusiasm for returning to dental practice. 'Doc', as he liked his friends to call him, was on a prolonged vacation and filled the idle hours making enquiries about the financial status of various young women around town. And when he settled on Clara Louise, the only daughter of an elderly millionaire drug manufacturer, John E. Peck, as his choice, he decided, surprisingly, to mount his main assault, not on the daughter, but on her mother, Mrs Hannah Peck.

'It was through mother that he gained consent to marry me,' Clara would recall. 'He paid little attention to me. His time was all for mother. He sat with her and told her stories of his accomplishments, and he had her completely won over in a short time. She suggested the marriage, telling me that it would be an excellent match and that I would be pleasing her if I consented. I was averse at first because father and Percy, my brother, were not favourable to the idea. We used to talk it over frequently, and then father and Percy gave in to mother's wishes, even though they slyly insisted that I should investigate his past. After a time, he began to lavish his attention on me, and with mother's helping influence, he succeeded in winning me.'

Clara Peck could not have investigated Dr Waite's background very thoroughly because, if she had, it is unlikely that her marriage to him on 3 September 1915, the social event of the year in Grand Rapids, would ever have taken place.

After the wedding, Waite proposed that they set up home in New York City, where he would have a chance to establish a more lucrative dental practice. In fact, after the couple rented a seven-room apartment suite in the Colosseum, at 435 Riverside Drive, Waite showed little inclination to do much beyond improving his tennis game. To explain his inactivity, he was soon telling people various stories. To some, he represented himself as a dentist trying to get his papers to practise in New York State, to others he was a medical doctor interested mainly in Wall Street speculations. He even deluded Clara into believing he had medical qualifications, leaving her one day parked outside a hospital while he went inside, he claimed, to perform an operation.

Even before his marriage to Clara, Waite had ingratiated himself not only with her mother, but with her aunt, Miss Catherine Peck, a wealthy woman who lived in the Park Avenue Hotel. He dined with her frequently, impressed her with his beautiful hymn-singing when he accompanied her to church, and convinced her of his business acumen. Soon Miss Peck was entrusting him, not only with treasured items of family jewellery, but with $40,000 that he was to invest for her, and was making it known that she planned to leave him a large bequest. Waite opened a $30,000 brokerage account and, reading in the Grand Rapids newspaper that his brother, Clyde, had resigned from the Bell Telephone Company, apparently under a cloud, he sent him a cheque for $10,000, with this surprising assurance: 'Don't worry, old man, there's a lot more where it comes from.'

When, from time to time, Miss Peck missed items of jewellery or fancied she had lost sums of cash, she did not connect it with her charming nephew by marriage. And when, one day, she tasted something gritty in her favourite marmalade, she simply returned the jar to the grocer.

At home, Waite played the affectionate husband and dutiful son-in-law, expressing pleasure when, in January, four months after the wedding, Mrs Peck announced she was coming for a visit. When she fell ill soon after arriving, Waite was indefatigable in his attentions. He sat with her, read to her, brought her flowers every day, and, when she complained of feeling cold, he went out and bought her a foot warmer. Only on one matter was he less than generous: when the doctor attending her suggested a night nurse, Waite said it really wasn't necessary. On Saturday 30 January Waite returned from a few sets of tennis to find his mother-in-law worse. In the morning, when Clara went into her mother's bedroom she found her dead.

With his wife in a state of shock, Waite insisted the body must be sent to Grand Rapids immediately. A casket lined with lavender satin was procured, and by 5:00 p.m. on Sunday they were on their way to Grand Rapids, where Waite persuaded the family not only that cremation was the sensible, modern answer to dispose of the remains, but that it had also been Mrs Peck's wish.

Back in New York, Dr Waite dedicated himself once more to tennis, to dashing around town in his automobile (garnering several speeding citations), and to adding to his collection of nearly a hundred suits. He also became a familiar figure in café society and a frequenter of the theatre, which was where he first saw Margaret Horton, a twenty-four-year-old performer more notable for her looks than for her voice.

Infatuated, he went to hear her day after day, arranged a meeting with her, and signed up for drama lessons with her, at which, appropriately, he read the part of Romeo to her Juliet. Impressed by his urbane manners, Mrs Horton, who was married to a man nearly twice her age, signed up along with Waite for French and German lessons at the Berlitz School of Languages. His next step was to set her up in a studio suite at the Plaza Hotel, which he reserved in the name of Dr and Mrs A. W. Walters.

There, Margaret Horton would assure sceptical listeners, they would pass their days platonically singing and, in the afternoons, practising their French.

'Dr Waite had an extraordinarily kind heart,' Mrs Horton would say. 'He loved all the fine sentiments and beautiful things of life. He used to say to me, "Margaret, when you sing you make me weep because you make me think of beautiful things." He loved music. It was that love of music that drew us together.' He painted her glowing pictures of his earlier life in London, England, where, he said, he had been in charge of a hospital, returning to the United States only because of the outbreak of the Great War. Perhaps when the war was over they would go together to London, he suggested.

He made no secret of the existence of Clara Waite. His wife, he assured her, was eager to meet her, although somehow the meeting never came off. But when some Peck relatives – Elizabeth C. Hardwick; her uncle, Dr Jacob Cornell; and her cousin, Arthur Swinton – happened to see Waite and Mrs Horton dining together at the Plaza on 22 February, he explained that he had just come from completing a major operation and, as a reward for his tireless nurse, Mrs Horton, he was taking her out to dinner.

Waite spoke, too, about money to his young protégée, telling her he expected soon to come into a large fortune. In fact, he was already viewing estates on the Hudson that might suit his new status. And her resources? Oh, she told him airily, she and her engineer-inventor husband had independent means. Both were indulging in a dance of deception: about this time her husband was filing for bankruptcy.

In February, too, the Waites invited Mr Peck, now lonely and disconsolate over the loss of his wife, to New York. His son-in-law spared no effort to cheer the old man up, going out for walks with him, and taking him for drives. When Mr Peck fell ill, Waite insisted he had the very medicine to make him better. At this time the old man had a lucky escape when Clara, coming into his bedroom, found someone had left the gas on. A servant was blamed. On 11 March Mr Peck experienced severe stomach pains, and Dr A. A. Moore was called. Believing his patient was suffering from only a minor digestive disorder, he prescribed a soothing remedy.

The same evening Dr Cornell, paying a visit, found Mr Peck's condition gave no cause for concern. As he was leaving, Waite came into the bedroom, carrying some medicine. Dr Cornell had the impression he had been waiting outside the door. He had the impression, as he stood in the hall, putting on his coat, that he heard the old man groan, but thought nothing of it. So, he was greatly surprised when he received a phone call from Clara early the following morning, informing him her father had died.

Dr Cornell hurried to the Waites' apartment

with his nephew, Arthur Swinton, but, when they rang the bell, Dr Waite blocked their way. 'What did you come for?' he asked with uncharacteristic brusqueness. 'I thought my wife called you up and asked you not to.' The two men finally insisted on coming in, and learned that Waite had already made arrangements for the body to be embalmed and dispatched the same day to Grand Rapids for burial. It would be noted later that both Mr and Mrs Peck had died on Sunday, when the coroner's office was closed, and that the bodies were on their way to Grand Rapids before the office opened again Monday morning.

At this point, it's legitimate to ask why on earth Cornell, Swinton, or other family members did not call in the police. The remarkable coincidence of two elderly people dying under such similar circumstances, and Waite's suspicious behaviour, should have set warning bells jangling all the way to Grand Rapids. But murder is not something that is supposed to happen among respectable folk living on Riverside Drive, and if there were doubts, they were generally put to rest by Arthur Waite's persuasive charm.

In Grand Rapids, though, Clara's brother, Percy, this time refused to allow cremation, and after the funeral the body was placed in the family vault. But he took no further action – until he received the mysterious telegram from 'K. Adams.'

Even as the first wisps of suspicions began to curl around Waite, he could not resist taking the next

261

step in his grand scheme. Clara had just inherited half her father's fortune – $500,000 – and, in their room at the Pantlind Hotel, in Grand Rapids, he suggested to her that, for their mutual protection, they should both sign wills, leaving each other their money in case anything happened. After all, the demise of her parents was a reminder of just how vulnerable we all are to fate. Clara, perhaps unsettled by her loss, began making out a list of bequests to her favourite charities. Oh dear me, sighed her husband, it wasn't necessary to be quite so generous, and he pruned the sum of her generosity to $18,000, with the balance going to himself. She copied it out at her brother's house, signed it and again at Waite's suggestion, it was sent to a lawyer's office.

At the same time Waite was telling old friends around town that his wife was not in the best of health and he did not expect her to live long. His words merited close attention: he had made similar predictions regarding his parents-in-law.

Did Waite realize that the game was almost up? Apparently not. With his father-in-law safely in the vault, he caught The Wolverine back to New York. It was only when he bought a newspaper on the train that he learned that an autopsy was to be performed on Mr Peck. By then, alerted by the Peck family, assistant district attorney Francis C. Mancuso and pathologist Dr Otto Schultze had already arrived in Grand Rapids from New York, and family members had engaged private detective

R. C. Schindler to track Waite's movements when
he returned to New York.

The autopsy revealed that Peck had died from
arsenic. For Arthur Waite, the result was an
admission of failure. He had planned to dispose of
his relatives using sophisticated new techniques
that would have defied the skills of the best pathologists. That he had finally had to resort to arsenic,
the easily detected poison of choice of the bumbling
amateur, was a come-down indeed.

Perhaps the idea had originally occurred to him
at some tedious lecture on hygiene at the University of Michigan, or maybe as he stood beside Clara
Peck at the altar. At any rate, it was an elegant
idea that anticipated the arrival of germ warfare
later in the century: how, Waite asked himself,
could murder be proved if he introduced the germs
of potentially fatal diseases like typhoid and pneumonia into the systems of his victims? Pretending
to be a medical doctor with a special interest in
bacteriology, Waite, soon after his arrival in New
York, was obtaining germs for typhoid, anthrax,
diphtheria, pneumonia, and influenza from the
Rockefeller Institute; the Willard Parker Hospital;
Bellevue Hospital; and Parke, Davis and Co., the
Detroit drug company. He also obtained disease
germs from Dr Percival L. de Nyce at the Flower
Hospital, but complained that they were not viru-
lent enough for his 'experiments'.

One person who followed the news of the autopsy
results in the newspapers with keen interest was

John S. Potter, the undertaker who had prepared Peck's body for transfer to Grand Rapids. If Waite was arrested, who would pay his bill? Potter presented himself at the Riverside apartment with a demand for payment. Wasn't it a bit early to be pressing for payment? 'It's the custom with out-of-town cases,' Potter lied blandly. Who had embalmed the late Mr Peck, Waite wanted to know. Eugene Kane, replied the undertaker. And had he used arsenic in the embalming fluid? Potter knew then that the bill for preparing the body might be a small matter compared with the sum Waite might be prepared to pay for other services. He would send Kane along to see him, he told Waite.

Next day, Kane, an embalmer of romantic inclination who had earlier been convicted for bigamy, found Waite in a nervous state. Could arsenic be used in embalming fluid? Yes, replied Kane, but that was illegal. If, when the police came to take a sample of his embalming fluid, arsenic could be detected, said Waite, he would give Kane enough money 'to set you up for life'. A figure of $25,000 was mentioned. Next morning, with police detectives shadowing him, Waite slipped into Gustave Cimiotti's garage, where he regularly had his car serviced, and asked Cimiotti if, as a favour, he would cash a cheque for $9,300 for him at the Corn Exchange Bank branch next door. Puzzled, Cimiotti went to the bank, but an equally puzzled bank official insisted on coming to the garage and identifying Waite before cashing his cheque.

Shortly afterwards, still under surveillance, Waite entered one of two telephone booths in a cigar store on Fifty-ninth Street. 'For God's sake, get the stuff into the sample,' he whispered to Kane, who was waiting in the adjoining phone booth. He stuffed the money into Kane's pocket before hurrying away. Police would eventually recover the money, buried in a can beneath a tree by a remote Long Island beach where the cautious Kane had hidden it.

The inevitable could not long be postponed. On 23 March detectives covered the exits of the Colosseum apartment building. Inside, they found Arthur Waite in a coma after taking an overdose of drugs. He denied later that he had been attempting suicide. I am inclined to agree with him. I don't believe he would have missed out enjoying his subsequent notoriety for anything!

In the apartment, police found a small medical library, including a book on poisons with a marker in the section on arsenic, as well as hundreds of microscopic slides containing what turned out to be the germs for potentially fatal diseases. No arsenic was discovered, but a check with drugstores in the area turned up a poison book bearing Waite's signature for a purchase of arsenic, which, he had told the druggist, he needed for putting down a cat. Shown the signature as he recovered in the Bellevue Hospital the following day, Waite, as usual, was not at a loss for an answer. 'I'll tell you, but you won't believe me,' he told the district attorney. 'Mr Peck was an old man and he was very despondent because of the death of his wife. He told me that he wanted to end his life and asked me to get some poison for him. I returned to the apartment with it and delivered it to Mr Peck unopened. I have no proof that he killed himself with the poison, but if they found arsenic in his body, I guess he did.'

As the district attorney left, Waite signalled to Schindler, the private detective working in the Peck family interest, to remain behind.

'I didn't poison the old man, I'm telling the truth,' he said.

'That's all well and good,' replied the detective, 'but how do we know you're telling the truth?'

'That's the trouble,' said Waite. 'But there's Dora Hillier, our servant. If you could see her you could tell her that I'll give her $1,000 if she will say she knows of her own knowledge that Mr Peck wanted to commit suicide.' True to his word he wrote out a cheque payable to Dora Hillier on a page of Schindler's notebook.

It was Waite's bad luck that he had not been able to read any newspapers. If he had, he would have known that Dora had already testified before the grand jury. Her story: that two days before Mr Peck died, her employer had come into the kitchen as she was ladling out the soup and had added some 'medicine' to his father-in-law's bowl. When he didn't eat the soup, Waite returned to the kitchen and added some more medicine to the old man's tea. By the following day, assistant district attorney John T. Dooling was claiming there was evidence that Waite had planned to poison his wife; his brother-in-law, Percy Peck; his aunt by marriage, Catherine Peck; and his mistress, Margaret Horton, and her husband. 'There seems to have been no limit,' said Dooling.

The two women in Arthur Waite's life reacted very differently. In Grand Rapids, Clara said the news that her husband was living with another woman at the Plaza was the last straw and that her love for him had turned to hatred. Not a penny of her newly acquired fortune would go to defend him, she said. Murdering her parents, apparently, was forgivable, but taking up with 'that woman' went beyond the pale. In New York, Margaret Horton, quick to capitalize on her notoriety, organized a small concert to which her lawyer invited friends and newspaper reporters. One critic described her voice as 'militant contralto'.

In Bellevue Hospital, Waite finally admitted to killing Mr and Mrs Peck, but insisted 'the man from Egypt', a sort of dual personality inside him, had made him do it. If he was hoping to convince a jury that he was insane, he hurt his chances by writing to Margaret Horton that he expected to be in an insane asylum for a while but then to recover his freedom. The letter found its way on to the district attorney's desk.

'My God, why can't I get this thing off my mind,'

Waite ranted in his hospital room to a detective named John Cunniffe.

'Who are you anyway?'

'I'm from the DA's office and I want to help you,' replied the detective ingenuously.

'You don't want to help me,' cried Waite. 'You, everybody, and the law are against me. I'm the worst scoundrel on the face of the earth!'

'Well,' replied Cunniffe, 'we all make mistakes.'

In Grand Rapids, Percy Peck was not prepared to take such a generous view. 'My one wish is to see Waite meet his merited end,' he said. 'His stories of my father's wish to commit suicide are absolutely false. He lies when he says it. The electric chair is too easy a death for my brother-in-law. If he were tortured it would be no more than fair.'

At the trial of Dr Arthur Warren Waite, which began on 22 May 1916, the identity of the mysterious 'K. Adams' who had first pointed the finger of suspicion was finally revealed. Taking the stand, Elizabeth Hardwick, Dr Jacob Cornell's niece, said she had taken an aversion to Waite from the beginning, and when she saw him with Margaret Horton at the Plaza she had no doubt from their behaviour that he was lying when he said she was his nurse. When her uncle told her of the reception he had received at the Waite apartment following Mr Peck's death, she was no longer in doubt about Waite's game: murder.

With Waite no longer making any attempt to deny his actions, the trail was remarkable for the complete reversal of roles between the defence and the prosecution. While the prosecution made every effort to make Waite appear sane and rational, the defence attorney, Walter R. Deuel, did everything in his power to portray his client as a devious and depraved monster in the hopes of getting him off on an insanity plea. In the witness box, Waite gave his attorney all the help he could, describing how, as a boy, he used to drown kittens, and how, in high school, he had begun the practice of stealing exam papers, a technique that got him through many of the hard spots in his university career. He had lost his first five jobs through dishonesty, he admitted, and in South Africa the firm for which he worked as a dentist had fired him when it was discovered he had been stealing from them. He did not love his wife when he had married her, he said, but was only interested in her father's fortune. But that did not stop him from stealing five dollars from his future mother-in-law's purse when he went on a trip down south with the family.

His first assay at murder, he said, was directed against Catherine Peck. 'Did you ever give ground glass to Miss Peck?' asked Deuel.

Waite smiled: 'Yes, I put some in her marmalade.'

'How did you give the marmalade to her?'

'Why, she had it there in the closet. I took it down from a shelf and put ground glass into it and left it there. She was fond of marmalade and ate it frequently.'

When that failed, he introduced germ cultures into a can of fish and presented it to her. Sometimes, he said, Miss Peck left milk and other foods out to cool in a window in the dining room, and every day or so he would empty half a test tube of germs into it. The germs were evidently not strong enough to bring down the redoubtable Miss Peck, so he turned his attention to his mother-in-law.

When she came to visit, 'I had everything ready for her before she arrived.' At their first meal together, he said, he went into the dining room ahead of the others and put what he believed were typhoid and pneumonia germs into her soup and other dishes. 'They acted on her immediately. She died within a week,' said Waite. The morning she died, he got up early to check that she was dead, then returned to bed, leaving the body for his wife to discover later.

But when Waite used the same techniques on Mr Peck, adding tubercular germs for good measure, they seemed to have no effect. Growing desperate, he gave the old man half a bottle of calomel (a compound of mercury and chlorine used as a laxative) at a time to make him sick, gave him pneumonia germs, took him riding in his car on cold days with windows open, and dampened his sheets before he went to bed. Nothing worked.

Then, said Waite, as one juryman finally gave way to laughter, 'I read in the paper how the soldiers in France were killed by chlorine gas. The paper said it was very effective, so I got some chlorine of potash and put hydrochloric acid in it and placed it inside his door. I fixed the electric heater with some stuff so it would smell as if varnish was burning if he woke up. But,' Waite shrugged, 'it didn't hurt him at all.'

'Did you give him anything else?' Deuel asked.

'Oh yes, I gave him arsenic along about Thursday or Friday.'

'How much?'

'All of it. A little at first, and then more until he had it all. I put it in food, oatmeal, rice pudding, hot milk, soup, and anything it seemed proper to put it in.'

The night Mr Peck died, said Waite, he had slept on the couch outside his room so that he could hear if anything happened. 'I slept a while and then I heard a groan. I went in and gave him chloroform.' When he returned to the room a few minutes later, there was no pulse. 'I wanted them to die,' Waite said in reply to another question. 'Why?' 'Because I wanted money,' was the reply. Was there any reason why he had killed Mrs Peck before her husband? Waite was silent for a moment. 'No, only that she was the first to come and see us.'

Several defence 'alienists', as psychiatrists were called then, claimed that Waite was a moral imbecile, in effect a psychopath who was not responsible for his actions. Mr Justice Shearn, in his address to the jury, demolished that argument. 'Moral depravity is not imbecility,' he said. At the conclusion of his five-day trial, Waite stood to hear the verdict with, as one observer noted, 'a pleasantly expectant expression on his face, as if some honour were about to be conferred upon him.' When he heard the 'guilty as charged' verdict, Waite did not give Percy Peck, sitting only a few yards away, the satisfaction of seeing him crumple. His composure intact, he returned to his cell and ate a hearty dinner.

Sentenced shortly afterwards to the electric chair, Waite passed his days on Sing Sing's death row writing poetry and giving interviews. 'I played the game and lost,' he told one reporter. He left his own contribution to the limited genre of death row verse with this, entitled 'Peace':

And when the sunshine plays along
The corridor to death,
Its light and shadows are but song
Unto my fleeting breath;
For where they play I soon shall pass
Down through the small death-door,
And I shall leave my failure there,
Forever more, forever more.

But when, after a medical panel finally ruled that he was sane, and the moment came to make that walk, Dr Arthur Waite was finally lost for words. 'Goodbye, boys,' he said, waving to the other prisoners on death row, and that was all.

THE DOCTOR WHO
MARRIED A MADAME

Now let's be serious. It's easy enough to chuckle over the case of the doctor who married the bawdy-house madame. The very notion of little Dr Robert Welsford Buchanan, twenty-nine and looking incurably naive behind his large, gold-rimmed spectacles, going to the altar with Anna B. Sutherland, a woman twenty years his senior, hair dyed orange, and with a large wart on the end of her nose, stretches our notions of romance past the breaking point. And when Dr Buchanan claimed afterwards that he simply had no idea the thrice-divorced Mrs Sutherland derived her fortune from the gentleman visitors who called nightly at her home on Halsey Street, in Newark, NJ, the snickers become guffaws.

But our sympathies should be firmly on the side of Mrs Sutherland. Because Dr Buchanan, appearances to the contrary, was a scheming scoundrel and, I am convinced, a murderer – not your average, blundering, spur-of-the-moment killer, but a thoughtful, ingenious craftsman who aspired to the holy grail of the homicide business: to commit the perfect murder. He was so clever, in fact, that the experts just couldn't agree on what, if anything, he had done to bring his wife's life to a premature end, and his arrest resulted in one of the classic poison trials of the last century.

Like the mass-poisoner Dr Neill Cream and a surprising number of the famous murderers of the nineteenth century, Buchanan was born in Scotland – on 17 October 1862. Presumably he must have emigrated with his parents because his first job was as a drugstore clerk in Halifax, a raw seaport and colonial outpost in Nova Scotia. An ambitious boy, Bob Buchanan went to Chicago to study medicine and graduated from the College of Physicians and Surgeons there in 1883, returning to Halifax to set up practice and marry respectable young Annie Bryce Patterson. A further period of study in Edinburgh preceded his arrival in New York in 1886.

He'd made the right move at the right time. A sober, hard-working young Scottish-born doctor was almost guaranteed success in that booming metropolis. But sober Robert Buchanan was not. Soon he was spending as much time carousing with his two closest companions, tavern-owner Richard Macomber and a retired British Army captain, William Doria, as he was at his office.

Buchanan was also a tireless womanizer who would eventually turn his friend Doria against him by persuading him to marry a young woman whom Buchanan, in the phrase of the day, had 'ruined'. But, in the days of their roaring friendship, there was nothing the trio enjoyed more than taking the train and ferry to Newark and passing a riotous evening with Mrs Sutherland's four brazen girls.

It may be that, in her cups, Mrs Sutherland was indiscreet about the money she'd made as a madame. Certainly, Buchanan set his eye on that fortune. Soon he was ignoring the girls and retreating to their employer's quarters, ostensibly to treat her for a kidney ailment. For fourteen years Mrs Sutherland had lived with James Smith, a handyman in her establishment, but he was soon kicked out in favour of the plausible young doctor. Both the discarded Smith and the outraged Doria would eventually play a part in the doctor's downfall.

But, for now, Buchanan was riding high, and soon Macomber was called in to witness a will in which Mrs Sutherland left nearly all her possessions to the doctor. And his side of the deal? On 12 November 1890 Buchanan divorced his wife, Annie, on the basis, if you please, of her adultery. Two weeks later, the owlish young Dr Buchanan and his ageing paramour exchanged their marriage vows before the Rev. Davis W. Lusk in Newark. The bride paid the $1,000 legal fees for the divorce as well as paying $9,500 for a house at 267 West Eleventh Street (in what is now Greenwich Village), the deed of which was in Buchanan's name.

Even before they married, the thankless Buchanan was protesting to his friend Macomber that it was Mrs Sutherland who was putting the pressure on him to marry although marriage to her would ruin his professional reputation.

Almost as soon as his new wife moved into the Eleventh Street house, which he shared with his mother and infant daughter, Buchanan was complaining about her behaviour. As a police surgeon and newly appointed Lunacy Commissioner, he had a position to keep up. But that was hard to do when his wife, who acted as his receptionist, was flippant and sometimes bawdy in greeting his patients, and shocked his more proper friends by telling outrageous stories and making blatant remarks about their sexual attractiveness or lack of same. (Frankly, Annie Sutherland sounds a whole lot more fun than her scheming husband.)

Soon, he was referring to his wife as 'the old crone' and 'the old hag', and, by the fall of 1891, he was confiding in Macomber his plans for getting rid of her. He would rent his practice to a younger physician and go to Edinburgh to continue his studies. The old woman had Bright's disease and would die in six months anyway, he said confidently. But a few days later, he had to report that when he had broached the topic with his wife, she had insisted on coming to Edinburgh too.

Anna Sutherland Buchanan was finally coming to her senses. She sent Macomber a note, 'Here it is one o'clock in the morning and the doctor is not at home. He is bad enough without any outside help. I do not wish you to call any more.' And Buchanan, who by now had an eighteen-year-old mistress, was soon telling his buddies that he was worried because his wife had been to a lawyer to enquire about recovering the money she'd given him. The doctor cannily paid the same lawyer $50 to look after his interests. 'He told me not to give up a cent, but to get rid of her any way I could,' he reported.

In March 1892 he told Macomber his wife was planning to return to Newark to reopen her house. She had also threatened to poison herself. 'Why don't you do so?' he replied. 'You know where my poisons are kept.'

The following month, Anna Sutherland indeed fell ill, collapsing in the dining room and experiencing excruciating pains in the head and difficulty in breathing. Buchanan carried her to her bed, then, if he was trying to do away with her, did something totally inexplicable: he called in the best medical help.

He enquired of Mrs Ida Brockway, the wife of a dentist to whom he was going to rent his house, whether she knew of a good nurse. Shortly afterwards, Mrs Brockway brought around Sarah Childs, who, everyone subsequently agreed, was an able and experienced nurse. They found Buchanan at his wife's bedside, giving her medicine out of a spoon. Mrs Brockway saw him administer two spoonfuls, but Nurse Childs saw him give her only one. His hands, the nurse noticed, were trembling.

Next, Buchanan called in two highly reputable physicians, Burnette C. McIntyre and Henry B. Watson. McIntyre, the first on the scene, found Mrs Buchanan fearful she was dying and wanting to see a lawyer. Her temperature was normal, her pulse rapid. He diagnosed a simple case of hysteria and prescribed bromide of sodium. The nurse would remember that Dr McIntyre casually sniffed the contents of the medicine bottle from which Buchanan had given his wife medicine, but that he had obviously noticed nothing unusual.

When he called back a few hours later, McIntyre found the patient worse, but prescribed only chloral, a relatively innocuous remedy. When he returned in the evening, Anna Buchanan was in a profound coma. Even when he slapped her face she did not respond. The doctor thought perhaps the woman was allergic to chloral, but Buchanan assured him that another doctor had earlier prescribed much larger doses for her. After a conference with Dr Watson, the two physicians decided the only plausible explanation for her symptoms was cerebral apoplexy. It was quite likely, said Buchanan, because his wife's father had died from the same cause.

The doctors stayed until after midnight, not because they could do anything, but out of courtesy to a fellow physician whose wife was dying. 'We thought she would die any hour,' McIntyre would say. 'It was a hopeless case.' When he called again at ten the next morning, she was still alive, although her temperature was 105° and her face florid. These symptoms only confirmed the diagnosis of cerebral apoplexy. That afternoon Buchanan told Nurse Childs he had to go out on urgent business. Shortly after he left, his wife died. The date was 23 April 1892.

Buchanan's 'urgent business' was cruising the taverns with Macomber. Later, after returning home and learning of his wife's death, he told Macomber he was checking into a hotel that night. Why? 'I wouldn't stay in that house with the corpse for $1,000,' he replied.

But, if Buchanan caused his wife's death, he again did an unlikely thing: he had her embalmed before burial at Greenwood Cemetery, thus preserving any evidence of wrong-doing. The day would come soon when he would tell a friend, 'Oh, if only I had had the sense to have the old hen cremated.'

On the way back from the burial a few days later, Buchanan told Macomber a great weight had been taken off his mind. The lawyer had reassured him that his wife had not changed her will. The two friends celebrated in a succession of taverns.

He collected the $50,000 due him under the terms of his wife's will, hired a private detective to make a daily check on his wife's grave to make sure it had not been disturbed, and left for a trip to Nova Scotia. And then Buchanan's luck ran out. The aggrieved James Smith learned of Anna Buchanan's death and went to see a coroner. Buchanan, he said, had married the woman only for her money, and her death so soon after was mighty suspicious. The coroner, Dr Schultz, dismissed Smith's suspicions as groundless. Mrs Buchanan's death certificate, showing cerebral apoplexy as the cause of death, had been signed by two of New York's most respected physicians, he pointed out.

But Isaac White, a reporter with the *New York World*, had overheard Smith's conversation with Schultz and, scenting a story, he followed the disgruntled Smith into the street, got more details, and went to see Dr McIntyre. At that time, the Carlyle Harris murder case, in which a medical student had been convicted of poisoning his secret wife, Helen Potts, with a morphine pill, was fresh in the mind of New Yorkers. Yes, McIntyre had to agree, some of the symptoms Mrs Buchanan exhibited were consistent with morphine poisoning. But, he explained to White, there was one infallible test for detecting morphine: the pupils contract. And he and Dr Watson had been careful to check the woman's eyes and had seen no sign of contraction, even though Buchanan had told them he had been treating his wife with morphine for a kidney ailment.

Undeterred, White went to see Buchanan's drinking buddies, Macomber and Doria, and learned of a significant remark the doctor had made at the time of the Harris trial. 'Harris is a fool,' he had told them. 'An amateur. He just didn't know how to disguise the symptoms of morphine.

Every acid, after all, has its neutralizing agent.' It wouldn't be hard at all, he said, to devise an undetectable poison.

Piecing together the story, White discovered that Buchanan had cancelled his trip to Europe just ten days before his wife was taken ill, and that Annie, his first wife, had also left New York for Nova Scotia around the time of her successor's death. Wiring the authorities in Halifax, White learned that Dr Robert Buchanan had remarried his first wife in Windsor, Nova Scotia, three weeks after the funeral of his second wife.

This was enough for the authorities: Anna Buchanan's body was dug up forty-three days after burial, and an autopsy was performed. The organs were all found to be healthy, there were no lesions suggesting a cerebral haemorrhage. And when the eyelids were lifted there was no telltale contraction of the pupils to indicate morphine poisoning. The doctors were perplexed.

Reporter White would claim that it was he who solved the mystery. When Buchanan returned to New York on 18 May, White tracked him down to Macomber's bar. But even after the journalist plied him with drinks, the doctor gave nothing away. It was while looking into Buchanan's thick-lensed glasses that White recalled that, at school, when a friend was having an eye examination, the doctor, to enlarge the pupil, had used a few drops of belladonna.

Buchanan, hounded now by reporters, made

preparations to flee. At his friend Macomber's suggestion, he gave him power of attorney to conduct his financial affairs – a deal that would certainly have operated in Macomber's favour if Buchanan had not been able to return. But, before the plan could be put into action, Buchanan was arrested and charged with poisoning his wife, either with morphine or with some unknown poison.

Buchanan would languish in the Tombs, New York's notorious prison, for nearly a year before his trial began on 20 March 1893. The prosecution, led by district attorney Delancey Nicoll, and the defence, led by a notable orator, Charles W. Brooke, used the time to marshal some top names in forensic science for one of the great courtroom confrontations of the era.

First, though, Nicoll spun a devastating web of circumstantial guilt around Buchanan, tracing his marital manoeuvrings, and his manipulation of Mrs Sutherland for his own financial ends. The prosecution's star witness was former friend Richard Macomber, who said he had become convinced of Buchanan's guilt after a conversation with that other former friend, Captain Doria. Macomber, a Yankee caricature with Vandyke beard, elegantly pointed patent leather boots, and a tendency to begin every answer, 'Wa-a-al', recalled Buchanan's talk of 'getting rid of the old woman'.

Buchanan, he said, panicked when the *New York World* started hounding him. Macomber was present when Buchanan's lawyer told him, 'If you did poison her, my advice to you is to get out and go as far as you can. If you did not, then stay here and face it out.' Buchanan made enquiries about countries that had no extradition treaties with the United States, then decided he was going to live in Milwaukee under an assumed name. If it all blew over and it was safe for him to come home, Macomber was to write him, 'Will ship goods at once.' If the contrary: 'Cannot ship goods.'

Buchanan was still in town the following day, however. He'd missed the Milwaukee train, he said. At another point, declared Macomber, Buchanan had said fearfully, 'My god, if they dig the old woman's body up they will find it full of morphine.'

In fact, Professor Henry P. Loomis, a world-famous pathologist who had conducted the autopsy, testified he had found no cause of death. And microscopic examination of the brain had revealed no signs of haemorrhage.

At this point the defence unleashed its secret weapon: William J. O'Sullivan, a brilliant young lawyer, barely thirty, who also had a degree in medicine from Yale and who had been preparing the case for six months. In half an hour, O'Sullivan had the renowned expert admitting he hadn't made notes of his findings, hadn't even examined some of the organs in detail for six months after the autopsy, and was unaware that the embalming fluid used on Mrs Buchanan contained arsenic and zinc, although the fluid might have caused changes in the brain. O'Sullivan, backed by his own team of experts sitting at the defence table with about a hundred medical volumes ready at hand, exposed inconsistencies in the autopsy report and, after Loomis had to admit there were diseases that could have caused death, but which he had not even thought of, he left the witness box with his reputation in tatters.

T. Mitchell Pruden, an eminent professor of pathology who had assisted Loomis, fared even worse on the stand. When a wax model of the human brain that Pruden was using to make a point proved inadequate, O'Sullivan handed him another brain. 'Why, this is a mere caricature,' said the witness scornfully. O'Sullivan smiled as he retrieved the object, which was, in fact, an actual human brain taken from the corpse of a man who had died of Bright's disease.

Although the district attorney had spoken of 'amazing amounts' of morphine being found in Mrs Buchanan's stomach, when Professor Rudolph Witthaus, an eminent toxicologist, took the stand, he had to admit that a series of elaborate tests had indicated the presence of only one-tenth of a grain. 'Let me see it,' demanded O'Sullivan. Witthaus said he could not, that his tests indicated only the presence of morphine. Witthaus had also put some of the contents of the stomach into the eye of a kitten. When this caused the pupil to dilate he inferred the presence of atropine, a product of belladonna that conceals the symptoms of morphine.

284

But O'Sullivan scored again when Witthaus had to admit other products of decay could have produced the same results.

The prosecution case was falling apart. Desperately Nicoll threw in more last-minute medical witnesses. O'Sullivan and his team of experts chewed them up. Then O'Sullivan fielded his own team of experts of even greater eminence and proceeded to destroy any lingering plausibility the prosecution case might have had. Victor C. Vaughan, counted America's greatest bacteriologist, actually set up a lab in front of the jury, re-created the tests that had been done for morphine, and, passing around the results among the jurors, showed that the original results had been totally meaningless.

O'Sullivan had done a remarkable job. The prosecution had been unable to prove that Anna Buchanan had been given a fatal dose of morphine, or, if she had, how it was given. But the defence had failed to take into account two factors: the unutterable boredom of the jury in the face of days and days of tedious technical evidence – some jurors slyly read newspapers while others dozed – and the insufferable vanity of Robert Buchanan.

If the jurors had not been paying much attention during the weeks of medical testimony, they sat up with a start when Buchanan, against all good sense and apparently against the advice of his counsel, went into the witness box. The doctor had been impressed by the fact that the medical student, Carlyle Harris, had failed to testify, and he had gone to the electric chair. Resolved not to make that mistake, Buchanan, outwardly composed, except for tapping his Masonic ring on the edge of the box, calmly denied having poisoned his wife and said he had never even prescribed any medicine for her after they were married.

For the prosecution, Buchanan in the box was a gift they couldn't have hoped for. 'Did you know [Mrs Sutherland] kept a house of prostitution in Newark?' asked Francis L. Wellman, a member of the prosecution team. 'I did not,' replied the witness as knowing smiles went around the courtroom. 'Did you not see girls at the Newark house?' He replied: 'Only the coloured servant and the one young woman who I understood was a friend.' After that, not even Buchanan's own mother would have believed a word he said.

And there was no stopping the man. As Wellman asked him about all the desperately incriminating evidence – paying a man to watch her grave; his hasty remarriage to his first wife; the fact that his wife's father had died of gangrene and not apoplexy, as he had told the doctors; the tasteless remarks about his older wife – Buchanan, not giving his counsel time to object, blurted out implausible denials.

It was that image of a lying scoundrel that the jurors carried with them into the jury room, and not those seeds of doubt so expertly sown by the young O'Sullivan. But there was to be a last surprise in this roller-coaster trial. When the jury asked to have some of the medical testimony read over to them again, Buchanan was confident he would be acquitted. The first Mrs Buchanan, a small, plump person with, like her successor, red hair, appeared in the courtroom ready to join her husband in his victory, and sounds of laughter came from the dock.

But the jury continued to deliberate. After twenty-eight hours, with some of them looking on the point of collapse, they adjourned for dinner to the Astor House Hotel after apparently having decided on a verdict. In the dining room, one of the jurors, a salesman named H. M. Paradise, collapsed, began bleeding at the nose and raving that he wasn't the murderer. A doctor living at the hotel revived him with infusions and injections of brandy and, at the urging of the judge, pronounced him fit to deliver a verdict. Paradise was half-carried into the courtroom, and his response when the jury was polled was inaudible. But the verdict was clear: guilty as charged.

Buchanan's lawyers objected furiously to the procedure. Paradise, they claimed, was an epileptic, and Buchanan had been tried by 'eleven men and one lunatic'. The appeals dragged on for more than two years. It was not until 2 July 1895 that Buchanan, who never confessed, went to the electric chair in Sing Sing. When his heart was found to be beating after the first charge, a second charge was administered. Police afterwards had to be called out to control the crowds that thronged to a funeral parlour where his body was put on exhibition.

That Buchanan was guilty of murder there is little doubt. Likely murder was not part of the scenario when he originally divorced his wife and married Mrs Sutherland for her money. He had obviously concluded she would not live long and then he would come into her money. That was his miscalculation. When she showed no sign of decline, and life with her became increasingly intolerable, Dr Buchanan turned his medical skills to deadly use. Luckily for the prosecution, Buchanan, like many murderers, was boorish and insensitive. The medical evidence fell far short of what was necessary to convict him. It was his loose tongue that did him in.

THE
CHARNEL HOUSE

Madame Ginas made small talk as she poured the
tea, but there was no hiding the nervousness of her
guests. Maurice Walbert, ignoring her invitation to
take a seat, stood fretfully before the window of the
concierge's little living room, glancing out at every
sound, while the teacup rattled audibly in his wife
Lina's hand before she found a spot on the crowded
side table to put it down. Adrienne Ginas had no
doubt at all that the Walberts – if that was even
their real name – had reason to be worried. As Jews
in Paris in this, the second year of the German
occupation, they were liable to arrest and deportation to an uncertain fate at any moment.

'Don't worry,' she reassured the couple, who were
accompanied by Maurice's elderly mother, Rachel,
'Dr Eugène will be here soon.'

For France's 350,000 Jews, a community that
dated its origins back to the first century AD, the
blinkers had finally come off in the summer of
1942. The Vichy regime's mounting harassment of

the Jews – many of them refugees from Germany, Belgium and the Netherlands – switched in July, with German prodding, to one of outright removal of the Jews.

On the morning of 16 July, French police raiding parties fanned out across Paris and by the following evening 6,000 Jews were lodged in Drancy, a half-completed apartment building used as an internment camp, while another, 7,000 including 4,000 children, were spending the first of many hideously uncomfortable and chilly nights on the benches at the Vélédrôme d'Hiver, a sports stadium outside Paris. The internees could not know that the two camps were only way stations on the road to Auschwitz where, in the next two years, 70,000 Jews from France would perish.

If they could not even imagine the horrors of that final destination, the Jews who still enjoyed a sort of freedom – although forced to wear yellow stars and denied their businesses, their jobs, even the privilege of shopping except in restricted hours – hid and dodged as best they could. Most vulnerable of all were the refugees, people like the Wolffs – for that was the real name of the trio waiting nervously in the concierge's living room at 10 rue Pasquier. Since Hitler had come to power nine years before, this wealthy lumber family from Königsberg, in Germany, had been more or less on the run, first to Amsterdam and now, after many scares, to Paris.

Madame Ginas' eyes widened at the tap on the

glass. She pulled the curtain back a crack, then, 'Come in, doctor, please come in.'

The first impression the Wolffs had of Dr Eugène was that of a butterfly in a dungeon. In drab occupation Paris, his well-cut double-breasted suit, the lavender bow tie and, most of all, the effusive manner and gracious hand gestures were reminders of a departed Paris. It was the doctor's eyes, dark, bold and utterly engaging, Maurice decided, that gave the physician his sense of magnetism. And, amazingly, almost before he'd found a seat and accepted a cup of tea, he was chatting away, not about their deadly serious business, but about Picasso and Ravel. The Wolffs, trying to contain their nervousness, followed his lead, and it wasn't until he'd accepted a second cup that Dr Eugène said finally, 'Well, well, I hear you would like my assistance.'

'Is it possible? Can you help us escape? We can pay,' said Maurice.

'Money, dear sir! That's of the least importance. I only do what I must so that people like yourselves can be saved from these Nazi bastards – begging your pardon, Mesdames. It's little enough, but it's my small contribution towards the day when France will be free again. Of course I can help. I seen no great difficulties. Within a few weeks, rest assured, you will be free and in South America or in any other part of the world that suits you.'

The Wolffs felt the cold steel around their hearts release. Only a few days before they'd had to flee

291

their hotel once again when the Gestapo had moved into the building next door. A chance connection had put them in touch with a Romanian Jewish woman, Eryane Kahan, who had not only found them a flat in her building at 10 rue Pasquier, but had offered to put them in touch with Dr Eugène, a French physician who operated his own underground Resistance group known as Fly Tox. And now, as he explained the details, the doctor seemed to offer them final release from their years of fear.

Yes, they could take all the money they wanted, he assured them, as well as two suitcases each. But they must make certain that their clothing contained no identifying labels. They should discard their old identification papers, but bring along ten photographs of each of them, five full-face and five profile. They would be hidden in a safe house for a few days while their documents were prepared.

'What were you told regarding the cost?' he asked.

'Madamoiselle Kahan said 25,000 francs (about £2,000 in today's currency) would be needed for each of us,' replied Maurice.

'That's good,' said the doctor, nodding. 'Some unscrupulous agents bringing me people have been asking 50,000 francs. It makes me furious!' His eyes flashed. 'That they would sully this noble work of humanity for low greed! Of course, I keep none of the money myself – it goes only to pay guides and document preparers and so on.'

The Wolffs were visibly more cheerful as the

doctor prepared to leave. 'I'll send a message and come and get you myself,' he said. Then, standing with the door open, 'A last thing. I'll have to give you innoculations to meet various international rules. Not afraid of needles, I'm sure?' All three smiled.

It was late in December when the Wolffs received word that Dr Eugène was to call for them that evening, but their preparations were already made. The women had sewn their jewellery into the shoulder pads of Maurice's suit, and their suitcases were packed with clothing and bedding for their new life in South America.

With mixed feelings of fear and anticipation they waited once again for Dr Eugène's knock. As they left, Madame Ginas watched them walk off down the street, Dr Eugène carrying two of the suitcases to relieve the women. No one ever saw Maurice, Lina and Rachel Wolff after that.

And then there were the Bastons, a Jewish family who, learning from their friends, the Wolffs, of Dr Eugène's miraculous escape route, summoned four of their relatives from their marginally safer hideaway in Nice so that they could all make their escape together. At that time safety lay mainly over the Pyrénées to Spain, but the crossing was desperately dangerous and guides would charge as much as a million francs, and then it's estimated only a third got through. Dr Eugène was unique in charging such modest prices and giving such convincing assurances of success.

And, in that dangerous summer, there had been the Knellers, Kurt, his wife Greta, and their son Rene, seven, who, after narrowly escaping being swept up in the July police raids, contacted Dr Eugène. Soon the doctor arrived at their flat with a handcart and accompanied by an elderly man. He had come to pick up suitcases belonging to the Knellers, who had already gone into hiding, he said. He played with Rene, who was being looked after by a friendly neighbour, as his assistant loaded the suitcases. He wanted to take the Knellers' furniture too, but their landlady wouldn't allow it.

And not just Jews. In the spring of 1943 Dr Eugène arranged for the escape of no less than nine underworld characters: pimps, prostitutes, thieves, Gestapo informers, people with colourful names like Jo le Boxeur, Adrien le Basque and Paulette la Chinoise (who told friends she was going to open a brothel in South America, and who took along her favourite black satin gown embroidered with swallows in gold thread), all of whom had reasons for escaping from the authorities. Several had even disguised themselves as Gestapo officers in carrying out robberies, so they too experienced feelings of relief when Dr Eugène met them by prearrangement at a barbershop on rue des Mathurins on a weekend morning and led them, like a cast call for *Guys and Dolls*, to his safe house in preparation for their escape.

Only one set of would-be escapers balked at the

last moment. Michel Cadoret de l'Epinguen, his wife Marie, a physician, and their son, were put in touch with Dr Eugène by Eryane Kahan in April 1943. He gave them the usual details about baggage, money, the need to stay hidden for forty-eight hours, and the injections. But when Marie, as a doctor, spoke to him about the availability of drugs in South America, she found his manner of speech odd and disjointed. His hands, unlike those of any doctor she had ever met, were dirty. Acting on her intuition, the family withdrew at the last moment and received their money back.

Dr Eugène's luck could not last indefinitely. In a city where informing had become a means of survival for many, not one but two German agencies were, unknown to each other, converging on Fly Tox, the doctor's escape network. Yvan Dreyfus, a wealthy Jew in the electrical business, had had the bad luck to fall into Nazi hands in 1940 while assisting the Resistance. With her husband liable to be deported to Germany at any time, Paulette Dreyfus handed over several million francs to French intermediaries to ransom her husband. As the final price for his freedom, Dreyfus was required to sign two letters – just a formality, he was told – implicating himself in helping the Germans. Once free, his note was called, and he was instructed to infiltrate Fly Tox by offering himself as an escapee to the mysterious Dr Eugène.

Dreyfus met the doctor at the barbershop on rue des Mathurins a couple of times to make arrangements. When, on 19 May, he made his final rendez-vous with the doctor, the two of them easily evaded the Germans following them, and Dreyfus, carrying the customary two suitcases, must have congratulated himself on the ploy that would soon see him free and far from Paris.

It was a Frenchman, Charles Beretta, already arrested once by the Germans, living in Paris with false identity papers, and whose wife was awaiting deportation to Germany from the camp at Drancy, who finally cooked Dr Eugène's goose. On Gestapo orders he offered himself as a candidate for Dr Eugène's underground railway and when, only two days after Dreyfus' disappearance, and carrying his travelling bag, Beretta met two of the doctors' accomplices, Gestapo men seized all three. It took only moderate pressure to force one of them, Raoul Fourrier, the sixty-one-year-old proprietor of the barbershop, to reveal 'Dr Eugène's' real identity and address. At an apartment on rue Caumartin, near the Galeries Lafayette department store, they burst in on Dr Marcel Petiot, his wife, Georgette, and, by chance, another of Petiot's accomplices, gangling René-Gustave Nézondet, forty-eight, a devious-looking man with one drooping eye who had been town clerk of Villeneuve-sur-Yonne, a town one hundred miles south of Paris, when Dr Petiot was its controversial mayor.

Petiot was kept in jail by the Gestapo for eight months and, I have no hesitation in saying, conducted himself like a hero of the Resistance. His treatment began with routine beatings. When these produced nothing beyond his admission that he was part of an escape network, but did not know the names of others in the organization, he was taken to the German army counter-espionage centre on avenue Henri-Martin. There he was submerged in a bath of freezing water to the point of drowning, his teeth were filed, and his head was squeezed in iron bands. All he knew, he insisted, was that the actual escapes were arranged by a man named Robert Martinetti – a name Petiot had apparently invented.

Lieutenant Richard Lhéritier, a French paratrooper dropped in occupied France and captured, shared a cell with Petiot for five months. Petiot had advised him how to withstand the brutal interrogation sessions, and the doctor's savage contempt for the Germans had inspired his fellow prisoners, the paratrooper would say. When the Germans demanded a large sum for his release, Petiot told them, 'I don't give a damn. I have terminal cancer so it doesn't matter.' His brother Maurice bargained the ransom sum down to a relatively modest 100,000 francs, and on 13 January 1944 Petiot walked free. Lieutenant Lhéritier would say there was nothing unusual about that, that having squeezed Petiot dry they simply hoped he would lead them unknowingly to other Resistance cells. Others have speculated that the Germans, now aware of an altogether darker side to Petiot's activities, were content to have him continue.

When Petiot, thin-faced and showing the signs of his rough treatment, was released, his wife Georgette and Maurice were there to accompany him back to Auxerre, the town of his birth, where he recuperated for a couple of weeks. And Georgette, trusting wife that she was, didn't think to disturb her husband by bringing up a matter mentioned to her by old family friend Nézondet (who had since been released by the Germans). A matter of some inconvenient corpses he had discovered. That was her story anyway.

When Petiot returned to Paris he resumed seeing patients at the apartment on rue Caumartin and life, on the surface at least, returned to normal. Until 6 March 1944, when a housewife, Madame Andrée Marçais, complained to her husband when he came home from work about the obnoxious smoke billowing from a chimney at 21 rue Le Sueur, across the street.

'I've been feeling sick all day with the stink. If you don't do something about it, Jacques, I will.' Marçais rang the bell and banged on the door without response. A faded hand-written note pinned to the door announced, 'Away for one month. Forward mail to 18 rue des Lombards in Auxerre.' By now, in the early spring darkness, Marçais could see the glow of flames in the smoke. The chimney must be on fire.

The call to the police came at 6:25 p.m. Two officers, Emile Fillion and Joseph Teyssier, who arrived on their bicycles shortly afterwards, had an equal lack of success gaining entry to the locked and shuttered house. A concierge next door had the name of the owner, Dr Marcel Petiot, and his phone number. 'Have you gone into the house?' Petiot asked when his wife called him to the phone. 'Don't do anything 'til I get there. I'll be there in fifteen minutes with the keys.'

The officers and, by now, firemen, watched the increasingly dense smoke with apprehension. Finally, with no sign of the doctor, a fireman broke in through a second-floor window. Minutes later one of the firemen emerged from the basement, leaned against the doorpost and vomited. In the basement Fillion and Teyssier found a coal stove blazing and almost red hot. From the open door drooped a hand, apparently female. A staircase was stacked with skulls, limbs, hands, feet, jaw bones, partial skeletons and mounds of flesh.

The two officers, taking deep breaths of air to expel that unforgettable odour, had barely phoned their superiors when a man whose piercing eyes they would remember rode up on a bicycle and identified himself as the brother of the owner of the building. He remained unmoved when shown the carnage in the basement. 'Are you Frenchmen?' he asked, you would think unnecessarily. He was the head of a Resistance group and the bodies, he said, were those of French collaborators and Germans. The policeman looked with a new respect at the man in the grey topcoat. He had better, Teyssier suggested, make himself scarce. Dr Marcel Petiot remounted his bicycle and, like the smoke still belching from the chimney, simply disappeared and was not seen again for eight months – eight momentous months during which, following the Normandy landings of 6 June, France would finally be rid of the German occupying army.

Meanwhile Commissaire George Massu – the policeman on whom George Simenon based his immortal pipe-puffing detective Maigret – assigned to the case late on the evening of the discoveries, had to make what he could of the charnel house at rue Le Sueur. The stylish house, off the avenue Foch near the Arc de Triomphe, contained fifteen rooms, and had formerly been the home of the actress Cecile Sorel. But it had been empty for some time when Petiot had bought it in the summer of 1941 from Princess Maria Colloredo de Mansfeld.

In spite of the grand, though now dilapidated, surroundings, Petiot made no attempt to convert the house to domestic use. He merely installed an extra stove, much larger than was needed, especially in a time of fuel shortages, had a high wall built at the back of the courtyard to prevent prying eyes, and set up a sparsely furnished consulting room in the garage with a corridor that led to the single most mystifying feature of the house: a small triangular room without windows, with one door which could not be opened from the inside, and fake double doors that opened on a wall. Eight iron rings were attached to one wall, and a peephole which, oddly, was covered on the inside with wall-paper, was designed to give an eye-level view from the outside of anyone secured to the rings. The floor of the garage next door to the consulting room was almost totally taken up by a pile of quicklime from which police sifted a butcher's display window of human parts, while a former manure pit in one of the stables contained stacked bodies again doused in quicklime.

The monstrous discoveries at rue Le Sueur were a preview on a minor scale of what the Allies would find when the Nazi death camps yielded up their secrets. Now it became easier to conjecture why Petiot, instead of being shot, as most arrested Resistance fighters were, had been released by the Nazis. It would be hard to believe the Gestapo had not discovered Petiot's slaughter house at the time of his arrest, and Petiot would have done his best to convince them that, in killing Jews, he was doing their dirty work for them. Again though we may be giving the Nazis too much credit, because in the early hours of the morning following the discoveries Massu was told of a telegram from the German authorities ordering him to arrest Petiot whom they described as a 'dangerous lunatic'. If the Germans wanted him arrested so badly, he couldn't be all that bad. As a good Frenchman, Massu went home to bed and, the following day, made no haste to get in touch with the doctor. When Massu arrived at the rue Caumartin apartment, the Petiots had departed shortly before.

Only gradually would the French authorities come to the view that Petiot, far from acting as a vigilante killing only Germans and collaborators, had been willing to kill anyone if there was money to be made. The hunt for the truth began with cataloguing the horrors at rue Le Sueur. In corners and closets the police found a pathetic array of items Petiot's victims had brought with them, expecting to use them in their new lives – toothbrushes, combs, lotions and pills. Paulette la Chinoise's pretty swallow dress, stained now, was found, along with a shirt with the initials K.K. still discernible that had certainly belonged to Kurt Kneller.

Dr Albert Paul, the chief coroner on the case, spent months sorting the human parts with the help of medical experts. The results were disappointing. Only ten bodies could be identified individually (and none of them by name) though three dustbins of charred bone fragments and five kilos of hair, including more than ten scalps and faces that had been surgically peeled from the victims, indicated a much higher total. Petiot would put the figure at sixty-three; others have estimated more than one hundred.

Understanding a man like Marcel Petiot, born on 17 January 1897 to Félix Petiot, a postal employee, and his wife, Marthe, would be expecting too much. His life, like that of most of the great evil-doers of history, leaves us confused and searching for answers. Police interviewed literally thousands of his patients and found them almost unanimous in their praise of the doctor who would cycle miles to see a sick child, and who would treat the poor free of charge.

People who'd known him as a child remembered (as people so often seem to remember in the case of great criminals) that he had been sadistic towards animals, torturing a kitten by dipping its paws in boiling water. Petiot's mother died when he was fifteen, and his schooldays were a series of scrapes and expulsions. But then, Winston Churchill's school record was nothing to be proud of either.

After being caught stealing mail in 1914, a court psychiatrist judged him 'abnormal' and of diminished responsibility due to psychiatric problems. It was as if Petiot had heard the theme tune for a life of delinquency. From then on he would play the psychiatric card whenever it suited his purpose.

It suited his purposes nicely in 1917 when, serving at the front in the First World War with the 89th Infantry Regiment, his foot was ripped open by an exploding grenade. When the injury was healed and it was time to return to the fighting, Petiot showed signs of mental disturbance. On other occasions he had a nervous breakdown, shot himself in the foot and went into convulsions, all to avoid returning to the front. In view of the terrible death toll in that war, we can only admire Petiot as a born survivor.

He left the military at war's end with a 100 per cent disability pension and destined for treatment in a mental hospital. Amazingly Petiot managed to switch his status from patient to medical student at the hospital, and capitalizing on speeded-up courses for ex-servicemen (and, the police suspected, some chicanery at exam time) he received his medical degree in December 1921.

Setting up practice in Villeneuve-sur-Yonne, twenty-five miles from his birthplace, Auxerre, the young doctor advertised shamelessly, flattered his patients, turned out at all hours for the sick, and gained a saintly reputation. His prescriptions though were sometimes deadly dangerous. ('What's the difference?' he berated a pharmacist who queried a prescription. 'Isn't it better to do away with this kid who's only pestering its mother anyway?') and he was steadily cheating the government medical-assistance programme.

The personable Dr Petiot who, people noted approvingly, lived modestly, put his reputation to the test when in 1926 he brought into his home a housekeeper-mistress named Louise or Louisette Bonet or Delaveau – the name is listed differently. Tongues wagged even more when Louise showed obvious signs of being pregnant. Then she simply disappeared. Someone remembered seeing Petiot loading a trunk into his car, and shortly afterwards a trunk was found floating in the river, containing the headless corpse of a young woman. The body was not identified and, amazingly, Petiot was never charged. By 1944, when police from the capital came to enquire, all police records of the incident had mysteriously disappeared.

With Petiot, always expect the impossible. The physician rebounded from this setback by running for mayor of Villeneuve and, after an especially dirty campaign, winning. His nine years in municipal politics were punctuated by allegations he had stolen municipal funds (with the connivance of his friend, the town clerk Réné Nézondet) and two court convictions, one for fraud, the other for stealing electricity to power his home. Petiot, like rascals before and since, claimed it was all an establishment plot and that only the people were on his side. And, indeed, he was remembered as the mayor who brought sewers to the town and accomplished many good works.

In 1930, though, the doctor was again suspected of murder after Henriette Debauve, the wife of the director of the town dairy cooperative, was found beaten to death, the premises set afire, and 235,000 francs missing. One man who announced his intention of speaking to the police about his knowledge of the crime died mysteriously after receiving an injection from Dr Petiot for his rheumatism.

Finally, in 1933, Petiot, evidently disgusted with the accusations that dogged him in his home province, moved with Georgette (the daughter of a leading Paris restaurateur and who he had married in 1927) and their son, Gérard, to the rue Caumartin premises in Paris. Even by the laxer standards of that day, the leaflet he sent out claiming to be able to treat or cure an extraordinary list of diseases, from senility to syphilis, was extravagant in its claims. Following the complaints of another doctor, he was forced to remove a brass plaque from the front of the building listing various fraudulent credentials. But patients flocked to him and years later they would still talk of the faithful physician who would ride fifteen miles on his bicycle at night to reach a sick indigent.

But trouble was never far behind Marcel Petiot. Following an incident when he stole a book from a shop and attacked the detective who accosted him on the street, Petiot retreated to a private sanatorium until the charges were dropped and he could safely resume his practice.

And then, in the spring of 1942, the doctor found a new outlet for his murderous talents. Among his patients were some one hundred drug addicts for whom he was legally prescribing narcotics in controlled amounts. The Vichy government, disguising its traitorous infamy behind the slogan 'work, family, fatherland', had cracked down on addicts, and Petiot was caught in the net, accused of over-prescribing narcotics. Four days before he was to testify at Petiot's trial, an important witness, Jean-Marc Van Bever, simply disappeared. Three days later, Martha Khaït, implicated in another relatively minor drug infraction involving Dr Petiot, told her husband she was going to see her lawyer, left a pan of water boiling for the laundry, and was not seen again.

As the story of Dr Petiot's bizarre career

unfolded, Commissaire Massu realized that the doctor must have laid the plans for his personal Buchenwald long before. Construction of the mysterious triangular room, the function of which would never be fully understood, and the other alterations at rue Le Sueur had been carried out by workmen in 1941, soon after Petiot purchased the property. So it's likely that Petiot, having discovered earlier how very convenient it was to dispose of awkward people, was simply on the lookout for victims when Van Bever and Khaït came his way.

Even so, there were obvious difficulties in operating a death factory in the heart of Paris, with neighbours to see the comings and goings. How could a man with no transportation other than a sturdy green bicycle have managed the matter of the quicklime? And then there was the question of the nine to twelve bodies recovered from the Seine, three of them believed to be the Kneller family, some of them displaying tell-tale wounds in the thigh where doctors dissecting would normally lodge their scalpels for convenience. One doesn't simply call a taxi, load aboard a corpse and direct it to the Pont Neuf.

Petiot in fact was assisted by his younger brother, Maurice. Neighbours remembered seeing a man they thought was the doctor coming and going even during the period Petiot was in prison. Maurice closely resembled his brother and he would admit that he had delivered quicklime for his brother – to kill cockroaches, he claimed. The neighbours also remembered seeing the same man removing a number of suitcases the previous summer. Traced to the attic of a friend's house near Auxerre, the 49 suitcases proved to contain 1,760 items, including 5 fur coats, 66 pairs of shoes, 77 pairs of gloves and 29 brassières. The Petiot's son, Gérard, had even been wearing one of the long-departed Adrien Le Basque's fancy silk ties when police had interviewed him.

As the dossier built up, the question remained: where was Petiot? The months went by, the Allies freed Paris, and the story faded from the newspapers. Had Petiot, like many Nazi war criminals, fled to South America? Massu didn't believe it. He knew his man by now. In October 1944 he leaked to a newspaper a dubious story that in 1943 Petiot had worn a German uniform and participated in actions against the Resistance. Rising to the bait, Petiot wrote to the newspaper furiously denying the claim. With their quarry still apparently in Paris, and, certain clues in the letter suggested, serving with the French forces, the police asked army security officers to watch for him. Among those assigned to the watch: Captain Henri Valéri, a counter-espionage officer.

A few days later Petiot, alias Captain Valéri, and now sporting a dark curly beard, was arrested by military officers in a Métro station. He had secured an army commission using stolen documents and the name of the doctor whose practice he had taken over when he moved to Paris in 1933. As with so many features of the Petiot story, his arrest too was a mystery. The officer who led the arrest team had acted on his own initiative, and it was only after he had disappeared that he was found to have been a notorious collaborator.

Until now we have seen Marcel Petiot through a haze. He has seemed almost superhuman, able to convince people, in the face of the most damning evidence, of his sincerity, able, it sometimes seems, to leap tall buildings in one stride. It is only as Petiot enters the courtroom, adopting heroic poses for the cameramen, seventeen months later to face twenty-seven counts of murder that we feel we are meeting the real man. In the intervening months, he has left the prosecution frustrated and in tatters. His brilliant claim is that, yes, he murdered people, but in the name of the Resistance. There are huge gaps in the case against him – no one ever saw the victims enter the house at rue Le Sueur, identification of the corpses has proven all but impossible, and the pathologists cannot even show the cause of death. Petiot's counsel, Maître René Floriot, one of France's leading lawyers, even has to force the reluctant state's hand in bringing his client to trial.

Now, as the president of the tribunal starts reading the long indictment against him, Petiot, who has been doodling and pretending boredom, takes over. He will dominate the trial to the very end.

'Let's stop this farce,' he tells the astonished

judge following one particularly silly accusation that Petiot long ago had stolen a cemetery cross. 'This is a story made up by fools and bigots in the country. That cross disappeared two hundred years ago. There must be a statute of limitations, isn't there, M. le Président?'

Shouting, interrupting, challenging every word, Petiot has soon reduced the judge to helplessness. 'What right do you have to talk,' Petiot yells at one of the prosecution lawyers. 'Defender of traitors and Jews!'

'Take that back,' the same lawyer cries when Petiot also accuses him of being a double agent. 'Or I'll knock your teeth in.' The society figures and journalists packing the courtroom howl with laughter. The Nuremberg war trials are taking place simultaneously, but it is Dr Petiot who commands the headlines in Paris.

Is he an anti-Semite? one lawyer asks. 'After all I've endured and done for the Jews,' said Petiot, mopping the tears and struggling to control his voice, 'and now, to see so many Jews against me. I'm beginning,' he says in a small voice of self-discovery, 'to be an anti-Semite.'

The Wolffs? He didn't know they were Jews, he says. They were just German spies sent to him by Eryane Kahan. But weren't they hiding from the Germans? Petiot smiles mischievously: 'They were hiding the way I did on my honeymoon. I pulled the sheet over my head and told my wife, "Try and find me!" '

But Kahan testifies that not only were the Jews she brought him not collaborators, they were deadly afraid of the Germans. Tellingly she says at one point of the Dr Eugène she had known, 'I worshipped him.'

At this trial, whenever the tension flags, the accused can be relied upon for laughter. When a medical witness brings up an obscure point about larvae in dead bodies, Petiot shows keen interest: 'Maybe I can drop by and discuss it with you further after the trial.'

A visit to the death house by the whole court turns into a farce as hundreds tramp through the rooms, lawyers pose before the lime pit holding human bones and, as they visit the mysterious triangular room, Petiot enquires impertinently, 'How would you go about killing someone in this little hole, M. le Président?'

The trial is perhaps unique. The question is not whether Petiot murdered the twenty-seven but whether, as the leader of Fly Tox, he killed, as he would say, 'for the glory of France'. Genuine Resistance heroes testify they have never heard of Fly Tox, and ridicule Petiot's claim that he had invented a secret weapon with which he had killed two German motorcyclists. Petiot's ignorance over the most elementary facts about plastic explosives, which he claims to have used in the Resistance, is easily exposed. But the testimony of Lieutenant Lhéritier, the possessor of impressive Resistance credentials, that Petiot acted heroically in prison and talked then of Fly Tox, is troubling to the seven jurors.

Maître Pierre Veron, representing some of the victims' families, summing up, finds the exact analogy. Petiot, he says, is like the shipwreckers of old – people who set lights on clifftops to attract ships on to the rocks so that they could plunder them. The sailors, never believing anyone capable of such evil, were led to their deaths, he said – as Petiot's victims were. He was . . . Vernon pauses for the words to make their impact, 'The false saviour.'

Maître Floriot, who during the evidence often appeared to be snoozing, gives one of the most brilliant speeches of his career, inviting his audience to consider the good side of Petiot. He had fought for his country as an infantryman; the police had interviewed two thousand of his patients without hearing a bad word spoken about him. Evidence showed that he had provided false documents to help Frenchmen avoid forced labour and to assist British parachutists to escape, and that he had warned Jews of impending raids. Petiot stands accused of twenty-seven murders, of which he admits to nineteen – all performed in the defence of his country. But the police, says Floriot, have tried to lay the blame for every missing person in Paris at Petiot's door.

Petiot is no ordinary man. 'He brought down his enemies, our enemies,' declared Floriot as the whole courtroom rises to applaud him. But when the cheers die down, the immense pile of suitcases, trunks and hatboxes belonging to Petiot's victims and now stacked against one wall of the courtroom seem to speak more eloquently than the counsel's words.

The lawyers, the journalists, expect it will take many hours or days for Président Michel Leser, the two magistrates who sit with him, and the seven jurors (who, under French law, must come to a verdict together) to sift through the twenty-seven cases. But in a little over two hours, and shortly after midnight on the trial's sixteenth day, the decisions are made. Petiot is found guilty of committing twenty-four murders. He is exonerated only in the disappearances of Van Bever, Madame Khaït and Denise Hotin, a woman who went to him apparently for an abortion. If the evidence is sketchy in individual cases, the sheer volume has convicted Petiot. After being condemned to the guillotine the physician, the last shred of charm gone, his eyes betraying the ruthless cruelty of the inner man, screamed, some thought to his wife, some thought to his brother Maurice, 'I must be avenged.'

But nothing is simple. We are not allowed to leave Dr Petiot in that ugly moment of self-revelation. There was always that confusing nobility about the man. Awoken in the pre-dawn darkness of 25 May 1946 with the traditional words, 'Petiot, have courage, your time has come,' he replied with an obscenity. No one could remember a man sleeping soundly the night of his execution, as Petiot

313

had. The coroner, who had attended many executions, would say he had never seen anyone as calm as Petiot. 'Gentlemen,' he said after the executioner had tied his feet and strapped him to the execution table, 'I ask you not to look. This won't be pretty.'

In the 1970s a young Philadelphia writer named Thomas Maeder, in the course of other research, came across an account of the execution of Dr Petiot in an old Paris newspaper. Petiot became his obsession. He dropped out of graduate school and spent several years tracking down official files and people with an involvement in the case. The book that resulted, *The Unspeakable Crimes of Dr Petiot*, did much to revive interest in this largely forgotten case.

It was the dual sides of Petiot's character that fascinated Maeder. Even into the 1970s, he said, there were still patients who swore by the doctor as the best they'd ever had. 'He had the makings of a hero,' Maeder said when I had a chat with him about the case, 'if he hadn't chosen evil.'